The Cinema of Mamoru Oshii

ALSO BY DANI CAVALLARO

The Animé Art of Hayao Miyazaki
(McFarland, 2006)

The Cinema of Mamoru Oshii

Fantasy, Technology and Politics

DANI CAVALLARO

McFarland & Company, Inc., Publishers
Jefferson, North Carolina, and London

LIBRARY OF CONGRESS CATALOGUING-IN-PUBLICATION DATA

Cavallaro, Dani.
    The cinema of Mamoru Oshii : fantasy, technology and politics
/ Dani Cavallaro.
        p.   cm.
    Includes bibliographical references and index.

    ISBN-13: 978-0-7864-2764-2
    softcover : 50# alkaline paper ∞

    1. Oshii, Mamoru — Criticism and interpretation. I. Title.
PN1998.3.O83C38   2006
791.43'34023092 — dc22   2006018554

British Library cataloguing data are available

Cover art: From the 1995 film *Ghost in the Shell* by Mamoru Oshii
(Manga Entertainment/Photofest)

Manufactured in the United States of America

McFarland & Company, Inc., Publishers
  Box 611, Jefferson, North Carolina 28640
    www.mcfarlandpub.com

For Paddy

Table of Contents

Preface

The rapidly expanding appreciation of Mamoru Oshii's caliber as one of the most intriguing personalities in contemporary cinematography invites sustained critical reflection upon his multifaceted career as a director, script writer, concept ideator and producer. This monographic study is intended as an introduction to Oshii's work for those who have not yet had opportunity to fathom the artist's graphic and conceptual universe, as well as an in-depth evaluation of Oshii's career, techniques and distinctive tropes for those who are already partially familiar with that world and wish to enrich their experience thereof.

Oshii has taken the animated medium to stylistic and intellectual reaches of arguably unprecedented complexity, while concurrently experimenting with live-action cinema in a highly imaginative fashion, thereby punctiliously exploring both the formal specificity of each and creative options for their mutual cross-pollination. Resolutely eschewing facile reductions of animation to the underprivileged category of child-oriented entertainment, Oshii has persistently maximized animé's proclivity to engage in the treatment of serious philosophical and ideological issues, and hence yield thought-provoking insights into realms of experience once deemed the uncontested province of live-action filmmaking. Simultaneously, he has endeavored to probe the animational potentialities of the live-action form itself, by bringing some of the acting and staging styles of animé to bear upon flesh-and-bone performers and their environments.

Throughout Oshii's oeuvre, one senses an unflinching determination to avoid consolatory resolutions. No ending, however promising it may seem, is ever devoid of a tantalizing element of open-endedness. Among the themes most assiduously revisited by Oshii's cinema are the nebulousness of the boundary between empirical reality and the oneiric domain; the condition of atomized solitude endured by virtually all living creatures— but most pointedly by humans—regardless of their membership in communities and professional teams; the rampant incidence of economic exploitation and political abuse in contemporary and futuristic societies; and the erosion of identity and, ultimately, even humanness resulting from

1

incrementally invasive technologies of cybernetic and biochemical derivation.

These themes are customarily articulated by recourse to a deft alternation of high-speed action sequences; dialogical or monological segments
in which motion is minimalistically curtailed and verbal meditation is
accorded priority instead; and methodically paced, wordless passages, normally accompanied by haunting melodies, which provide memorable picture galleries and pauses for reflection. Cinematographically speaking, this
characteristically Oshiian mix tends to rely on the systematic employment
of montages, long takes, sequence shots, scrolling pans, distorted perspectives, exaggeratedly low and high camera angles, and a dexterous manipulation of the interplay of light and shadow, reflections, refractions, and color
gradations. Equally recursive are numerous images drawn from the natural world, used as metonymic correlatives for metaphysical notions and
preoccupations. Above all, Oshii's cinematography is marked by an adamant
avoidance of theatricality as an end in itself, as a result of which the most
enduring memories from his productions come to be associated with studiously simple and elegantly unobtrusive details and gentle chromatic variations, aural modulations, gestural clues and allusive textures rather than
the clamor and pomp of operatic set pieces.

Oshii's films draw on a variety of inspirational sources supplied by
Eastern and Western traditions, as well as diverse historical eras, ranging
from Shinto mythology to cyberpunk, from indigenous animistic beliefs and
rituals to global expressions of advanced technocratic regimes. At the same
time, the director's creative trajectory evinces unusual versatility in the
handling and personal re-elaboration of a range of generic codes and conventions. This renders the survey of Oshii's cinematic output over the past
two decades a uniquely captivating journey across the realms of comedy,
romance, visionary science fiction, dystopian speculation, action adventure, the epic saga and the detective tale. Along the way, these disparate discourses—which verge on irreverent slapstick humor, at one end of the
spectrum, and on the murky depths of existentialist or absurdist drama, at
the other—felicitously partake in processes of reciprocal redefinition,
thereby mapping and remapping themselves onto one another to the point
that their initial diversity metamorphoses into reciprocally enhancing com-
plementarity.

Part One, "Oshii's Cinema: An Analytical Survey," provides a
panoramic assessment of Oshii's corpus in the context of the medium of
animé and of its cultural significance, outlining the principal stages of the
filmmaker's career and focusing on the most characteristic traits of his signature at the levels of imagery, thematic concerns, animation techniques
and approach to cinematography. In Chapter 1, "Background: Develop-

ments in Animé," key moments in the history of Japanese animation and in the cognate medium of *manga* (comic books or graphic novels) are examined to help the reader situate Oshii's opus within the broader perspective of indigenous graphic traditions. The topic of animé's impact on Western audiences is also inspected. Chapter 2, "Oshii's Creative Trajectory," traces Oshii's evolution from his budding interest in filmmaking, fueled by the veritably avid consumption of disparate movies of Eastern and Western — and especially European — derivation, through his early forays into animation in numerous capacities, to his progressive assertion of a highly personal style and attendant expeditions into increasingly complex ideological issues.

In Chapter 3, "Themes, Imagery and Symbolism," the discussion concentrates on recurring narrative and iconographic aspects of Oshii's work that range from his innovative employment of diverse mythological frames of reference at the diegetic macrolevel, to his consistent use of treasured visual tropes at the pictorial microlevel. Chapter 4, "Cinematography and Animation Techniques," evaluates in detail, and with illustrative reference to appropriate productions, Oshii's adoption of particular camera moves and choreographing techniques in the construction of his typical conception of *mise-en-scène*. The specifically animational strategies brought to bear on the formulation of his characters' personalities and of his settings' unique moods are concurrently discussed.

Part Two, "Oshii and the Carnivalesque," examines Oshii's allegorical engagement with the carnival as a philosophical and visual phenomenon affording almost limitless opportunities for the constellation of radically destabilized worlds, by recourse to the exuberantly ludic and the disturbingly surreal in turns. Chapter 5, "Concepts of the Carnival," offers an assessment of cultural and philosophical theorizations of that phenomenon, addressing both its definition as the traditional locus of temporary disruptions of order intended to provide salutary release mechanisms, and its recent adaptation to the socioeconomic imperatives of the adventure (or experiential) society. Chapter 6, "*Urusei Yatsura: The TV Series*," Chapter 7, "*Urusei Yatsura Movie 1: Only You*," Chapter 8, "*Urusei Yatsura Movie 2: Beautiful Dreamer*," explore Oshii's contributions to the sensationally popular animé universe of *Urusei Yatsura* (1983–84) as paradigmatic illustrations of the carnivalesque at its most flamboyant. Chapter 9, "*Urusei Yatsura Movie 4: Lum the Forever*," focuses on a post–Oshii production (directed by Kazuo Yamazaki in 1986) within the same animational domain as a means of assessing the ongoing legacy of Oshii's distinctive take on the carnivalesque. Chapter 10, "*Angel's Egg*," and Chapter 11, "*Twilight Q2: Labyrinth Objects File 538*," offer appraisals of those two productions (executed in 1985 and 1987) as instances of Oshii's flair for transmuting bizarre playfulness into Kafkaesque disreality.

Part Three, "Oshii's Technopolitics," tackles Oshii's treatment of grave political and historical dilemmas through the lenses of committed science fiction, concentrating on his highly original appropriation and reinvention of the *mecha* (giant robot) subgenre of animé and on his articulation of the complex interactions governing individual and collective patterns of conduct. Chapter 12, "Visions of Power in Live-Action and Animé," supplies a panoramic survey of Oshii's distinctive approach to those questions. At the same time, it also considers the director's sustained efforts to articulate a rich dialogue between live-action cinema and animé by recourse to a range of stylistic codes and a markedly personal interpretation of notions of stylization, exaggeration and minimalism.

Chapter 13, "Dallos," examines Oshii's engagement with the aforementioned issues in the original video animation (OVA) of that name (1983–84). Chapter 14, "*Mobile Police Patlabor*, OVA 1," Chapter 15, "*Mobile Police Patlabor*, TV Series and OVA 2," Chapter 16, "*Patlabor 1: The Mobile Police*," and Chapter 17: "*Patlabor 2: The Movie*," explore Oshii's incrementally sophisticated treatment of analogous themes in the context of his involvement in the *Patlabor* franchise between 1988 and 1993. Related productions that have been more or less overtly influenced by Oshii's take on the *Patlabor* universe and its spin-offs are then considered in Chapter 18, "*Patlabor WXIII: Movie 3*," a study of the feature film of that name directed by Fumihiko Takayama in 2002, and in Chapter 19, "*Minipato*," which looks at a collection of animated shorts directed by Kenji Kamiyama in 2001.

The discussion then concentrates on Oshii's subsequent elaboration of one of the axial issues first articulated in the *Patlabor* movie: that is to say, the unresolved tension between the zealous protection of justice on the part of the guardians of law and order and the descent into brutality to which this may lead if taken too far. This crucial aspect of Oshii's oeuvre is probed with reference to his live-action "Kerberos" trilogy (1987, 1991, 1992) in Chapter 20, "*The Red Spectacles*, *Stray Dog* and *Talking Head*," and further pursued in Chapter 21, "*Killers: .50 Woman*," an examination of a live-action short produced in 2002 and included in an omnibus project. Chapter 22, "*Jin-Roh: The Wolf Brigade*," focuses on the one — and arguably most impressive — "Kerberos" feature executed through the medium of animation, directed by Hiroyuki Okiura in 1998, for which Oshii penned the screenplay.

Part Four, "Humanity/Virtuality: Oshii's Post-Robotic Vision," addresses Oshii's treatment of his most inveterate concerns— what *makes* us human? what does it mean to *live as* a human?— with reference to a range of features varyingly influenced by developments in cybertechnology and, relatedly, by cyberpunk aesthetics. In tackling those intertwined questions, the director simultaneously throws into relief the inextricability of the organic from the artificial, with a focus on the infiltration of either the sensorium or the physical organism in its entirety by virtual-reality equipment and biotechnological extensions. Chapter 23, "Approaches to Cybersociety," proposes that the films included in this part are primarily distinguished by an adventurous amalgamation of traditional and innovative animation techniques, and that this fusion of the ancient and the modern is thematically paralleled by their consistent return to time-honored myths even as they focus on the fate of identity and humanity in advanced technological milieus. Hence, cybersociety is posited as an eminently hybrid cultural formation that cogently encapsulates the intractably composite nature of contemporary subjectivities at large.

Chapter 24, "*Blood: The Last Vampire,*" Chapter 25, "*Avalon,*" Chapter 26, "*Ghost in the Shell,*" and Chapter 27, "*Ghost in the Shell 2: Innocence,*" varyingly document the above proposition, arguing that it is in the productions studied in this part (and released in 2000, 2001, 1995 and 2004) that Oshii's cinema reaches something of an apotheosis as a symphonic ensemble of technical adventurousness, pictorial opulence, and a profound commitment to defending the right to ethical and emotional integrity on behalf of all creatures. Chapter 28, "*Ghost in the Shell: Stand Alone Complex,*" examines related aspects of the *Ghost in the Shell* world with a focus on the television series of that title directed by Kenji Kamiyama in 2003 and 2004. Chapter 29, "Post-*Innocence* Developments," finally, provides a survey of projects in which Oshii has been engaged in the aftermath of his completion of the second *Ghost in the Shell* feature — particularly, his design of a pavilion for the Japan Expo 2005 devoted to "Nature's Wisdom," and his direction of the live-action feature *Tachigui — The Amazing Lives of the Fast Food Grifters* (2006), based on his novel of the same title.

The textual discussion is complemented by stills from three productions that could be deemed representative of as many key stages in Oshii's career:

- *Patlabor 1: The Mobile Police,* the film which Oshii has described as the work that *made* him (Oshii 2003), and in which his deeply ingrained anxieties regarding the collusion of technological, economic and broadly social issues are challengingly foregrounded;
- *Ghost in the Shell,* a movie now granted a cardinal position in the Olympus of epoch-making cyberpunk classics alongside seminal titles such as Ridley Scott's *Blade Runner* (1982) and Larry and Andy Wachowski's *The Matrix* (1999); and

- *Jin-Roh: The Wolf Brigade,* the feature that most dispassionately attests to Oshii's ongoing apprehensions concerning the ineluctably equivocal nature of notions of loyalty and justice.

My discovery of Oshii's work was somewhat fortuitous, as research into the background to the Wachowski brothers' cult movie *The Matrix,* undertaken in the course of writing a book on cyberpunk and cyberculture,[1] incidentally led me to realize that *Ghost in the Shell* had not only deeply influenced the American directors' project and stylistic preferences but also been instrumental in helping them get an apparently baffling concept past a slew of doubtful prospective sponsors. Having thus been prompted to familiarize myself with that seminal instance of animé, I proceeded to explore the whole of Oshii's opus. I became incrementally intrigued with the sheer variety of characters, situations, generic formulae — and corresponding moods and styles — which that body of work seemed capable of evoking.

Increasingly systematic investigation on my part of the medium of animé, conducted both as a corollary of a general fascination with that art form and its concurrently cultural and technical distinctiveness and in specific conjunction with my production of a book on Hayao Miyazaki and Studio Ghibli,[2] eventually led me to conceive of a monograph devoted to Oshii himself.

Published materials on the director's work are scarce, at least in the West, and this entailed that electronic and archival searches had to be depended upon quite substantially in the drafting of this study. However, it is thanks to a steadfast dedication to the experience of watching the films themselves, and indeed engaging in several repeat viewings with a capacious disposition towards their multiaccentual messages, that the present book has come into existence and that my interest in Oshii's cinema may ultimately be communicated to other readers and spectators.

Part One

OSHII'S CINEMA: AN ANALYTICAL SURVEY

The animated cartoon has made little progress except in America, but the popularity of Disney films, rivaled in universal appeal only by the films of Chaplin, gives reason to hope that there will be a world-wide development in the field of animation, each country adapting the techniques of animation to its own artistic tradition.

— *Taihei Imamura*

Ever since the late 19th century there have been attempts to expose the West to many aspects of Japanese culture such as theatre, architecture, gardens, the tea ceremony, calligraphy, print arts, and more. These have had some success but have tended to convey a view of Japan as a refined and artistic culture — and also as rather formal and even boring. Then animé and manga made their way across the seas, and many who had tired of the higher arts, or had no interest in them anyway, discovered Japan in a different light. What was intended as popular entertainment for domestic consumption became a worldwide phenomenon. Because of animé and manga more and more non-Japanese are being exposed to a culture with which they have been only vaguely familiar, and they are starting to ask questions about what they see.

— *Gilles Poitras, p. vi*

1

Background:
Developments in Animé

Over the past few decades, *manga* and *animé** have ruptured the cultural boundary supposedly dividing East and West, growing into a global lucrative enterprise and, concurrently, redefining conventional perceptions of Japan. Japanese animation resolutely eschews the stereotypical Hollywood proposition that animated films are "kids' stuff" and assiduously addresses social, political and psychological issues of considerable gravity. Nevertheless, it could scarcely be denied that the actual number of animated productions aimed specifically at reflective adults is somewhat limited, and that the number of movies that deploy animation as a vehicle for philosophical commentary is even paltrier. The intrinsic nature of animation, as both an art form and a medium requiring the active involvement of scores of practitioners at virtually all stages of the production process, would seem to banish any leeway for the formulation of an individual vision or indeed of a meditation on contemporary society. Approached from this perspective, the duskily speculative and technically refined films of Mamoru Oshii are of singular significance, insofar as they defy the torpid formal premises of much traditional Western animation while concomitantly supplying a highly individual and cogent commentary on the permutations of both individual and collective identities in the twentieth and twenty-first centuries.

With the international success of *Ghost in the Shell* (*Koukaku Kidoutai*, 1995) and the enthusiastic reception of its sequel *Ghost in the Shell 2: Innocence* (*Koukaku Kidoutai 2: Inosensu*, 2004), culminating with the latter's nomination for the *Palme D'Or* (Cannes 2004), animation director Mamoru Oshii has established himself as a dexterous builder of concurrently tantalizing and harrowing universes. The escalating popularity of Oshii's productions among film critics and historians, members of the animation industry and the cinema world at large, as well as multigenerational lay

These two terms are now fully accepted in English and will not be italicized hereafter.

audiences the world over, would seem to provide ample justification for dedicating a monographic study to this director.

Importantly, Oshii's artistic caliber has increasingly been attracting global attention and gaining recognition in the guise of legion accolades not exclusively on the basis of the aforementioned productions—cinematographically ground-breaking and philosophically pivotal though they indubitably are. In fact, Oshii is also being incrementally hailed as the versatile creator of stylistically and thematically diverse features, comprising both animated and live-action movies, as well as TV series and OVAs. Indeed, *Dallos* (1983–84) was the first Original Video Animation ever produced and it is hardly an exaggeration to claim that the history of animé since the 1980s would never have been the same in the absence of that epoch-making initiative.

The arguments proposed in this book proceed from the tested premise that today few animé viewers (including those who do not situate "serious" animation at the top of their list of preferences) would deny that Oshii's cinema has enterprisingly redefined the parameters of animation by dealing with issues of global cultural relevance, and by engaging equally confidently with comedy, romance, science fiction, political critique, surrealist experimentation, crime and horror, thus generating an utterly novel cinematic synthesis and correspondingly invigorating vision.

Oshii's cinema epitomizes the sheer breadth and complexity of which contemporary Japanese cinema is capable more eloquently than that of any other indigenous filmmaker — with the exception, of course, of Hayao Miyazaki's. At the same time, it exposes the often limited and even blinkered grasp of Japanese animation to which Western audiences are generally disposed. Due to the West's initially limited exposure to animé, many people have tended to associate this art form exclusively with tumultuous action, pornography and gore. Hence, numerous videos have received X ratings merely on the basis of their having originated in Japan, even if the product in question was no more grisly or sexually graphic a film than *My Neighbour Totoro*. The reason behind this rather narrow perception of animé is, quite simply, that a large proportion of titles originally imported into the West in the early 1980s had male teenagers with a passion for science fiction, action adventure and horror as their primary targets. As a result, animé has been stigmatized as the repository of weird plots, explicit sex and gratuitous violence, which has served to preclude the very plausibility of a thoughtful and stylistically sophisticated utilization of that medium. Oshii's accomplishments squarely counter this view, and hence invite a more commodious approach to animé. It is hoped that the present study will contribute, however modestly, to furthering this very cause.

Although manga are conventionally considered as the equivalent of Western comic books or graphic novels, they are actually deeply different from either in both stylistic and thematic terms. Manga represent a significantly more commanding facet of Japanese culture than comics do in Western milieus, being hailed as an honorable art form and prominent constituent of popular culture. Japanese *manga-ka* (manga writers) write for all age groups and cater for a wide range of interests, which almost automatically ensures that practically everybody reads them. In assessing manga's specific visual style — the result of codes and conventions that differ quite profoundly from those usually associated with mainstream American cartoons— it is crucial to acknowledge the specificity of Japanese art and its traditions. As argued in some detail later in this section, what is noteworthy for the purpose of the present study is Japan's ubiquitous penchant for stylization. Ritual masks, Noh theater, Kabuki theater and Bunraku ("puppet") shows exemplify that trend. So does Japan's intrinsically pictographic worldview, encompassing calligraphy and the constant collusion of image and text, line and meaning, painting and poetry.

Animé is intimately connected with manga not solely because several animé movies are based on plots recounted and illustrated in manga but also by virtue of their stylistic features. The shooting techniques used in the animé world are explicitly inspired by the pictorial style peculiar to manga. Indeed, animé assiduously embraces the comic-strip formula inviting viewers to use their imagination as a means of nudging or propelling the narrative along. At the same time, the films abound with tracking shots, long-view establishing shots, pans, uncommon point-of-view camera angles and extreme close-ups, where Western animation tends to capitalize on an action-driven middle-distance. Concurrently, as Gilles Poitras points out, "[m]uch of the action in animé is framed as if it had been filmed with actual cameras ... backgrounds are more likely to be in motion and to change and turn [than in U.S. animation].... Not all animé uses a dynamic background, but much of it does, along with other cinematic effects such as pan shots, angles, distance shots, scenes where the focus between the foreground and the background changes" (Poitras, pp. 57–8).

Like live-action cinema and the manga behind it, animé features a great variety of genres, including science fiction (e.g., *mecha*— or giant robot — stories, android-based stories, cyberpunk, war sagas, political epics); fantasy (e.g., stories based on both Asian and Western traditions, tales of the supernatural, myths and legends); comic fantasies; superhero or super heroine-based adventures; comedy (ranging from the quasi-lyrical evocation of fabulous domains to blunt slapstick); romance (tailored for different age groups); crime; action adventure; historical drama; horror; children's stories; humanoid animal tales; stories based on martial arts; stories based on sports and team activities; adaptations of literary classics; medical dramas; epics; adult dramas (often war stories); erotica; softcore porn; and hardcore porn.

Furthermore, animé's thematic variety is matched by a no less eclectic approach to the pictorial and cinematographical dimensions. As Lee Server has observed, "[w]ispy pastel impressionism, the dense storybook look and anthropomorphism" of the Disney productions and "slick hyperreality" coexist, in a veritable glut of "cinematic extravagance," with "free-floating cameras climbing skyscraper walls or hurtling into space at will, and state-of-the-art sonics" endowing the movies with "the ability to totally envelop the viewer in their sensory spells" (Server, p. 87).

Animé practitioners often tackle issues deemed off-limits by Western animators, feeling less constrained than their Hollywood counterparts by the budgetary imperative to appeal to the widest possible public, especially children. Indeed, animé productions are not, by and large, aimed exclusively (let alone primarily) at the very young, and even when they are, they frequently evince a refreshing respect for the ability of budding audiences to handle complex themes and plots. Furthermore, while animé is undoubtedly a phenomenon of popular culture, it also, as Susan Napier comments, "clearly builds on previous high cultural traditions. Not only does the medium show influences from ... Japanese traditional arts ... but it also makes use of worldwide artistic tools of twentieth-century cinema and photography" (Napier, p. 4). Animé's visual ancestors can be traced back to the Edo period (1600–1868) and even further back to mediaeval Zen cartoons. No less profoundly influential have been the themes and imagery prevalent in the Bakumatsu and Meiji periods (1868–1912), and specifically their keenness on the representation of supernatural occurrences and tendency to indulge the public's craving for icons of the bizarre, the grotesque and the macabre. Furthermore, in spite of animé's basic definition as a popular cultural phenomenon, the issues it explores by recourse to characteristically convoluted and multilayered storylines are often akin to those tackled by the most respected forms of live cinema. Nowhere, arguably, is this proposition more eloquently corroborated than in Oshii's output.

Animé's detractors have tended to focus on three principal stylistic categories in the pursuit of their arguments, maintaining that (1) animé makes excessive use of static frames that impair the action's dynamism; (2) animé's character designs lack a tangible sense of mass and hence convey an impression of virtual weightlessness; (3) animé is incapable of communicating a satisfying feeling of mimetic illusionism and dramatic naturalism. Animé's promulgators, conversely, propose that these criticisms hold a modicum of validity only as long as Japanese animation is assessed by the presumed yardstick of Disney-oriented animation, and that the assumption of such a referential criterion is itself groundless and misleading. According to these sympathetic commentators, animé actually constitutes an art form *sui generis*, seeking to convey *alternative* perceptions of dynamism, space and time to those fostered by Western animation and not, therefore, a mediocre attempt to emulate Hollywood-based approaches to the rendition of satisfying motion.

Within this frame of reference, animé's predilection for static frames is held to embody reflective proclivities over and above action-driven drama, and its indifference to the feeling of mass is seen as a corollary of an aesthetic that posits the line, not sculptural three-dimensionality, as the most appropriate vehicle for the depiction of movement. As for animé's ostensible lack of realism, it may be beneficial to reflect that not many *real* people move in the way American animated characters do—i.e., in an overly energetic and flamboyantly exaggerated fashion — and that animé's slower sequences, often featuring characters merely sitting or standing while carrying out a conversation, are, in a sense, truer to life than frisky hyperactivity.

Ultimately, animé's distinctiveness can only be adequately grasped in the context of a specifically Japanese approach to storytelling, representation and staging wherein Western notions of realism and dynamism are simply irrelevant. Stylization plays a pivotal part in each and every Japanese art form, from landscape gardening to cuisine and the graphic traditions of the *ukiyio-e* (woodblock print) and the *e-maki* (picture scroll), from origami (paper-folding) and ikebana (the art of flower arrangement) to poetry (especially as exemplified by the poetic form known as haiku) and theater. The most traditional Japanese performance arts, such as the aforementioned Kabuki theater and Noh theater, operate primarily on the basis of highly stylized and intrinsically allusive representational codes rather than of naturalism of the Western variety for their dramatic and diegetic effects. Concurrently, the flow of the action is considered secondary to its formal features, as borne out by Kabuki's emphasis on symbolic poses which the lead actors hold for an often protracted duration to the audience's uttermost glee, and on stylized sword fights that are actually more akin to dance than to action sequences in the Western sense of the phrase.

Animé is heir to this tradition, as evinced by its prioritization of dramatic postures and gestures, sometimes intensified to comically melodramatic extremes. At the same time, it abides by conventions which may feel utterly alien to a Western spectator but are perfectly commonplace for Japanese viewers. For instance, an indigenous audience would find it quite acceptable for a sequence dramatizing childish behavior on the part of an adult character to display a grotesquely deformed infantile version of said character, even though many Western viewers would be baffled by such a visual strategy. Before dismissing it as preposterous, however, we should remember that Western animation, too, relies on conventions which could be deemed absurd — such as shots of characters hanging in mid-air and only plunging into a precipice once they have realized that their feet have indeed left the cliff.

In emphasizing animé's cultural specificity, it is nonetheless important not to lose sight of its concurrently international dimension. Firstly, it should be noted that even though the West's initial assessment of animé was almost overweeningly derogatory, audience responses to Japanese animation have been changing quite radically in recent years. As Michael Arnold has observed, "the animé-to-Hollywood ratio in U.S. cinemas keeps tipping toward what you might find on a multiplex screen in Tokyo," with ample evidence for the "enthusiastic support of viewers of all races and genders" (Arnold). Secondly, it is crucial not to underestimate the impact of Western conventions on animé's thematic choices, whereby the medium has been increasingly delivering hybrid tales in which typically Japanese elements such as references to local mythology, religion and lore fluidly crisscross with echoes of Western fairytales, cyberpunk novels and *film noir*.

Thirdly, close attention should be paid to the role played by the West's intervention in distribution deals, a number of titles having reached American and European stores from the early 1990s onwards only thanks to the assistance of U.S.-based distribution companies such as AnimEigo and Manga Entertainment. The proposition that animé is not an unproblematic expression of national individuality is confirmed by the fact that one of the most pivotal moments in its evolution is marked by a close cultural collaboration between East and West. This consists of the production of the weekly TV series based upon Osamu Tezuka's futuristic manga *Tetsuwan Atom (Astro Boy)*, which debuted on New Year's Day, 1963. The show, stylistically influenced by Western designs, was eagerly picked up by the American television industry, and Tezuka subsequently worked on productions explicitly executed with U.S. distribution priorities in mind. *Janguru Taitei* (1965, released in the U.S. as *Kimba the White Lion* in 1966) was produced in color specifically so that it would appeal to Western audiences, a domestic release alone being unlikely to have covered the exorbitant production costs. It was the infusion of dollars into the venture, in other words, that enabled Kimba to become the first Japanese color TV series. Following *Astro Boy*'s phenomenal success, the 1960s witnessed a veritable explosion of TV science-fiction or action-adventure animé movies. By the 1970s, the range had expanded considerably and studios were busily churning out mystery dramas, soap operas and Western classics such as *Heidi, Girl of the Alps* and *The Diary of Anne Frank.*[1]

2

Oshii's Creative Trajectory

Born in Tokyo on 8 August 1951, Mamoru Oshii was already an avid movie consumer while attending primary school, and hence proceeded to garner an encyclopedic knowledge of world cinema, marked by a deep fascination with directors as diverse as Andrei Tarkovsky, Chris Marker, Andrzej Wajda, Jeray Kawalerowicz, Andrej Munk and Ingmar Bergman. At the same time, Oshii's films have been increasingly providing influential sources of inspiration for numerous Western directors, including Stanley Kubrick, James Cameron and Andy and Larry Wachowski. (It is highly unlikely, incidentally, that *The Matrix* would have come into existence at all had the Wachowskis not shown *Ghost in the Shell* to their potential sponsors so as to allay their skepticism in the face of the brothers' daring concept.)

Following his involvement in revolutionary politics in the late 1960s and early 1970s — an activity that resulted in parental opprobrium and in his eventual alienation from the student movement — Oshii graduated from the Fine Arts Education School of the Tokyo Liberal Arts University (Gakugei Daigaku) in 1976, and presently committed himself to sustained experimentation with photography and cinematography — even though limited finances forced him, for a while, to *shoot without film.*

Oshii's first fleeting engagement with animation took place in 1977 with his production of the storyboards for one episode of the animated series *One-Hit Kanta* (*Ippatsu Kanta-kun*). Oshii obtained his first actual job in the animation industry at Tatsunoko Productions in 1977. His artistic responsibilities included the creation of storyboards and contributions to the direction of several animé series. In 1980, he moved to Studio Pierrot, where he worked with Hisayuki Toriumi on the series *Nils's Mysterious Journey* (*Nirusu no Fushigi-na Tabi*) and met the artist Yoshitaka Amano (who had also previously worked for Tatsunoko as an animator), with whom he would embark on challenging collaborations in later years. Oshii soon became involved in the production of the hugely popular TV series

16

Urusei Yatsura, a romantic sci-fi comedy based on the manga by Rumiko Takahashi, in a directing role (1981–82). He further directed the *Urusei Yatsura* features *Only You* (*Urusei Yatsura: Onri Yuu,* 1983) and *Beautiful Dreamer* (*Urusei Yatsura: Byuutifuru Dorimaa,* 1984), where he began to move away (particularly in the second production) from the TV series' jocular mood and slapstick dimension, in the direction of a more serious exploration of the relationship between appearance and reality.

At this stage in his career, Oshii revolutionized the universe of animé by inventing the concept of OVA (Original Video Animation, also known as OAV, Original Animated Video). *Dallos* (1983–84), a space opera revolving around factions of Moon-based colonists and rebels, was the first production created by Oshii in this format. In late 1984, wishing to develop an original aesthetic vision that would transcend the boundaries of the *Urusei Yatsura* world to which he had hitherto been committed, Oshii set himself up as an independent director. In this capacity, he created the OVA *Angel's Egg* (*Tenshi no Tamago,* 1985)—a mesmerizingly surreal parable— in collaboration with Amano.

During the execution of *Angel's Egg,* Oshii met producer Toshio Suzuki, a founder of Studio Ghibli alongside Hayao Miyazaki and Isao Takahata. Suzuki and Studio Ghibli would later abet Oshii in the production of *Ghost in the Shell 2: Innocence* (*Koukaku Kidoutai 2: Inosensu,* 2004). Shortly after the launch of *Angel's Egg,* Oshii encountered Miyazaki himself and the two artists began to work on a movie provisionally titled *Anchor,* which Oshii would direct and Miyazaki write. Stylistic and aesthetic divergences caused the project to be aborted just after the planning stages. (Artistic disagreements between the two directors survive to this day despite their mutual admiration and frequently proclaimed respect: Oshii finds Miyazaki excessively idealistic, whereas Miyazaki believes that Oshii prioritizes philosophy over entertainment.)

In 1987, Oshii directed his first live-action film, *The Red Spectacles* (*Akai Megane*). This was the first installment of a trilogy (which would eventually also include *Stray Dog* and *Talking Head*) in which Oshii supplies dark critiques of despotism and mendacity, interspersed with elements of action adventure, romance and moving reflections on the relationship between dogs and humans. In the same year, Oshii also created the OVA episode *Twilight Q2: Labyrinth Objects File 538* (*Towairato Q2: Meikyuu Bukken File 538*), a simple yet subtle dramatization of the inextricability of the illusory from the actual.

As investors and sponsors became less and less inclined, throughout the 1980s, to work with individual directors and increasingly interested in studios, the animé team "Headgear" was formed, and Oshii was invited by the screenwriter Kazunori Itoh to join it in the positions of director and writer. The result was the *Patlabor* franchise and attendant elaboration of a complex technopolitical saga comprising several OVA and TV episodes as well as feature-length movies. Oshii contributed significantly to this project with the direction of the first *Mobile Police Patlabor* (*Kidou Keisatsu Patoreibaa*) OVA series (1988) and of the two feature-length productions *Patlabor 1: The Mobile Police* (*Kidou Keisatsu Patoreibaa*, 1989) and *Patlabor 2: The Movie* (*Kidou Keisatsu Patoreibaa 2 The Movie*, 1993), as well as the script for a number of TV episodes (1989–90) and for parts of the second OVA (1990–92). In the "Headgear" phase, Oshii also directed a prequel to the aforementioned live-action movie *The Red Spectacles*, namely *Stray Dog: Kerberos Panzer Cops* (*Stray Dog Keruberosu Jigoku no Banken*, 1991), and a further live-action film entitled *Talking Head* (1992), centered on the mysterious disappearance of an animation director during the production of a heavily anticipated release.

The turning-point in Oshii's career was *Ghost in the Shell* (*Koukaku Kidoutai*, 1995), an irrefutably unique interpretation of cyberpunk that constitutes both a ground-breaking intervention in the developing art of CGI and a narratively and philosophically enterprising adaptation of Masamune Shirow's popular manga. The film was released simultaneously in Japan, the U.S. and Europe, and although its domestic reception was initially lukewarm, it was immediately successful everywhere else, hitting the top of the U.S. Billboard Video Chart in 1996. Having gained global recognition, *Ghost in the Shell* rapidly rose to the status of a cult movie and was indeed hailed as very possibly the most seminal sci-fi production of the late twentieth century. (The ethos and aesthetics of cyberpunk are examined in some detail in Chapter 3.)

Oshii's unrelentingly innovative and thought-provoking movies have continued to attract both professionals and amateurs the world over, as demonstrated by the screening of a retrospective of the director's work at the Rotterdam International Film Festival (2000), by the projection of the live-action and digital animation hybrid *Avalon* (2001) at the Cannes Film Festival in the year of its release and, as noted, by the selection of *Ghost in the Shell 2: Innocence* (*Koukaku Kidoutai 2: Inosensu*, 2004) for the *Palme D'Or*. *Avalon* offers a chilling dramatization of the aberrations spawned by the unchartered virtualization of the real with reference to a lethal VR game and its hapless players, deftly interweaving throughout the ludic and the uncanny.

Innocence, a daunting reflection on people's endless quest for the genesis of their identities and memories, constitutes both a problematization and a compendium of Oshii's most inveterate technical and thematic concerns. The cyberpunk component already pivotal to *Ghost in the Shell* is here retained but Oshii's preoccupation with the meaning of humanity and with the plausibility of love in an exhaustively technologized world reaches utterly novel levels of complexity. *Innocence*'s standing as one of the only five animations ever nominated at Cannes eloquently attests to its international recognition, making it an indisputably momentous phenomenon in the history of not merely Oshii's cinema but animé at large.[1]

Oshii has also supplied the screenplay for Hiroyuki Okiura's *Jin-Roh: The Wolf Brigade* (1998)—a superbly animated rendition of the "Kerberos" universe already brought to the fore by the live-action features *The Red Spectacles* and *Stray Dog*—and the visual concepts for Hiroyuki Kitakubo's *Blood: The Last Vampire* (2000), a lusty horror story set against the backdrop of the Vietnam War, as well as a pioneering experiment with digital cinematography. Just prior to the release of *Innocence*, Oshii's principal projects included the production of the script for *MiniPato* (2001), a series of self-parodying shorts set in the *Patlabor* universe directed by Kenji Kamiyama; the direction of a segment of the live-action thriller anthology *Killers*, namely *Killers: .50 Woman* (2002). In the post–*Innocence* phase, Oshii has engaged in the design of an interactive pavilion for the Japan Expo 2005, combining state-of-the-art technology with a trenchant ecopolitical statement, and in the direction of the film *Tachigui — The Amazing Lives of the Fast Food Grifters* (*Tachiguishi Retsuden*, 2006), based on his own novel of the same title.

It is Oshii's unique directing style that renders his worlds acutely resonant, yet worthy of repeat viewings. This factor exhibits itself most strikingly when one assesses some of Oshii's best-known productions to date — e.g., *Urusei Yatsura Movie 2: Beautiful Dreamer*, the two *Patlabor* features and the *Ghost in the Shell* movies— against the animé and manga texts upon which they are based. Thus, while the original *Urusei Yatsura* productions tended to capitalize on fast-paced farce, *Beautiful Dreamer* is pervaded by a latently ominous— though not uniformly tenebrous— atmosphere. The *Patlabor* films are likewise permeated by baleful premonitions. The *Ghost in the Shell* movies, finally, marginalize the humorous banter and overall conviviality that characterize Shirow's manga (despite the latter's undeniable engagement with serious philosophical, political and economic issues) in order to evoke a mood of concurrently intriguing and forbidding ambiguity reminiscent of Kubrick at his most challenging.

3

Themes, Imagery and Symbolism

In her essay "Myths for the Millennium: Japanese Animation," Antonia Levi maintains that

> Japan ... never abandoned its mythology.... This was not necessarily a good thing. The Meiji government which came to power in 1868 justified the overthrow of the Shogun through the use of ancient Shinto mythology, and twisted its creation myths to justify an imperialistic, ultra-nationalist autocracy that terrorized Asia and nearly led to Japan's destruction in World War Two.... The misuse of Japan's creation myths did have one positive aspect, however. It kept alive not only the myths themselves, but also an understanding of what mythology was. Even at the height of Japanese ultranationalism in the 1930s and 1940s, Japan never confused mythological truth with rational truth. Shinto creation myths were taught as fact in the public schools, but Darwinism was also taught.... [M]anga and *animé* ... resurrect ancient mythologies and use them to create new myths, myths better suited to the needs and realities of postmodern Japan and, it would seem, most of the world [Levi, pp. 33–4].

Oshii's films fully corroborate Levi's hypotheses insofar as they abound with images and symbols drawn from diverse mythological traditions—including Shinto, Buddhism, Christianity, ancient Japanese lore and Arthurian legends—as well as with reconfigurations of such materials in the light of contemporary exigencies and experiences. Numerous variations on the inseparability of illusion and reality, virtuality and actuality, facts and dreams are arguably the most insistently recurrent component of Oshii's signature. Mythological references contribute crucially to the dramatization of this dominant idea, as do symbolic incarnations of the director's existential, psychological and affective concerns. These include images of feathers, birds, angelic beings and gigantic fish which are persistently employed as metaphors for spiritual elevation, and images of trees and plants which, conversely, are meant to convey the sense of a creature's grievous anchoring to an earth-bound and deterministic universe.

In evaluating Oshii's use of the dream topos in his films, it ought to be borne in mind that Japanese cinema dramatizes the oneiric dimension with almost obsessive regularity, and with dozens of variations on the themes of escape and haunting. Dreams, accordingly, are used to symbolize alternately an allegorical transcendence of existential or societal malaise, and an occasional immersion in portentous situations. In both cases, the experience is posited as *temporary* (and, ideally, cathartic). In Oshii's oeuvre, the oneiric acquires novel resonance since it is presented as a *permanent* (and by no means unequivocally enlightening) condition. Nobody can ever be certain, within the parameters of Oshii's universes (be they ludic as in *Urusei Yatsura*, surreal as in *Angel's Egg*, politically engaged as in the *Patlabor* franchise or metaphysically disposed as in the *Ghost in the Shell* productions), that what one perceives as the real world actually obtains in an empirical sense.

A number of mediaeval Japanese legends, such as the collection of tales known as *Uji Shui Monogatari*, utilize dreams consistently in ways that are more or less overtly echoed by Oshii's film plots. Hayao Kawai proposes that the treatment of oneiric experience in Japanese folk literature and mythology features three principal recursive elements: "the free interpenetration of this world and the dream world" (Kawai, H., p. 15); the undertaking of a journey to "the land of death" (p. 17); and the notion of "multiple realities" (p. 19), which conceives of the world as many-layered and therefore highly variable, depending on the nature of the layer inhabited at any one point in time. Oshii's suspension of the boundary between the empirical and the hypothetical gains considerable momentum from the portrayal of mutually permeating dimensions, whereby his characters' grasp of their spatial and temporal coordinates becomes painfully tenuous. Accorded absolute prominence in *Beautiful Dreamer*, this approach is also employed, in varying degrees, in the "Kerberos," *Patlabor* and *Ghost in the Shell* movies.

Kawai also posits the coalescence of self and others as a key feature of dream-centered Japanese narratives. This element finds expression in the Japanese language itself due to its distinctive — and at times baffling — designation of individual and collective identities: "[t]here are many terms for the first person singular, such as *watakushi, boku, ore*, and *uchi*. The choice depends entirely on the circumstance and the person being addressed. In this respect it can be said that the Japanese finds 'I' solely through the existence of others" (pp. 23–4). However, what we are presented with is not a scenario that utterly negates the possibility of individual autonomy, since relationality is actually believed to require an active understanding of one's inner self. Hence, it only operates adequately when the individual subject forsakes passivity and endeavors to internalize the principles of respect, honor and memory *through actions*.

The relationship between the individual and the group is an axial component of Oshii's opus. Oshii's characters typically operate within a group regulated by particular rules — e.g., the Special Vehicle Division 2, Section 2, in the *Patlabor* films, the VR game in *Avalon*, Section 9 in *Ghost in the Shell*. This aspect of the director's work could be seen as a reflection of a defining component of Japanese tradition and culture, namely their emphasis on the importance of group affiliation from childhood onwards, and on the related imperative of loyalty. At the same time, however, Oshii's take on the notion of the group carries global, rather than merely regional, relevance insofar as it also constitutes an implicit critique of postcapitalist dispensations wherein grouping people together by recourse to homogenizing strategies such as the fashion system and commodity fetishism belies people's actual atomization and disconnection. Indeed, Oshii's protagonists are invariably isolated and solitary individuals even as they appear to occupy technological networks characterized by rampant communicational saturation. In order to convey a palpable impression of the individual's isolation in contemporary society by cinematographical means, Oshii has developed a characteristic approach to the issue of *eye contact*. In an interview with *Fluctuat.Net*, the director has elaborated this idea with specific reference to his first epoch-making feature:

> In *Patlabor* ... the characters converse but never look at one another. They are never facing one another but always face the viewer. The characters only communicate to a screen. I have found this device to express my idea of people's loneliness. I believe that throughout history, intersubjective communication has been far too often privileged. We have never explored the relationship ... that may obtain between a human and a dog, or a human and a machine. If humans do not yet know themselves, it may be because they have always approached the human person in relation to other human beings. I am concerned with other types of relationships [Oshii 2002].

The tension between the concept of loyalty to a group, on the one hand, and the notion of subjectivity as coterminous with a state of existential disconnectedness, on the other, tends to remain unresolved. Moreover, the groupings portrayed by Oshii are themselves marked by a sense of isolation in virtue of their adoption of team-specific rules that often come into conflict with the demands and sense of decorum treasured by the wider social web. For example, *Patlabor*'s Section 2 are frowned upon by the general public and the Metropolitan Police alike due to both their personal idiosyncrasies and to the rather unpalatable nature of their law-enforcing missions.

An analogous fate befalls the Kerberos Panzer Cops in the live-action films *The Red Spectacles* and *Stray Dog: Kerberos Panzer Cops* and in the animation *Jin-Roh: The Wolf Brigade*. The game players in *Avalon*, for their part, are unequivocally ostracized as criminals. At the same time as dramatizing the ordeals of individuals doomed to a destiny of loneliness even though they belong to a group, Oshii also portrays the predicament of characters who are repeatedly forced back into communal structures even as they actually yearn for solitude. Major Kusanagi and Batou of Section 9 in the *Ghost in the Shell* features, Ash in *Avalon*, Captains Nagumo and Gotoh in the *Patlabor* movies, Fuse in *Jin-Roh*, Ash in *Avalon* and Saya in *Blood: The Last Vampire* appear to incarnate this modality in varying degrees. We are thus presented with the double paradox of isolation-in-commonality and commonality-in-isolation.

In order to grasp the cultural import of these thematic preoccupations, it is vital to remember that in Japanese society, togetherness plays a key role. The reason for this is, to a certain extent, straightforwardly demographic, Japan being a country where approximately the equivalent of half the population of the entire U.S.A is concentrated in the territorial breadth of California, Washington and Oregon alone. Hence, the very notion of privacy has traditionally carried connotations that are profoundly different from those it habitually carries in the West, and the feeling that one is never quite alone has accordingly preserved psychological and emotional dominance for the Japanese. Traditional architecture corroborates this proposition through its extensive use of partitions (e.g., sliding doors between rooms or closets—*fusuma*—and wood or paper screens) that represent more of a connecting tissue within the household than actual dividers. The aforementioned predilection for the concept of interpenetrating worlds in Japanese lore and even contemporary fiction and cinema could be said to mirror this very mentality.

Where the theme of relationships is concerned, Oshii's representation of love is no doubt one of the most remarkable (albeit almost undiscernibly so) traits of his entire register. So unobtrusive is his approach to this theme that many viewers have tended to assume that Oshii simply steers clear of romantic plots altogether. In fact, the director's works do deal with love assiduously and, once the spectator has grown accustomed to his very personal cinematic language, in a very touching fashion. This is clearly evinced by the awkward and unresolved relationships involving Captains Nagumo and Gotoh in the *Patlabor* films, Kei and Fuse in *Jin-Roh* and, most enigmatically, Major Kusanagi and Batou in the *Ghost in the Shell* features. An aura of melancholy and a pervasive sense of missed or lost opportunities ("all the years we have wasted," as the theme song of *Innocence*, "Follow Me," puts it) surround the love element at all times, yet do not render it any less warm or poignant. Oshii's sentimental plots come across as elusive because they do not pander to the dictates of either romantic or courtly adoration, to either erotic titillation or brazen carnality, but celebrate instead the principles of respect and friendship, as corollaries of both devotion and self-awareness.

According to Kawai, Japanese lore also repeatedly suggests that there is "no distinct demarcation" between "man and Nature":

> Throughout European history, Nature has been a concept which stands in opposition to culture and civilization, and continues to be objectified by human beings. The word "Nature" was translated into Japanese as *shizen*. Prior to this we did not have a concept of Nature. When we Japanese wish to talk about "Nature," we use such expressions as *sansensomoku*, which literally means "the mountains, rivers, grasses, and trees" … before the encounter with the West … [*shizen*] is not even a noun … [but rather] an adverb or adjective … that expresses a state in which everything flows spontaneously. There is something like an ever-changing flow in which everything — sky, earth, and man — is contained. Because it is like a continual process, it can never be grasped spatio-temporally, and strictly speaking, cannot be named [pp. 25–7].

The culturally specific approach to the humanity-Nature dyad posited by Kawai should be borne in mind when assessing both Oshii's treatment of ecological issues and his take on the ceaseless cycles through which identities materialize and dissolve in society and Nature alike.

Already evident in a few *Urusei Yatsura* episodes, Oshii's concern with technology's impact on the environment acquires incontrovertible centrality in the first *Patlabor* film, whose plot unfolds against the backdrop of the rampant urbanization of Tokyo Bay. Throughout the *Patlabor* saga, Oshii makes sustained references to environmentalist protests, and Section 2 includes two characters who harbor passionate ecological agendas: Noa, who repeatedly fights for animal rights, and Hiromi, who tends a small greenhouse and breeds chickens. These themes are complemented by recurring images of numerous non-human species: dogs, cats, birds, fish and, in a couple of OVA episodes, even an albino alligator who lives in the sewage system underneath the Section's base.

Oshii's preoccupation with the role played by technology in the shaping of both personal and collective definitions of humanity, sentience and responsibility is located within a nexus of primarily philosophical and ideological considerations. Like many science-fiction authors, the director exhibits an ambivalent attitude towards technology, critically acknowledging its implementations as simultaneously beneficial and detrimental. He captures this uncertainty in images that at times point unequivocally to the evils of technology, and at others allude poetically to its mixed blessings. The image of the tank is particularly prominent as a flagrant icon of bellicosity — for instance, in *Beautiful Dreamer*, *Angel's Egg*, *Patlabor 2*, *Ghost in the Shell* and *Avalon*. The image of the screen is no less conspicuous. This manifestation of technology frequently epitomizes the strategies of manipulation, distortion and semiotic violence relentlessly perpetrated by the media in their dissemination of adulterated images (this theme is axial to *Patlabor 2*). Nonetheless, the screen concurrently carries positive connotations, insofar as it may function as a reminder of the ubiquitously halluci-natory nature of the world we inhabit at all times, and hence as a poten-tially invigorating awakener of otherwise dormant psyches.

The images deployed by Oshii include both literal screens (e.g., tele-vision monitors and computer terminals) and metaphorical ones (e.g., reflective or semi-reflective surfaces such as mirrors, windows, fish tanks and glass cages). The latter serve to present the characters themselves with quasi-cinematic renditions of their actions and settings, thereby making them not only the actors but also the spectators in the lusterless spectacle of their daily experiences. At the same time, these symbolic screens repeat-edly double, split and indeed *dismember*, in a psychological sense, the char-acters' identities, eroding any consolatory sense of wholeness to which they may strive to hold on. It should also be noted, however, that Oshii's reser-vations about technological advancement does not prevent him from indulging with a refreshingly childlike gusto in the meticulous representa-tion of military hardware, surveillance mechanisms and intricate cyber-netic equipment.

To the theme of technological abuse Oshii often allies that of terror-ism. Hoba in the first *Patlabor* feature, Tsuge in the second, the Puppet Master in *Ghost in the Shell* and Kim in *Innocence* are all, in varying degrees, portrayed as terrorists intent on undoing the sociopolitical fabric by recourse to cybertechnology and to the raw urban chaos to which its reck-less deployment is capable of leading. *Blood: The Last Vampire* also alludes to terrorism, despite its generic affiliation with the classic vampire tale, since the squad of U.S. special agents sent to Japan to vanquish the blood-suckers tend to regard their enemies as political traitors hell-bent on pre-venting troops from being conveyed to Vietnam. While anarchic tendencies are undoubtedly one of the defining traits of Oshii's terrorists, it is note-worthy that analogous proclivities may also be detected in characters puta-tively committed to the maintenance of law and order. Captain Gotoh from the *Patlabor* films, in particular, repeatedly urges his colleagues not to worry excessively about rules, and Section 2 itself is something of a world-within-a-world governed by its own rather idiosyncratic code.

Animals are pivotal to Oshii's symbolic repertoire. Dogs are repeat-edly brought into play as unprejudiced witnesses, capable of observing human behavior with impartiality and candor. This topos reaches a crown-ing achievement in *Innocence*, where the dog is a genuinely pivotal charac-ter and the world is perceived largely through his eyes. In the interview with *Fluctuat.Net* referred to earlier, the director has commented thus on his fascination with dogs: "[the dog] is the greatest mystery in my view. If I could fathom this mystery, I might direct an actual movie about dogs. But since the answers I have are only partial, I am satisfied with inserting dogs in my films in supporting roles. Thus far, films that deal with dogs have merely humanized them, which is not a proper way of doing them justice" (Oshii 2002). At a broader level, Oshii's tendency to allot key roles to animals (and indeed to other non-human or only partially human species such as dolls and cyborgs) attests to his deep aversion to anthropocentrism as an arrogant, conceited, and ultimately quite fallacious creed that barely assuages human beings' deep-seated uncertainties and doubts.

Other recurrent images and styles that have come to be regarded as Oshii's trademarks include characters' reflections on watery surfaces— generally employed to allude to moments of introspection; desaturated (i.e., nearly black and white) palettes in the depiction of spaces of strife and peril; and crushed perspectives as means of evoking a stifling atmosphere. An important aspect of Oshii's architectural imagery resides with his emphasis on ruins. Pondering the metaphorical implications of cinematic images of crumbled buildings and even whole conurbations, it could be argued that such images evoke a Gothic fascination with decay which substantiates William H. Fox Talbot's comments concerning "the camera's special aptitude for recording 'the injuries of time'"— and specifically, as Susan Sontag has observed, the ineluctable destiny of "buildings and monuments" (Sontag, p. 69).

Oshii's take on the themes of devastation and degeneration also corroborates Jonathan Jones's account of major historical shifts in the perception of wreckage: "[i]n the eighteenth century, ruins were objects of contemplation, reverie and sober enjoyment. They were an opportunity to reflect on the passing of empires and the vanity of human effort. Yet in an age abandoning its religion, they were also reassuring images of what survives, what remains of us.... [A]rtists took delight in ruins. They drugged on decay" and were acutely drawn by "the broken sensuality of the past." In the twentieth and twenty-first centuries, by contrast, ruins carry substantially different connotations due to the very means by which they tend to come about: "there's a difference between a ruin that is the product of slow centuries, the richly rotting fruit of time, and a building whose ruin takes place in a moment: the difference between dying of old age and murder" (Jones, pp. 12–13). What Oshii's movies emphasize is not merely the illuminating potential of people's confrontation with dilapidated structures but also the iconic significance of ruins as tenacious mementos of the human propensity for both ideologically triggered and utterly gratuitous destructiveness.

No less noteworthy is the director's assiduous deployment of themes and imagery associated with cyberpunk, a cultural movement that found inception in the mid-1980s (primarily through the writings of William Gibson and Bruce Sterling) and still signals a drastic shift from older science fictional modalities. In cyberpunk, the shiny hardness of metal, of sturdy and imposing machinery and of industrial technology at large (hardware) favored by traditional sci-fi cinema and literature gives way to the murky softness of junk-infested urban settings and of often undependable post-industrial technology (software). Furthermore, if in the 1960s and 1970s fantastic texts mainly tended to depict squeaky-clean and decontaminated worlds in which human *minds* were controlled by machines, in the 1980s and 1990s the emphasis falls on the eternal night of the apocalyptic megalopolis wherein abjection and monstrosity are written on the *body*. Indeed, cyberpunk offers insistent intimations of the greater and greater confluence of machines and bodies (largely due to the increasingly miniaturized dimensions of cybernetic apparatuses), whereby the human organism is both physiologically and psychologically reconfigured by invasive forms of biotechnology.

In this respect, Oshii's cinema subtly documents the transition from pre-cyberpunk science fiction to full-fledged cyberpunk: in the *Patlabor* movies, technology complements and augments the human body in an essentially prosthetic manner, remaining palpably separate from the flesh itself in the guise of an exoskeleton; in the *Ghost in the Shell* films, conversely, technology increasingly infiltrates the characters' living tissues to the point that ascertaining their humanity becomes well-nigh impossible. A variation on the latter modality is supplied in *Avalon*, where a ludic configuration of cybertechnology penetrates the sensorium in its entirety, and the travelers in hyperreality may become so utterly engulfed in the technological simulation as to be unable to return to the so-called real world. Technologies initially intended to guarantee incremental degrees of both affective and material *returns* actually end up transforming their users into *non-returners*.

Oshii's cinema further embraces a world view typical of Gibsonian cyberpunk by underscoring the provisional status of many conventional definitions of value, rationality and truth in a radical rejection of the Enlightenment ethos. Moreover, it amalgamates in frequently cryptic ways the rational and the irrational, the new and the old, the mind and the body, by integrating the hyper-efficient structures of high technology with the anarchy of street subcultures. It is important to remember, in this regard, that if the *cyber-* component in the term cyberpunk alludes to the fact that the point of reference of this branch of science fiction is cybernetics rather than spaceships and robots, the *-punk* element, for its part, hints at a defiant attitude based in urban street culture. Cyberpunk's characters are people on the fringe of society: outsiders, misfits and psychopaths, struggling for survival on a garbage- (*gomi-*) strewn planet which is always on the verge of dissolving into a quagmire of muddy dreams.

On one level, Oshii's cinema could be seen to consist primarily of situations and environments pervaded by dense lyricism and cryptic introspectiveness through which the director seeks to capture the floating substance of reality and chillingly toylike nature of the human. On another level, and in a fashion reminiscent of David Lynch's cinema, the meditative and intensely symbolic dimension of Oshii's universe is counterbalanced by rapid-fire action sequences, and the elusively oneiric component by a lucidly dispassionate dissection of ideological, metaphysical and ethical preoccupations. Averse to the contemplation, let alone promotion, of totalizing visions, Oshii's films consistently return to the representation of worlds permeated by not merely pluralism but also, at times, skeptical relativism.

4

Cinematography and Animation Techniques

Oshii's cinematographical style evinces a marked preference for *long takes*. The long take designates a shot produced by one uninterrupted run of the camera that continues for an unusually lengthy time. Rare in silent cinema, the long take became more significant in the 1930s and 1940s, notably as used by Jean Renoir and Orson Welles. It soon asserted itself as a common technique in films throughout the world. (This technique is germane to the so-called *plan-séquence* [sequence shot], a French term for a scene handled in a single shot, usually a long take.) Oshii makes most memorable use of this technique in sequences—such as the ones punctuating the *Patlabor* and the *Ghost in the Shell* movies—that evoke an intensely allusive sense of space by methodically training the camera across alternately bustling and subdued cityscapes replete with legion atmospheric details.

Oshii is also an assiduous practitioner of the *cut-back*—namely, a return in time to an earlier event in the story—and of the *cut-in*—that is, the intermingling with cutting motions (intercutting) of disparate portions of a story occurring in different locations. Both *Jin-Roh: The Wolf Brigade* and *Ghost in the Shell 2: Innocence* exploit these techniques to maximum effect in order to dramatize their protagonists' changing perceptions, as their so-called realities are incrementally infringed upon by hallucinations and mirages induced by self-persecutional guilt, in one case, and by cybernetic brain-hacking, in the other.

Most importantly, both the animated and the live-action films employ a number of imaginatively varied shots to muster up momentum and impart a particular sequence with a characteristic visual and affective atmosphere. Especially noteworthy, in this regard, are the devices deployed in the more dynamic sequences, such as those depicting battles, chases and instances of physical conflict in general. Although Oshii introduces such sequences sparingly and somewhat prudently, their cinematographical distinctiveness is unmistakable and instantly recognizable, regardless of whether they dramatize comical confrontations in the characteristic *Urusei Yatsura* vein or whether they depict grisly onslaughts as they tend to do in *Innocence*. In all cases, the director typically resorts to the *swish pan* (a.k.a. *flash* or *zip pan*, namely a very rapid horizontal move of the camera producing a blurring effect); *rack focusing* (a.k.a. *selective focusing*, namely a dimming of focal planes in sequence that compels the spectator's eyes to travel with the images which remain in sharp focus); and sometimes *reverse motion* (the photographing of images with the film reversed) for recapitulative purposes.

In such scenes, tension is built through subtly choreographed *soft-focus* shots which serve to suspensefully eclipse everything except one desired plane of a shot — normally the plane where some climactic or disturbing action will occur. Suspense is also conveyed through images which suggest that something is going on in a portion of space which the audience cannot see at that point or, conversely, show the audience a source of danger or cause of impending surprise of which the pivotal character in the scene is not aware, thus emphasizing his or her vulnerability.

Close-ups are used discriminately in order to draw the viewer into the action and *extreme close-ups*, in particular, are extremely useful — mainly in the handling of facial expressions — to convey through a succinct and instantly recognizable pictorial code feelings of urgency, apprehension or solace. (A close-up of Noa's face at a climactic juncture in the first *Patlabor* feature, for example, is capable of communicating the situation's overall pathos more eloquently than an entire action sequence conceivably could.) Concurrently, *establishing* shots help the viewer form an overall picture of who is where (and perhaps also why) in a given scene, while *cutaways* are employed to isolate shots of small details, such as ornamental objects defining the style of a setting, or of movement focusing on an individual part of the body. These shots often succeed in conveying more visual information and emotional momentum than protracted stretches of dialogue ever do.

Oshii's cinematographical style also emphasizes *PoV* (point-of-view) shots which show the audience what characters perceive from particular angles (both spatial and affective) and consistently motivates such shots by supplying some premonition of what it is — or might be — that is holding the characters' attention, drawing them into the action or repelling them from it. Often, several of the elements outlined above operate in mutually sustaining ways. For instance, the artist may present us with something which a character cannot immediately see and then use a PoV shot which shows how the character is reacting to what we have already been familiarized with. In such a case, the audience's and the character's perceptions are encouraged to follow parallel trajectories — which may or may not, eventually, coalesce — instead of being forced together by a dominant authorial hand.

Oshii's approach to space gains much from the use of intrepid camera angles that depart from the customary tendency to make the camera's point of view level with the human eye and show an even horizon, and experiments instead with disorienting and mystifying perspectives. These are created by recourse to extreme *high-angle* and *low-angle* shots that capture characters and settings from above or below respectively, in preference to visually and psychologically stabilizing eye-level shots; *deep-focus* shots that allow all the distance planes of a setting to remain in equally sharp focus, and accordingly unsettle the spectator by investing disparate levels of reality at once with perplexing cogency; *oblique-angle* (or *tilt*) shots, whereby the capture of a subject by a tilted camera will make the subject itself appear slanted across a diagonal plane when the film is projected; *wide-angle* lenses that enable the camera to photograph a wider area than a normal lens would afford and hence convey the impression of an exaggerated perspective; and *zoom* lenses that permit the transition from wide-angle shots to *telephoto* shots in which the lens literally operates like a telescope, magnifying the size of objects situated at a great distance from the foreground.

Already evident in embryonic form in the vertiginous architectures proffered by *Dallos* and *Angel's Egg* and in the constellation of the oneiric ambience wherein *Beautiful Dreamer* unfolds, the techniques described above gain increasing prominence in the *Patlabor* movies, and come to literally dominate the screen in the *Ghost in the Shell* productions. The latter, moreover, maximize the overall sense of spatial dislocation by consistently resorting to *depth-of-field* effects, namely shifts of focus between the foreground and background that serve to emphasize the features of different and often contrasting portions of a scene — e.g., idyllic peacefulness and intimidating magnificence, allusions to the picturesque at its dreamiest and tamest and to the sublime at its most harrowingly awesome, baleful embodiments of a callous and exploitative technology and glimpses of a nurturing and regenerative Nature. Feelings of hesitation, apprehension, fear or grief are frequently communicated by means of *freeze-frame* shots (shots composed of a single frame repeated several times on the film strip to convey the illusion of stillness), while disorientation is often marked by *jump cuts*, namely abrupt transitions between shots.

Throughout Oshii's opus, changes in the weather and other atmospheric variations are effectively conveyed by animating the natural environment by recourse to techniques that vibrantly emphasize its vitality and dynamism, such as the *wave* and *whip* effects. These are based on two sets of drawings executed separately and then interleaved in order to evoke wobbly, quivering or shaking patterns of motion. Such pictures may consist, for instance, of a set of curves oriented from right to left interleaved with another set of curves oriented from left to right. Alternatively, they may consist of a set of drawings simulating the lines traced by a whip as it is raised and another simulating the lines traced by a whip as it descends.

One of the most instantly recognizable aspects of Oshii's cinematographical style resides with his inclination to linger on appealing images in *montages* (sequences of rapidly edited images) where no overtly significant event takes place. These images, which include recurring shots of flocks of birds and of basset hounds akin to Oshii's own (Gabriel), are not intended to contribute dynamically to a film's narrative but rather constitute underscoring pauses which allow the audience moments of reflection instead of rushing them relentlessly from one action sequence to the next. Their visual function is to effect a deliberate suspension of the text's momentum. Such sequences fully validate Roger Ebert's contention that one of the most special formal features of *animé* consists of its employment of the graphic equivalent of the *pillow words* used in Japanese poetry. As the critic explains, a pillow word "represents almost a musical beat between what went before and what comes after." Its cinematic correlative is the "pillow shot" so typical of Japanese cinema — as borne out, for example, by the films of Yasujiro Ozu. In Ebert's terms, this is a transitional, often quite unexceptional, image situated at the end of a "phase" before the next segment of the action commences. It thus functions as a kind of "punctuation," as well as "a form of silence," which is fundamentally a way of saying "let's not rush headlong from each scene to the next scene." When implemented in the specific context of animation, pillow shots invest this form with a sense of "thoughtfulness." Furthermore, insofar as the images on which they pivot are frequently "inconsequential" in plot terms, the fact that Japanese animators should be "willing to go to the trouble" of drawing and animating such moments with no less care than main sequences fully attests to their total dedication to their art (Ebert).

No less conspicuous, where cinematography is concerned, is Oshii's use of action sequences in the opening segments of his movies, often situated ahead of the opening credits. By and large, such sequences dramatize a past occurrence that will later be revealed to be axial to the film's narrative present (e.g., *Only You, Ghost in the Shell*), or else serve to introduce the viewer to an imaginary domain entirely of the director's conception (e.g., *Angel's Egg, Stray Dog*).

Oshii also handles with remarkable sensitivity the dialogical sequences of a fundamentally philosophical nature, of which one encounters a veritably cornucopian profusion throughout the director's career. Aware that their content and allusions are complex, multi-accentual and sometimes quite unpalatable, the director constellates the filmic narrative so as to ensure that those speculative dialogues are followed by slow-paced and visually lyrical sequences that afford the spectator time to take in their import and ponder their implications. Kenji Kawai's soundtracks contribute vitally to the overall effectiveness of these poetic passages through their concurrently haunting and soothing melodies. Moreover, the soundtracks are ingeniously harmonized with other sound effects, with the result that the cumulative aural ensemble plays a pivotal part in investing Oshii's movies with unmistakable cinematographical qualities. Simultaneously, acoustic effects are industriously correlated and juxtaposed with dynamic and chromatic elements, both the music and cognate sounds being repeatedly deployed in order to amplify the inscrutable lure of natural and urban settings alike.

The animation is also characterized by a keen sensitivity to the importance of combining specific types of action and movement with appropriate chromatic palettes. Thus, a peaceful and reflective mood tends to be matched by a suitably restrained, cool range of hues. By contrast, violent action sequences are customarily accompanied by aggressively hot, bright colors. Interestingly, however, the contrast between the two types of action and corresponding moods is not abrupt but emerges gradually by means of gentle color gradations, light modulations and subtle moments of transition.

Animals play a crucial part in several of Oshii's most memorable sequences, and exhaustively attest to the director's devotion to the achievement of a seamless fusion of realism and fantasy. Moreover, Oshii's approach to the representation of animal motion fully confirms Richard Williams's proposition that even though "cartoon animals" are essentially "designs, mental constructs," their effectiveness depends on the animator's commitment to the study of the "animal figure to understand its structure and movement" for the purpose not of "realism" as such but of "believability" (Williams, p. 34). Oshii's animals work convincingly precisely because of his painstaking grasp of kinesiology — the discipline devoted to the study of movement according to a body's individuating structure — and deep awareness that ultimately no amount of CGI can replace the animator's hands. Thus, even as the mouse and monitor come to play increasingly pivotal roles, enabling the production of photorealistic renders that are practically indistinguishable from reality, paper and pencils remain vitally important.

Animal motion in Oshii's films bears witness to a rigorous understanding of each body's structural pivots and resulting twists, turns, kinks and quirks. Furthermore, meticulous attention is paid to each animal's specificity — to the very factors that make it a dog, seagull or wolf, say, and cause its movements to be just as they are. Finally, Oshii's animals potently remind us that the term *animation* is etymologically rooted in the Latin *anima* — "soul," "spirit" — and that the power to animate resides exactly with the ability to instill a sense of aliveness into even the most obdurately inanimate entity.

Another pivotal aspect of Oshii's style of animation consists of his handling of facial flexibility. The films earnestly demonstrate how important it is, in the frame-by-frame orchestration of a change of expression, to stagger the modifications instead of going from A to Z, as it were, in one single transition. Facial animation in Oshii's productions exemplifies this tenet by concentrating on facial sections— eyes, nose, mouth, ears, hair — and creating frames with *overlapping* elements, securing that no stage of the change is hurried or out of synch with the overall pattern of motion. According to Williams, the overlap "gives us action *within* an action ... movement *within* a movement" (p. 222), reflecting the natural mechanisms whereby *"everything does not happen at the same time"* but some parts actually *"'drag'"* in the wake of the "main action" (p. 226). In this regard, it is most important to focus on the *follow through*, i.e., the staggering of the terminating portion of an action. Different parts of the face or body complete their parts of an action at different times and at different rates: for example, in a walk, the hip tends to lead, followed by the leg and then by the foot. As the part of the action performed by the hip is completed, other parts lag behind and move further. To have all components come to a halt simultaneously would inevitably produce an implausible pattern of motion.

Applying the principle of segmented fragmentation, it is possible for the animator to have an action work its way down or up the face, as well as capitalize on ironic contrasts by having the two halves of the face appear to convey conflicting emotions. The effects achievable by this method are aesthetically more satisfying, as well as more convincing, than any obtainable by having a character switch in the space of just two frames from a calm to an agitated state, say. For instance, to shift elegantly from a joyful smile to a cheerless expression, the animator may opt, in the transitional stages, for anything from surprise to false confidence, disappointment to revulsion, or resignation to ire. At the same time, by accommodating the possibility of capturing antagonistic moods simultaneously, segmented fragmentation allows for the communication of a graphically wider and psychologically more complex range of emotions.

Preeminently useful, as a means of evoking compelling emotions while also avoiding formulaic shifts from one expression to another, is the *elongated in-between*— an intermediate drawing between two keyframes that deliberately distorts the character's face by lengthening it unnaturally in the traveling position, so as to impart a smoother and more realistic pace to the motion. One of the forms of elongation which Oshii's animation employs most proficiently is the *zip turn*, where the transitional drawing between the image of a head facing right and that of the same head facing left is a grotesquely distorted visage incorporating elements of both of those images as well as a frontal view of the face. Equally effective is the movies' use of *over-extension* in the animation of various parts of the body. This refers to a technique whereby the drawing connecting two images of a normal-sized hand or foot, for instance, lengthens said hand or foot to an intentionally anomalous extent so as to make the movement appear more fluid and, if appropriate to the situation, even solemn.

The technique just mentioned underscores the importance of the *transitional frame* (also known as *passing position, middle position, intermediate position* or *breakdown drawing*) between any two extremes and, specifically, its profound impact on characters and actions alike. Even though, strictly speaking, this position remains unseen, any understanding of the art of animation and ability to genuinely appreciate the visible results of both facial and bodily motion will depend precisely on the ability to recognize its value. Generally, the interest generated by a sequence increases in proportion to the intensity of the sense of change effected by the transitional frame.

Segmentation is also dexterously employed in the dramatization of changes that engage not just the face but the entire body in order to limber up and add verve to a character's performance without, however, sacrificing the figure's overall solidity and stability. Once again, Oshii's films show how crucial it is, in this respect, to decide carefully where to place the passing positions between keyframes, for it is in these liminal places that a character's movement comes to life as individualized and unique, and it is here that suppleness is introduced without the character's gestural and physical consistency being compromised. To achieve this aim, the animation uses in tantalizing ways what practitioners refer to as the *breaking of joints*— namely, the deliberately exaggerated articulation of elbows, shoulders, wrists, hips, knees and ankles in order to suggest a heightened impression of flexibility. This technique enables animators to create supple and plastic bodies by effecting curvilinear motion on the basis of incremental clockwise and anticlockwise rotations of straight lines around a fulcrum (e.g., a character's elbow), rather than through the use of arcs—which would inevitably end up conveying the impression that the character is not actually lissome but *rubberized*. Walks, moreover, are used most effectively as a means of investing the characters with unique personalities and to evoke particular emotions, states of mind and proclivities.

A vital role, concurrently, is played by *accents* and *takes*. The term *accent* generally refers to the moment in a shot at which a character conveys an extreme emotion. This is not, ideally, a sudden and totally unexpected occurrence but is actually prepared for, and made part of a gradual —however brief—process. "A 'take,'" as Williams explains, "is an anticipation of an accent which then settles" (p. 285). For instance, it is possible to display the transition of a character's whole body from a feeling of mild surprise, through an anticipation suggesting bewildered disbelief, to an accent showing utter shock or alarm, which may then settle once the character has had a chance to take the scene in. The settling position is often a stationary and relatively relaxed version of the attitude displayed in the anticipation, and indeed conveys in a composed fashion what the anticipation conveyed in dynamic form.

Takes are a truly invaluable way of building up momentum, creating suspense and varying the rhythm of an action. The extent to which the manipulation of takes, anticipations and accents yields effective outcomes will depend largely on the animator's skill at delaying actions and intensifying their "vitality" by incorporating an apposite number of passing positions between extremes without, however, "overanimating" for the sake of it (p. 292). Moreover, as borne out by the *zip turn* technique discussed earlier, animators "shouldn't be afraid of distortion in the *interior* of an action. Our drawings or images may look strange, but we only really see the start and end positions. We *feel* the distortion within and that's what counts" (p. 290).

The evocation of credible movement requires great dexterity in the handling of a character's or object's *mass* within an action. All manner of both living and inanimate entities are likely to misshape as they move — e.g. by flattening if squashed or stretching if extended — and in conveying these deformations it is vital to conserve the entity's initial volume and resist the instinctive temptation to make it look smaller when squashed, say, or longer when stretched. The rendition of coherent and plausible motion is further abetted by the definition of *arcs* that clearly delineate the visual paths traced by an action over a number of frames, and by a lucid grasp of *tension*, namely the cumulative momentum that controls the pace of an action through principles of continuity or discontinuity depending on the desired effect (for example, smoothness as opposed to abruptness, a graceful flow as opposed to a staccato cadence).

The techniques described above, which Oshii's films ubiquitously deploy in order to evoke both facial and bodily flexibility by means of segmentation, distortion, elongation, fragmentation and a daring handling of mass, are instrumental to the infusion of a distinct personality into each of his characters. This is equally true of relatively caricatural types such as the monk Cherry in the *Urusei Yatsura* films and the parental figure in *Twilight Q2: Labyrinth Objects File 538*, of the naturalistically rendered adults featuring in the *Patlabor* movies and in *Jin-Roh*, and of the palpably artificial yet engrossingly sentient cyborgs of the *Ghost in the Shell* productions.

At the same time, Oshii's works potently confirm the hypothesis—central to numerous practitioners' take on their art — that the manipulation of time constitutes the truly pivotal factor among the defining traits of animation. Indeed, it is at this level of the creative process that one may fully capitalize on animation's irreverent disengagement from the laws of not only gravity and inertia but also, ultimately, logic. Animators are under no obligation whatsoever to mimic normal time. For example, they may deliberately accelerate the motion in order to evoke a frantic sense of activity or slow it down to convey feelings of dignity and ponderousness. In the timing of action sequences, specifically, Oshii consistently evinces a tendency to avoid ordinary beats and experiment instead with intentionally accentuated impressions of either celerity or sluggishness. Additionally, the films industriously juxtapose superdynamic scenes — breakneck runs, adrenaline-pumping chases and explosive climaxes — and meditative moments, including lofty panoramas of drifting cloud banks and majestic water expanses. Some of the most memorable sequences, moreover, are quite dialogue-free, thus faithfully embodying *anime*'s emphatically un–Western tendency to accord silence a vital role and hence incorporate numerous scenes that contain no human voices whatsoever.

On the technical plane, an increasingly important component of Oshii's cinematic universe resides in the deployment of numerous computer-centered tools and methodologies, including digital composition and layering, 3D rendering, morphing, particles systems, texture mapping, digital painting, ray tracing and computer-generated atmospheric effects. However, they are unflinchingly committed to the judicious integration of traditional animation and CGI, demonstrating that Japanese animation still regards pens and paintbrushes as pivotal tools of the trade. The technowizards behind the digital marvels of Oshii's films are Production I.G, the studio founded in 1987 by Mitsuhisa Ishikawa and Takayuki Gotoh and situated in the Kokubunji district of Tokyo that achieved international recognition in the wake of Oshii's *Ghost in the Shell*. Over the past fifteen years, the company has created a number of acclaimed feature films, TV series, OVAs and videogames, including — beside several of the films here examined — the movies *Neon Genesis Evangelion: Death and Rebirth* and *The End of Evangelion* (dir. Hideaki Anno, 1997), as well as *Sakura Wars: The Movie* (dir. Mitsuru Hongo, 2001) and the animated segments of *Kill Bill, Vol.1* (dir. Quentin Tarantino, 2003).

Ultimately, Oshii's works eloquently proclaim that although the animation process involves highly demanding and labor-intensive schedules (as evinced by several documentaries covering the making of Oshii's movies), the rewards it yields are considerable. As Jenny Roche points out, "the visual challenges of animation are immense," yet the freedoms it affords are potentially limitless for "there is no set which is too expensive or exotic;

there is no stunt which is too difficult ... the scientific laws of physics, biology and chemistry are no restriction either" (Roche, pp. 137–8). The joy of animation lies precisely in its flouting of the conventions and expectations of mimetic art.

Animation is famously divorced from the aesthetic and ideological demands of mimetic realism. Indeed, it has a unique adeptness at creating its own worlds instead of passively recording existing ones. Moreover, it often accomplishes this tantalizing task by recourse to strategies that enable characters to emote much more expansively than is commonly the case with live-action cinema. In Oshii's domain, this is most true of animals, insofar as these creatures are invested with a much greater — and ultimately even more convincing — acting potential than real ones ever could be. Animation, therefore, could be said to shun the restraints of realism as a representational agenda not in order to escape reality but rather to supply a metadiscourse, a series of critical reflections upon realism and reality alike. As Paul Wells points out, in this respect, "[a]nimation ... prioritizes its capacity to resist 'realism' as a mode of representation and uses its various techniques to create numerous styles which are fundamentally *about* 'realism'" (Wells, p. 25; emphasis added).

This salient feature of the medium of animation deserves special attention in the present context since both animé generally and Oshii's cinema specifically tend to take the suspension of realism — at least in the sense accorded to this term within Western cultures— to arguably unparalleled and undeniably compelling extremes. Oshii's films emphatically remind us that neither images nor propositions nor thoughts represent reality intrinsically: as Ludwig Wittgenstein once remarked, a picture of a man walking uphill could also be a picture of a man sliding backwards downhill (Wittgenstein). Nothing inherent in the picture *per se* makes either reading more valid than the other. Hence, a representation is only *capable of representing* to the extent that it is available for interpretation, and can ultimately be said to depict absolutely anything which it has the power to evoke or even merely intimate — that is to say, it carries an indefinite repertoire of potential representational messages. The concept of representation, moreover, is inextricably intertwined with that of repetition insofar as both verbal and non-verbal signs are representations which only manage to garner certain meanings insofar as they may be recursively deployed, literally *re*-presented.

These ideas have been increasingly advocated, in recent years, by numerous visual artists and fiction writers, historians and geographers, linguists and anthropologists, sociologists and psychologists, filmmakers and designers, eager to emphasize the ubiquitous feelings of uncertainty and unease that promiscuously consort with our perception of things and, concomitantly, with our orchestration of what we perceive in the guise of visual or verbal texts. Within this world view, so-called reality cannot be represented accurately and neutrally for the reason that it is not a fact but rather an effect of how it is experienced from disparate perspectives. The real as such is arguably unattainable beyond the mediating agency of texts, images and stories and these, in turn, never mirror reality transparently and objectively but actually represent it according to the codes and conventions of particular cultures. By and large, these principles are so deeply embedded in a society's fabric that their constructed and fundamentally arbitrary status is no longer recognized, and they are therefore adopted as though they were natural tools rather than the products of context-bound ideological deliberations.

The representations conceived through the deployment of those codes and conventions are accordingly naturalized as their status as constructs is squarely effaced. In the vast majority of Western cultures, the process of naturalization has been assiduously sustained by the logic of realism as the dominant philosophy of representation. Indeed, realist techniques ensconce the process of construction of an image or text so as to lure us into unproblematically accepting that representations simply reflect the world, that they provide a keyhole view on a solid and consistent reality shared and recognized by each single member of the same culture. Representations thus serve to bolster the distinctive ideologies concocted by that culture in order to assert its legitimacy and regiment its subjects in the name of ideological stability.

The cardinal message conveyed by the realist ethos is that reality is immutable, for negating the notion that something has been made in the first place amounts to denying that it could ever be *un*made. Norman Bryson terms this stance the "natural attitude": a suppression of "history," of the possibility of change, and of the specific cultural milieus within which representations are created and consumed which can only be challenged once "the real" is "understood not as a transcendent and immutable given, but as a production brought about by human activity working within specific cultural constraints" (Bryson, p. 5). Simultaneously, it is necessary to question the assumption that "visual experience" is "universal and transhistorical" (p. 10), for the ways in which we receive and perceive representations are no less historically contingent than the representations themselves. A recognition of the immanently cultural and social character of all representations, therefore, also implies an acknowledgment of the viewing subject's own cultural situation.

The positions outlined above hopefully demonstrate the validity of the postulate that realism is not an innocent representational mode but an ideologically determined and culture-bound phenomenon. When applied specifically to the sphere of animation, this contention is confirmed by the fact that this art form is not intrinsically espoused to the realist ethos. In fact, realism came to be regarded as animation's primary aim in a very specific time and place, and for particular cultural reasons—namely, as a consequence of Disney's endeavor, from the 1930s onwards, to attract large audiences to animated movies by competing directly with live-action cinema. To achieve this aim, Disney Studios sought to emulate as faithfully as possible the three-dimensional solidity instinctively associated by spectators with live-action productions, striving to choreograph deep-focus effects in the rendition of space, to paint backgrounds that would resemble film mattes (in contrast with the panel-like look of comic strips) and to exhibit the characters' exposure to the impact of gravity with often spectacular results. (This approach was in sharp contrast with the New York Style dominant in the 1920s, epitomized by Otto Messmer's *Felix the Cat*.) Hollywood's idolization of realism does not, however, make it a universally treasured goal: as observed earlier, it is by no means as pivotal to Japanese aesthetics as it is to the West, and Oshii's cinema fully exemplifies this culturally individuating factor.

Finally, all the technical and stylistic components discussed in the preceding paragraphs are instrumental to the overarching imperative of the *mise-en-scène*, namely, the means by which the director communicates his vision through performance, lighting, setting, costume and camera placement; the *mise-en-cadre*, namely, the organization of various elements within any one frame; and, more generally, what David Bordwell terms the *staging*: that is to say, "a perspectival projection of space" through which the director "can guide our attention across a complex visual field, play hide-and-seek with our expectations, summon up expressive qualities like delicacy or dynamism, and participate in a broader narrative patterning" (Bordwell, p. 16). Throughout Oshii's output, the director's staging strategies evince a marked predilection for temporal distension, structural repetition, long takes, the subtle alternation of harmony and dissonance, and sustained tracking shots and cut-ins that enable him to orchestrate unique poetic patterns of visuality by means of spatial, compositional and chromatic rhymes and rhythms of arresting vigor.

Part Two

OSHII AND THE CARNIVALESQUE

What is suspended [in carnival] first of all is hierarchical structure and all the forms of terror, reverence, piety, and etiquette connected with it.... During that moment the normal constraints and conventions of the everyday world are thrown off ... commoner and aristocrat rub shoulders in the marketplace and all social distinctions are erased.... The fool reigns.... Essentially, the carnivalesque ... aims at social change by uncovering the truth about the emperor's new clothes: the difference between king and peasant is arbitrary, relative, and merely an accepted convention. But, of course, in reality, such conventions of difference are enforced with a variety of powerful means, from public opinion to actual weapons, which often make the egalitarian urge at the core of the carnival nothing more than an idle daydream. Nevertheless every representation produced by the carnival spirit shows traces of the utopian ideal of a democratic society that lies at the heart of the urge to ridicule authority, even when literally no chance of unseating such authority exists.
— *Tom Sobshack*

... false beliefs and superstitions are rejected by the critical side of the SF [science fiction] intellect, but on the other side SF writers and fans are attracted to magic because it presupposes as yet unknown and unpredictable changes in our reality system.
— *Casey Fredericks, p. 153*

5

Concepts of the Carnival

The term carnival generally designates a topsy-turvy world wherein everyday rules and norms are more or less flamboyantly transgressed, yet the notion of order is not entirely obliterated insofar as the transgression is itself calendarized and hence societally sanctioned. The world of *Urusei Yatsura* may be described as carnivalesque on two counts: as a literal dramatization of varyingly extravagant festivals, parties and revelries, and as a metaphorical reflection upon the elusiveness of the boundaries separating the real from the dream, responsibility from escapism, duty from indulgence in the Pleasure Principle.

Oshii's constellation of the carnivalesque echoes Mikhail Bakhtin's theories on the subject as advocated in *Rabelais and His World* and *Problems of Dostoevsky's Poetics*. For Bakhtin, the carnival is not just an event within the domain of folklore but actually an elaborate textual formation whose language and rhetoric are informed by the interrelated discourses of corporeality, the burlesque and collective sentiment. Thus, the carnivalesque does not merely manifest itself at the level of ritual spectacles such as pageants, masquerades, fairground curiosities and street theatre but also at the level of disparate linguistic constructs—for instance, humorous verbal compositions such as satires, parodies and pastiches, popular oaths, curses, proverbs and blazons—and, by extension, the witty repertoires and word games to be habitually found in both stage-based and screen-based comedic forms. Concurrently, the carnivalesque erodes conventional hierarchies and attendants notions of propriety by encouraging interactions among people who would normally operate in quite distinct sectors of society. This breakdown of etiquette is paralleled by flamboyant misalliances that afford scope for the coalescence of the sublime and the ridiculous, the sacred and the profane, the lofty and the humble, the wise and the droll.

These suspensions of honored behavioral codes no doubt constitute something of a debasement of a culture's dominant values, yet it must be stressed that they occur at agreed times and in agreed locations and do not, therefore, belong in the league of anarchically random perversions of the norm. In other words, they represent ritualized forms of participation in disruptive acts which may ultimately contribute to the legitimation and consolidation of the status quo. It is by allowing temporary suspensions of order that the system most effectively asserts its stability, permanence and invulnerability to transgressive forces. Moreover, whenever the value of an exalted object or concept is debunked within the logic of a planned event, one is concomitantly reminded of its privileged status by its ability not merely to tolerate profanation but also to survive it unscathed. At the same time, the carnival serves to bolster an overarching sense of continuity, even as it appears to foster discontinuity, by evoking the enduring rhythms of existence: primarily, the recurrence of life-and-death cycles, the alternation of the seasons and even the human body's recurrent functions, down to their most blatantly scatological.

Ambivalence is pivotal to the carnival: what is permitted inside its boundaries is licensed only insofar as it is couched in ludic terms. Nevertheless, there is something indubitably refreshing about the carnival, and this resides, ultimately, with its status as a discursive challenge to ideologies that thrive on the valorization of sealed systems of belief and conclusive outcomes. By contrast, the carnival celebrates becoming, renewal and ongoing metamorphosis, thereby shunning any crystallized notion of finitude or immutability. Grotesque imagery consistently reinforces this disruptive thrust by mocking the authority of balanced, polished and rational forms of expression and performance through the foregrounding of visual signifiers of both physical and psychological dislocation.

In assessing Oshii's articulation of these ideas in the *Urusei Yatsura* universe, it is noteworthy that emphasis is persistently placed on the notion of the carnivalesque as a complex textual construct — not simply a matter of festivities and parties, even though these play an undoubtedly axial and highly entertaining dramatic role. Especially memorable, in this context, are the sumptuous (and repeatedly aborted) nuptials depicted in *Only You*; the annual school festival, the fireworks parties and ritual summertime events pivotal to *Beautiful Dreamer*'s plot; and the majestically staged *hanami* (blossom-viewing party), costumed pageant, and ceremonial journey to the underworld presented in *Lum the Forever*. This is fully borne out, as argued in depth in a subsequent section, by the structural sophistication and gamesome handling of multiple twists and turns evinced by *Beautiful Dreamer*'s prismatic plot. The post-Oshii feature *Lum the Forever* will embrace this stylistic approach and deliver a no less unsettling storyline. By contrast, and in consonance with its generally less seasoned outlook, *Only You* gives precedence to the content level of carnivalesque occurrences over the formal subversion of diegetic logic. This is fully evinced by its keenness on comedically exaggerated ceremonial spectacles. In all three films, significantly, conventional hierarchies are flagrantly flouted as unorthodox collusions of the grand and the bizarre come into play.

The concept of order is not totally suspended, insofar as both the visual and the discursive forays into the carnivalesque offered by the *Urusei Yatsura* films are somewhat sanctioned by the particular societal context in which they take place, and the characters, accordingly, are ongoingly restrained by specific codes of conduct. Thus, even when logic appears to have forsaken their worlds altogether — most portentously in *Beautiful Dreamer*— they react to their predicaments by assuming subject positions that are ultimately congruous with their basic roles within the *Urusei Yatsura* realm. Furthermore, the disruptions they experience are eventually contained by their location within an intelligible, though possibly perverted, structure of meaning: a lie in *Only You*, a nightmare in *Beautiful Dreamer*, a myth in *Lum the Forever*. However, the carnival's invigorating displacement of rigid ideologies is ultimately kept alive by the films' varyingly radical erosions of traditional reality markers, and related inauguration of scenarios of potentially unlimited change which no recuperative gesture may reliably control. As a result, audiences are invited to ponder the affective implications of *any* temporary suspension of the real — both within and outside the auditorium — and the potentially energizing import of their own exposure to imaginary obfuscations of the empirically verifiable of precisely the kind to be consistently encountered in Oshii's cinema in its entirety.

From a sociological point of view, the carnival could be seen as a predecessor of the modern holiday culture, even though the unbridled explosions in which folk humor was capable of indulging from Roman times through the Middle Ages to the Renaissance were doubtlessly well in excess of today's average manifestations of calendarized fun. Indeed, nowadays the carnivalesque spirit appears to have been watered down and rendered virtually anodyne by its chemical dispersion through the entire cocktail that constitutes, cumulatively, the so-called *experiential* or *adventure* society. Following the sociologist Gerhard Schulze, Regina Dahmen-Ingenhoven has described this type of societal organization as a structure "subject to a kind of experiential imperative. To be deemed contemporary, you must experience something. Those who do not experience anything have only themselves to blame."

The willingness and ability to experience are hence considered absolutely vital attributes in contemporary postindustrial cultures, and the failure to do so is automatically stigmatized as a severely disabling defect. It is therefore important, in the logic of Dahmen-Ingenhoven's argument, to invest buildings with an eminently interactive character. While this feature of today's architecture is especially salient in the context of edifices designed for the purposes of leisure (e.g., theme parks, amusement parks, sports centers, restaurants), it is becoming increasingly evident in quite different types of buildings, too: for example, museums, banks, shopping malls and airport lounges. The common objective of all these various architectural formations is to stimulate their users and visitors, create a stirring atmosphere, and thus elicit a sense of adventure — in other words, to animate them. The formal language and expressive registers of comics and animation is accordingly applied to the articulation of contemporary architectural registers. Animation, in this context, refers to an extra dimension, an element of excess over normal discourse, and is hence considered an ideal tool in the capture and fuelling of heightened emotive responses: "[a]nimation has infiltrated everyday life and has left its mark on architecture in a manner that is no longer marginal.... Today, everything and everyone is exposed to animation and there is no escape: a bank is no longer a bank but an experiential finance department store. The same is true of train stations and airports, which have long since ceased to be mere sites of travel" (Dahmen-Ingenhoven, p. 12).

The prototype of the kind of animated space theorized by Dahmen-Ingenhoven is, without a shadow of doubt, Disneyland. Walt Disney understood from the early planning stages of his seminal project that to summon up an authentically adventure-driven atmosphere, he must rely on people that were fully conversant with the theoretical principles and pictorial discourse of animation: "[Y]ou know," he once said, "the only way I've found to make these places is with animators— you can't seem to do it with accountants and bookkeepers" (quoted in Dahmen-Ingenhoven, p. 90).

Dahmen-Ingenhoven's hypotheses are particularly relevant to the context of this discussion as a felicitous marriage of the logic of the carnival and the art of animation. Specifically, Oshii's representations of festivities, ritual ceremonies and the spaces wherein these unfold could be said to incarnate those propositions by simultaneously dramatizing the carnivalesque spirit on the thematic level, and experimenting with the language of *animé* on the technical level.[1] In constellating his carnivalesque locations, Oshii congenially turns the technical ingredients of animation into reality, deploying most forcibly those animational techniques (here described in the introductory chapter) that thrive on exaggeration, distortion, disorientation, over-extension and even grotesque deformation. In both *Only You* and *Beautiful Dreamer*, these traits are most evident in scenes that depict disconcerting transitions from familiar pockets of quotidian life to the futuristic cityscapes of distant galaxies, and from a relatively well-groomed suburban architecture to dystopian scenarios of chaos and decay.

Thus, the *Urusei Yatsura* productions encapsulate the proclivity to invest buildings with carnivalesque energy but not exactly in the vein theorized by Dahmen-Ingenhoven. While the spaces described by the critic domesticate the notion of entertainment by containing it within seemingly carefree but also thoroughly regimented structures, the *Urusei Yatsura* stories take quite a different course of action. Locations such as the playground in *Only You*, the everyday streets and edifices in *Beautiful Dreamer*, or the shopping mall in *Lum the Forever* are carnivalesque by virtue not of their proclivity to package "adventure" for uncritical consumption by their users but rather of their flair for transmuting familiar urban settings into deeply unsettling social milieus. Moreover, the seemingly most solid and stable architectural structures—such as the Tomobiki High School in *Beautiful Dreamer* and Mendou's family mansion in *Lum the Forever*—are prey to profoundly displacing metamorphoses whereby both depth and height tend to disintegrate into a vertiginous proliferation of intricate mazes, fathomless shafts and optical tricks.

After a panoramic survey of *Urusei Yatsura*'s origins in the culture of manga and its initial life as a TV series, the sections that follow examine Oshii's *Only You* and *Beautiful Dreamer* with reference to the articulation of the carnivalesque in concurrently spatio-temporal and psychological terms.

6

Urusei Yatsura:
The TV Series

Urusei Yatsura[1] began life as a manga by Rumiko Takahashi.[2] *Urusei Yatsura* was Takahashi's first series and in many ways set in place graphic and narrative elements destined to become central to her stylistic cachet — principally, the collusion of romance, comedy and detailed characterization methods. Making its debut in 1978, the manga instantly asserted itself as a sensational success, earning its creator the prestigious publisher Shogakukan's Best New Artist Award. While Takahashi, as yet somewhat inexperienced at the mere age of twenty-one, could only manage sporadic production in her salad days, by 1980, *Urusei Yatsura* had become a serialized weekly comic in *Shounen Sunday*— a weekly comic anthology of phonebook proportions issued by Shogakukan that is unequivocally considered one of the giants in manga publishing. It there reigned unchallenged until 1987, when Takahashi decided to draw the series to an end. *Shounen Sunday* featured fifteen-page *Urusei Yatsura* episodes drawn almost exclusively in black and white, as is customarily the case with manga, but occasionally contained a few introductory pages in color designed to lure the reader into the flow of the narrative.

Like other very successful series, the *Urusei Yatsura* comic was also released in the form of *tankoban* (graphic novels) including clusters of sequential chapters from the weekly serialization. A novel-size paperback, the *tankoban* would compile eleven weekly installments into a single volume. By the end of the series, *Urusei Yatsura* had been collected into thirty-four volumes, amounting to about six thousand pages of strips. In the early 1990s, to mark the manga's tenth anniversary, the *tankoban* was superseded by the *wideban* (wide edition) format, consisting of volumes that contained twenty-five installments each, eventually leading to a total of fifteen volumes. About ten years later, the enduring popularity of the series led to the publication of Takahashi's stories in the *bunkoban* (pocket edition) format. To satisfy the requirements of the more casual ranks of manga readers, the episodes were also made available as cheap *My First Big* editions for sale in general bookstores.

Urusei Yatsura was published in North America by Viz — a subsidiary of Shogakukan — from 1989 in the guise of monthly releases in translation, with each issue incorporating two stories. After a hiatus of a few years, *Urusei Yatsura* was later serialized in Viz's *Animerica* magazine under the title of *The Return of Lum* up until 1998. *Urusei Yatsura* has also been translated into Italian, Spanish and Cantonese. Its fan base has been persistently strong worldwide and the range of ancillary merchandise which it has spawned constitutes a paradigmatic example of contemporary media synergy across the globe. (This point will be returned to in the assessment of *Urusei Yatsura*'s evolution beyond Oshii's involvement in the franchise in the context of Chapter 9.)

This brief survey of the manga's publishing history explicitly demonstrates *Urusei Yatsura*'s enduring popularity, and it would indeed be fair to state that the series is one of the most passionately cherished *animé* creations of all times, and not exclusively on home turf. This is primarily a result of Takahashi's unique style as an inspired fusion of the mellow and the vigorous and, relatedly, of her ability to capitalize on graphic minimalism yet also to deliver highly detailed and mimetically accurate designs ranging from cartoonish exaggeration to pictorial realism.

Animationally, *Urusei Yatsura* came into being as a TV series developed by Kitty Animation, based on Takahashi's exceptionally popular manga. The series debuted on 14 October 1981 and instantly became a record-breaking success held by many to have altered the very face of *animé*. Indeed, in acknowledging *Urusei Yatsura*'s popularity, it is also important to pay homage to its originality. As Makosuke (Marc Marshall) has pointed out,

> [m]any of its plot devices (gender bending, multiple girls after the same worthless guy, weirdoes from outer space ...) have become *animé* staples, but you might remind yourself as you're watching it that in many cases they're classic *because* of *Urusei Yatsura*. It's the originator of so many *animé* clichés that I have to wonder what *animé* today would've looked like without it for inspiration. That alone makes it a seminal work the likes of which few things outside of Tezuka's little robot can boast of [Makosuke].

Urusei Yatsura is certainly one of the most irreverently carnivalesque and exuberantly bizarre animated realms ever ideated either within or outside Japan. While employing an adventurously barmy and even ribald tone, generous doses of slapstick, whimsically edgy comedy and overtly ludicrous situations, it is also capable of yielding lovable and psychologically credible characters — in spite of their physiognomic preposterousness and warped identities — and a pervasive sense of dramatic empathy, rendered by recourse to a subtle oscillation between unblemished radiance and dusky chagrin in the depiction of the protagonists' facial expressions and body language alike.

Furthermore, the series derives considerable verve and wit from its audacious proclivity to parody all manner of established genres and cinematographical conventions, as well as countless aspects of ancient mythology and
contemporary pop culture alike.

The contributions to the show made specifically by Oshii and by the
talented Studio Pierrot team played a vital part in helping *Urusei Yatsura*
transcend the farcical style adopted by the parent manga and become a
unique world in its own right. To begin with, each show comprised two
12-minute episodes aired back to back, which imparted a somewhat frantic rhythm to the viewing experience as a whole. The format was soon
modified to one single half-hour episode, which enabled the creators to
concentrate to a greater degree on plot development and imbue the action
with a more varied and dramatic mood. Greater prominence was concomitantly accorded to originally peripheral characters. The early episodes
evinced a deliberately childlike style, marked by bright colors, cute characters, bouncy tunes and altogether simple animation. Yet, they contained
sophisticated humor and elaborate scripts, and were therefore able to appeal
extensively to both kids and grown-ups.

Oshii aimed at enhancing this serious— or at least semi-serious—
dimension of the show and hence at developing a more mature animation
style. In the process, graphic and thematic elements destined to become key
parts of the director's unique signature over the following two decades
began to emerge. While Oshii may have overstepped the limits of what
could be considered thematically and conceptually acceptable as an adaptation of a fundamentally comedic universe, the endeavor to polish up *Urusei Yatsura* continued beyond the director's involvement with the venture,
and his legacy can indeed be detected in subsequent productions, most
notably the feature film *Lum the Forever* (dir. Kazuo Yamazaki, 1986).

In the TV series, the story arc as a whole deals with the adventures of
a group of teenagers based in Tomobiki-cho (Tomobiki Town), a fictional
district in the Nerima ward of Tokyo, alternately depicted as a semirealis-
tic urbanscape and a preposterously surreal habitat. The town is named
after *Tomobiki*, a day in the complex lunar calendar used in Japan until the
nineteenth century the literal meaning of which may be translated as "taking along friends." People are discouraged from holding funeral services
on this particular day in the belief that the concept of "taking along friends"
will cause another such ceremony to be necessary in the very near future.
This superstition is relevant to the world of *Urusei Yatsura* insofar as no
peculiar or menacing event that takes place in Tomobiki-cho is ever an isolated incident, and whenever a character is caught up in some mishap, many
more members of the cast are inexorably swept along in its wake. In articulating this idea, the series also harks back to the principle of interconnect-

edness, pivotal to both Buddhism and Shinto, according to which no natural (or indeed supernatural) occurrence can ultimately be extricated from a far-reaching web of seemingly discrete phenomena.

The story's premise is laid out in the first episode, where a young man named Ataru Moroboshi — who is famed for his unquenchable lecherousness and preposterously bad luck[3] — is charged with the task of saving the Earth by competing in a game of tag with the alien beauty Lum, a princess of the Oni endowed with supernatural powers, tiger-skin underwear, horns and a capricious temper that frequently results in the emission of mighty electrical waves. Ataru may only beat Lum by touching her horns — an ostensibly unattainable goal which he eventually achieves by causing the princess's bikini top to drop through a dirty trick, and thus leaving her momentarily exposed and vulnerable.

Although Ataru's accomplishment removes the danger looming over the Earth, it does not put an end to the hapless character's personal ordeals. Indeed, he has gained the motivation to take the game seriously after a series of spectacular defeats only because his longsuffering girlfriend Shinobu has promised she will marry him if he wins. But when, having vanquished Lum, Ataru proudly declares, "Now I can get married," a momentous interplanetary misunderstanding ensues: the Oni princess takes his words as a proposal addressed to her very self. Despite his eagerness, at first, to cop a feel off an extraterrestrial bimbo, the fickle Ataru has by now lost all interest in Lum, even though she is madly, inexplicably and irrevocably besotted with her human "Darling." Ataru's recalcitrance springs simply from the fact that accepting Lum as his future bride would undesirably curtail his amorous exploits. However, as an interim arrangement, Lum goes to live with Ataru and his parents, attends his high-school lessons, endlessly plans their wedding, and punishes him by means of electric shocks whenever his lascivious nature comes to her attention. Such happenings by no means exhaust the spectrum of the ill-fated boy's misadventures, for he is also at the receiving end of his human sweetheart's ire due to his inordinate hormonal drives, resented by school-mates who fancy Lum for themselves, and is shunned by his parents. Thus, amid the farce, one can clearly sense a potentially serious undercurrent cursing through Takahashi's story right from the start of the series.

After the TV series had ended, 11 Original Video Animations were made. The first of these was arguably the only noteworthy contribution to the *Urusei Yatsura* universe. Titled "Inaba the Dream Maker," the first OVA delivers a delectably moving tale in which Lum, Shinobu and Ataru catch glimpses of their plausible destinies, and the intriguing character of Inaba is introduced as a potential romantic interest for Shinobu. The remaining productions are essentially the equivalent of additional TV episodes and though they are undeniably entertaining, they do not quite live up to the standards set by first one.

Beside Lum, Ataru and Shinobu, *Urusei Yatsura* contains a vast and varied gallery of supporting characters, the dizzying diversity of which is hardly attenuated by the one crucial factor they all share — namely, a flamboyantly carnivalesque weirdness. At the same time, however, the characters are rendered markedly convincing by their multi-facetedness and resolute avoidance of any clear-cut segregation of heroes and villains. All cast members ultimately harbor contrasting dispositions— and therefore behave with realistic inconsistency — as they forge on amid spiraling conflicts, grudges, animosities and misunderstandings. One of the most refreshing aspects of *Urusei Yatsura*'s main players is their ingrained childlikeness, a trait that makes them unrelentingly inquisitive, passionate and, by and large, guileless. Takahashi treasures the concept of innocence throughout her oeuvre and indeed uses the image of a baby chick as a visual refrain to symbolize that state. Interestingly, her own given name encapsulates the idea of an everlasting childhood since it consists of the *kanji Ru* (to stay), *Mi* (beautiful) and *Ko* (child).

The series steadfastly celebrates the undimming hopefulness of a more lively and less callous world, yet often hints at the perils inherent in its characters' reluctance to grow up, portraying this as potentially synonymous with immaturity and irresponsibility. In so doing, it captures the duplicity inherent in the carnival itself: indeed, like the latter, it rejoices in the suspension of the Reality Principle but simultaneously reminds us that the assumption of codified adult mentalities and related subject positions is finally an inescapable fate.

Makosuke's comments on the series' characters are especially useful in highlighting one further facet of the *Urusei Yatsura* world to which the stories owe much of their uniqueness:

> After 30 or 40 episodes ... the series gets into its groove, taking on an everyday air that other *animé* rarely has the length and depth to make work as effectively. The small group of high school friends are involved in sufficiently wacky escapades, but they really do feel like a group of friends despite their bizarre backgrounds.... Of particular visual note is the everydayness of Lum; although she can and almost always does fly or hover around, it's portrayed in a natural-seeming way that makes it feel sort of normal. Lum also makes for a bit of an ongoing fashion show, with all manner of interesting outfits appropriate to the setting. When you put the two together, you pretty much get what makes the whole series so much fun: a green-haired girl with horns, dressed in hiking gear or a school uniform, hovering around her boyfriend ... and it just seems entirely natural [Makosuke].

The sense of naturalness exuded by the character of Lum springs largely from the fact that in spite of her preternatural powers and possession of advanced technological wonders such as time-traveling machines, shrinking beams, cloning guns and contraptions capable of providing portals to alternative dimensions, she is paradoxically humanized, rather than dehumanized, by her otherness. Indeed, her not-at-homeness on Earth is recurrently alluded to, even as she appears to fit in smoothly with Tomobiki-cho's quotidian merry-go-round, by her naive responses to the host planet's customs, mores and, above all, language. Not only do Lum's speech patterns abide by the grammatical and syntactical rules of an outlandish dialect, she is also frequently perplexed by her friends' use of words, with frequently momentous repercussions (as in the case of the aforementioned first episode). This aspect of *Urusei Yatsura*'s universe would seem to corroborate the proposition that subjectivity is molded primarily by language and by the structures of thought and behavior to which verbal signs arbitrarily assign meaning. Ironically, and in full consonance with Takahashi's subtle humor, Lum's diction also evinces the traits of an actual and contemporary discursive trend: namely, the employment of a saccharine mode of delivery normally associated with real Japanese girls struggling to sound cute.

It should also be noted that the identities of several of the *Urusei Yatsura* characters are consistently defined with reference to aspects of Japanese tradition, mythology, religion and lore. Thus, though sensitively normalized and hence rendered appealing to today's audiences, they nonetheless strike their roots in time-honored legends. This strategy bears witness to what could be regarded as a cardinal feature of Japan's prismatic culture, whereby the incorporation of global trends and the country's attendant modernization have never quite erased the ancestral vestiges of narrativity's imbrication with the past — with an inveterate and even nostalgic fascination with the "Once-Upon-a-Time" (*Mukashi Mukashi*) attitude to storytelling.

Parodic references to religion abound, mainly by virtue of the creepy Buddhist monk Sakuranbo (obsessed with being addressed as "Cherry") and his penchant for portentous predictions and dark omens. A more positive character also associated with religion is the highly talented Shinto priestess Sakura, Cherry's niece but by no means his ally. Stunningly beautiful in an imposing yet never haughty way, Sakura also serves, in a twist of logic typical of the *Urusei Yatsura* world, as the high school's patient and resourceful nurse. Ancient Chinese mythology and popular culture meet and merge in a curiously harmonious fashion in the supporting character of Benten, an extra-terrestrial motorbike punk babe who is also loosely based on the Chinese Goddess of Luck. Another dramatis persona closely connected with ancient lore is Kurama, the princess of the *Karasutengu* (Crow Goblin), powerful mountain spirits featuring in numerous tales of old. Oyuki, the graceful Queen of Neptune, is likewise associated with a vintage piece of mythology that harks back to the Legend of the *Yuki-Onna* (Snow Woman), an ostensibly ethereal and placid beauty endowed with the power to breathe mortally frosty air onto unsuspecting humans.

Most important, within *Urusei Yatsura*'s mythical infrastructure, is the presence of the Oni, Lum's race. Although there are instances of non-aggressive, genial and even protective Oni in Japanese tradition, it is common to regard these creatures as malevolent figures.[4] Some old texts indicate that the term *Oni* refers to all sorts of demons and specters, while others propose that people who specifically died as a result of famines and epidemics, as well as wronged women driven by jealous rage, were the most likely to turn into Oni. The majority of Japanese legends and folktales, however, tend to posit the Oni as exceptionally strong, ferocious and hideous monsters endowed with horns and fangs and only clad in tiger hides, capable of undoing at will the very fabric of humanity. Takahashi's manga adopts the central ingredients of this popular version of the Oni, considered by most scholars to be a relatively recent development within Japanese lore. However, she felicitously morphs the vestigial demon image into something veritably rich and strange, through the infusion into the mythological frame of reference of numerous elements associated with sci-fi extra-terrestrials and other cherished stereotypes of action-adventure cinema.

7

Urusei Yatsura
Movie 1: Only You

The huge success enjoyed by the TV series led to the production of six feature-length movies, of which Oshii directed the first two: *Only You* and *Beautiful Dreamer*. In the first film, Ataru is required to marry the alien Elle due to his stepping on her shadow in the course of yet another fateful game of tag played in early childhood (in Elle's culture, such an act is regarded as a marriage proposal), and the rest of the plot concerns Lum's endeavor to prevent the union. Some of the film's most memorable sequences are the transportation of Ataru and his high-school mates to an exotic planet against a full-blown space-opera setting; the brief idyll which Ataru enjoys with Elle in her palace before discovering her true predatory nature; and Lum's initiatives to abort the nuptials, including breakneck chases and mock-heroic battles conducted with genuinely carnivalesque fervor. Clownish overacting and consistent forays into the phantasmagoric realms of both literal and metaphorical masquerades fittingly garnish the carnival-flavored fare. No less striking, however, is the prologue (to be returned to later in this section) in which the children playing tag are portrayed in simple silhouette and by recourse to an effectively minimalistic chromatic palette.

As the plot takes the characters back and forth in time, from their provincial suburb into the galaxy's far reaches and back again, the animation is consistently characterized by remarkable fluidity, detailed design and energizing vitality. Fluid transitions are especially remarkable, most notably in the articulation of Lum's frequent shifts from regular human motion to flight and vice versa —for instance, in the film's first sequence, where she and Ataru walk to school amid droning gossip about the mysterious Elle. The animation concurrently evinces a typically Oshiian fascination with meticulously executed mechanical designs for the film's myriad vehicles and gadgets, as well as a nascent tendency to use reflections as a means of conveying a variety of psychological and emotional states. For example, the specular play between Lum's face and its reflection in the window of the café where she sits, lonely and dejected, after Ataru's desertion serves to communicate both succinctly and effectively the character's inner sense of displacement. (It is noteworthy, incidentally, that the venue is named Pierrot, presumably in homage to Oshii's animation studio at the time.) Later in the film, Ataru's and Elle's reflections in the pond adorning Elle's sumptuous garden allude to the conventional meaning of the mirror image as an icon of deception as a means of elliptically commenting on the two characters' duplicitous natures and hidden agendas.

By the time *Only You* was released, *Urusei Yatsura*'s alien heroine already enjoyed a strong following in Japan as a result of the tremendous popularity surrounding both the parent manga and the TV series. Thus, Oshii had to confront the problem — analogous to the one faced by directors involved in feature-length adaptations of comics and graphic novels such as the *X-Men*, *Sin City* and, of course, *Superman*, *Spiderman* and *Batman*, to mention but a few — of having to incorporate the conventions put in place by his source materials, which established fans would expect to find and warmly respond to, and yet develop an independently compelling narrative for everyone to savor. *Only You* succeeds in accomplishing precisely such a balancing act by integrating supporting characters that fans would love to behold on the big screen without these figures becoming so central, however, as to make their roles impenetrable for the uninitiated, and maintaining the focus primarily on Lum and Ataru.

Only You's aforementioned opening sequence is one of the most intriguing animational experiments in Oshii's entire oeuvre: the setting's details, including the paths and steps traced by the child versions of Ataru and Elle in the game of shadow tag, do not preexist the characters but actually materialize and dissolve in accordance with the patterns of their movements through space. Such a space, importantly, is intensely abstract and yet characteristically Eastern and specifically Japanese due to its chromatic composition. White and red (the colors of the Japanese flag) predominate, while yellow (a hue deemed symbolic of life and energy, or *ki*) is used for several of the principal architectural elements, and a touch of blossom-pink (again a color readily associated with Japan) is introduced for the image of the rose petal (a metonym for the female child's romantic prospects) floating against a charmingly simple black-and-white landscape redolent of the graphic style immortalized by the indigenous *ukiyio-e*. The scene displaying the receding spaceship taking Elle back to her native planet evinces the traits of a gigantic, sculpturally detailed floral motif that also echoes traditional Eastern iconography.

As the film proper begins, the pivotal theme is instantly introduced: Ataru is to marry Elle — a figure nobody, Ataru included, knows anything about. Mistrusted by his mates, Ataru is subjected to torture in the guise of intolerable tickling, and further exposed to both the rage of his human sweetheart Shinobu and massive electric treatment at the hands of Lum — the latter being conducive to the near disintegration of the clocktower wherein Ataru's ordeal is taking place and to the attendant metaphorical suspension of time. (This motif will gain novel, and more sinister, relevance in *Beautiful Dreamer* by recourse to the very same architectural fixture.) The fracas is brought to an end by a portentous magnetic storm and concomitant appearance of an alien ship from Planet Elle meant to convey Ataru to his betrothed. This sequence is undoubtedly one of the most striking in the whole movie: varied palettes and chromatic contrasts matched by an appositely inspired soundtrack evoke an atmosphere of awe as a deluge of rose petals descends upon Tomobiki-cho, the clouds split open, and the gigantic ship itself finally materializes.

Whereas Ataru is only too happy to indulge in this precious opportunity for interplanetary dalliance with an unearthly beauty, and is hence looking forward to his imminent departure, Lum is utterly disheartened and rendered somewhat pathetic by the realization that no amount of high-voltage current may work to her advantage once her "Darling" has been enveloped in a protective "shield" unique to Planet Elle. As the mammoth vehicle withdraws, its captain having pledged to return to collect the intended on the morrow, the stylized image of the ship presented in the prologue is reproposed with the addition of more realistic details and a visually ambivalent character whereby it comes to resemble a rose (Elle's recurring symbol) or a toy windmill, depending upon the angle from which it is viewed. Sakura's lines following the departure of the ship from Elle are a memorable illustration of *Urusei Yatsura*'s humorous vein at its most ironic: "[t]he universe is truly vast. To think that someone could compete with Lum's bad taste in men."

Lum is shaken out of her maudlin torpor and coaxed into action by her extra-terrestrial friend Benten, as a result of which Ataru, his parents and the weird monk Cherry are abducted by Lum with the aid of a "suction device" (suitably decorated with tiger-skin patterns), and with the objective of taking the group to Lum's parents so that the Oni princess and Ataru may finally be wedded with all due pomp. Benten, for her part, hires a "Space Taxi" to kidnap Ataru's school friends and convey them to the wedding as so many — signally uncooperative — guests. The action swiftly moves to Lum's parents' massive ship, where we witness the reunion of various parties. An engagingly hectic sequence ensues as Lum knocks out Ataru with a mallet, and Elle's envoy, Rose, knocks Lum out with her own "supersonic hammer" after emerging from the statue of a notoriously metamorphic species, the *tanuki* (raccoon), takes on Lum's identity and kidnaps Ataru. Having bombastically embarked on an "all-out" war at the news of the future bridegroom's abduction, the Oni bathetically give up when it becomes clear that Ataru is perfectly happy with the outcome of his adventure.

The story rapidly advances towards its climax as the action shifts to Ataru's and his mates' arrival on Planet Elle. Ataru would very much like to turn the place into his "ultimate harem," unaware that Elle has already achieved a similar goal for herself by constructing an "inner sanctum" that houses her private "refrigerator of love": namely, a crypt-like container wherein all the handsome men who have ever loved her are eerily suspended in cryogenic sleep. (An uncanny anticipation of Steven Spielberg's 2002 sci-fi thriller *Minority Report* might be detected in this portion of the film.) It soon becomes obvious that Elle has something other than marriage in mind and, intrigued by Mendou's good looks, aims at making him the 100,000th addition to her collection. Elle's nefarious schemes are finally disrupted, as is the sealing of her and Ataru's wedlock thanks to Lum's timely rapping on the church's stained-glass window (in an delightful spoof of *The Graduate*) just as the exchange of vows is about to be sealed by one fateful kiss.

Only You's dénouement discloses that Ataru's apparent marriage proposal was never actually valid insofar as he had merely *pretended* to step onto Elle's shadow in the course of their childhood game. This revelation gives rise to a quintessentially surreal sequence, which stylistically anticipates *Beautiful Dreamer*, in which Ataru's teenage self berates and rather brutally beats up his infantile incarnation for having caused so much trouble in the first place. The absurdist humor of the episode derives considerable momentum from its graphic literalization of the theme of psychological conflict, by transposing the warring internal parties onto the outer and emphatically visible plane. Though undeniably hilarious, the scene nonetheless carries latently harrowing connotations in virtue of its exposure of the dodging of personal responsibility and of the unscrupulous preparedness to abuse the younger and weaker in the service of callous egoism as nefarious encroachments on communal harmony and well-being.

Only You is a relatively juvenile exploit within the broad context of Oshii's opus, yet it already evinces the signs of a highly individual and enterprising take on storytelling and cinematography. This is borne out by the sophisticated amalgamation of an approach that favors stylization and pictorial minimalism, on the one hand, and a graphic discourse informed by realism and tangible three-dimensionality, on the other. At the same time, the film's mood benefits consistently from the careful juxtaposition of conflicting images — e.g., in the graphic contrast between the deluge of rose petals suggestive of a mellow fairytale atmosphere and the coldly metallic alien ship evocative of technology at its least genial, as well as in the oscillation between representations of the alien venues as resolutely outlandish locations and as familiarly suburban.

Concurrently, *Only You*'s occasional incursions into wacky melodrama do not ultimately efface its deeper concern with the issues of militarism, heroism, nationalism and related cultural values. This preoccupation is vividly foregrounded in the sequence where the Oni rulers claim to want to vanquish the armies from Planet Elle for the sake of "honour" and "glory" yet their lofty intent is farcically dwarfed by the carnivalesque preposterousness of their entire culture, mores and somatic attributes. A discreet critique of the notion of war-as-spectacle is also provided, as Ataru and his mates are shown watching the military operations through a spaceship window as though it were a television screen and, rebuked by the stern Shinobu, vapidly state, "of course we're happy — now we're 'children who know war,'" in a rather disturbing reference to the Japanese protest song "Children Who Don't Know War." Further opportunities for poking fun at the military are supplied by the clumsy "army" protecting the colossal estate inhabited by Mendou — supposedly the wealthiest boy on Earth — and his family, while Mendou himself comes to constitute the fulcrum of a dispassionate critique of prosperity and power as he is portrayed theatrically posing as a latter-day samurai.

Simultaneously, while the romantic entanglements, misunderstandings and betrayals are often used as pretexts for unbridled slapstick, Oshii also provides numerous hints at the depth and authenticity of the characters' emotions as the twists and turns of the plot steer them back and forth between elation and dejection, self-satisfaction and moroseness. The dispassionately unsentimental realism of the psychological states captured by *Only You* is epitomized by the sequence in which Ataru, driven exclusively by his proverbial lecherousness, hypocritically states that "romance is not all there is to life" and that he is ready to "sacrifice" himself and surrender to the gorgeous Elle *only* to prevent the war. Also remarkable, in this respect, is the dungeon scene in which Ataru claims to feel profound remorse at his ill-treatment of Lum in the past while stuffing himself all the while with gargantuan fervor. He later appears genuinely relieved by the discovery that Lum has not, as initially suspected, been killed by the activation of afterburners on a malfunctioning fighter ship but has managed to eject safely, even though minutes earlier he had incontrovertibly equated life with Lum to "hell" and Elle's emissary, Rose, to an "angel" and a "saviour."

Ultimately, *Only You* works, diegetically and cinematically, thanks to Oshii's determination to take the *Urusei Yatsura* universe seriously, and accordingly juggle both plot convolutions and character interactions with unprecedented sensitivity and warmth even amid zany banter and tacky romance. Concurrently, the comedic complications favored by the series are dexterously streamlined into punchy strings of jokes, cameos and vignettes that cumulatively amount to an uplifting visual ride. Oshii's direction plays a key role in enabling the story's ubiquitous sense of whimsy to cohere in an aesthetically satisfying whole while also preserving an element of inconclusiveness—a stylistic tactic destined to become pivotal to the director's signature. Hence, although the movie may seem a rather peripheral accomplishment compared to subsequent Oshii productions, it holds the undeniable virtue of demonstrating that animation is an utterly unique medium in its ability to surprise, and that in competent and adventurous hands, its tools enable even the most fatuous of concepts to be molded into engaging entertainment.

8

Urusei Yatsura Movie 2: Beautiful Dreamer

Oshii was not satisfied with *Only You*, and in the next production, he strove to invest the *Urusei Yatsura* universe with an original tone and a style of his personal formulation. If *Only You* had afforded some leeway for the treatment of troubled emotional states, its overarching mood had nonetheless tended to capture the carnival's pleasure-seeking proclivities. In *Beautiful Dreamer*, Oshii's take on the carnivalesque is markedly more somber, insofar as the film emphasizes the untenability of any long-term suspension of societally ratified responsibilities, and the transcendence of prescribed forms of conduct is accordingly posited as an ephemeral — and by no means unequivocally pleasurable — state of affairs. This proposition will be elaborated further later in this chapter.

As a result of Oshii's darkening of the manga's original tone, Takahashi came close to rejecting the script for the movie as too distant from her own story. With the second movie, there is no doubt that Oshii's aesthetic and cinematographical vision has begun to acquire an incontrovertibly distinctive shape. The utilization of slow-paced, meditative scenes compounded with lengthy verbal disquisitions, bound to become a central trait of later productions, is already evident in *Beautiful Dreamer*. At the same time, the film abounds with references to folklore and legend, as will also be the case with the director's most seminal works (i.e., *Ghost in the Shell, Avalon* and *Ghost in the Shell 2: Innocence*). In the second *Urusei Yatsura* feature, the complexity of Oshii's burgeoning world picture is encapsulated by his handling of the image of the labyrinth, which fully attests to the director's keenness on conceptual dichotomies at the levels of both cinematic representation and philosophical speculation. Indeed, the image allows Oshii to allude simultaneously to notions of bewilderment, disorder and imprisonment, and to prospects of self-regeneration, labyrinthine locations being traditionally used as settings for religious practice and spiritual enhancement.

In *Beautiful Dreamer*, the characters are caught in a temporal and spatial warp whereby their school environment appears stuck in a perpetual yesterday, while the external world has moved on unaccountably and turned into a dark, postapocalyptic environment replete with maze-like structures and halls of mirrors. In the face of this disorienting aporia, they have to juggle two conflicting options: namely, either accept that a cataclysm has indeed occurred and that its effects are irreversible, or hold on to the past and its pleasures in a stubborn rejection of their predicament. Moreover, they have to contend with the ultimate challenge of having to ascertain the extent to which their experiences are real and the extent to which they just amount to an especially tenacious dream.

The narrative pattern delineated by *Beautiful Dreamer* actually resembles that of a dream by constellating various characters' transitions from a familiar location to an alternate, phantasmatic dimension, symbolizing the shift from one mode of consciousness to another, profoundly and disconcertingly different one. In keeping with the codes and conventions of exhaustively recorded oneiric narratives both within and outside Japanese tradition, the alternate realm disclosed by the dream's metaphorical transcendence of the quotidian sphere presents the dreamer with challenging facets of the self, generally distorted and rendered incrementally daunting by their precipitation in puzzling or even overtly inimical environments. In *Beautiful Dreamer*, the oneiric experience is exponentially intensified by the fact that — with the exception of the actual dreamer — the characters are by and large not aware that they are living out a subconscious vision, that they are indeed fulfilling their roles as designated dramatis personae within a narrative beyond their ken and control. To this extent, the film resembles a carnivalesque occasion in which the revelers are caught inadvertently, without any chance of anticipating its occurrence: a carnival, as it were, beyond the recognized calendar, law and ultimately reason.

The entire narrative trajectory traced by *Beautiful Dreamer* eventually turns out to be a dream belonging to Lum and granted by Mujaki, the Dream Eater,[1] in order to help her "live happily ever after" in a perpetual Neverland. The problem with Mujaki is that he is ultimately driven not by generosity but by spiteful anger, his reason for wishing to create an eternal dreamworld being that he seeks revenge upon Baku, the Nightmare Eater who invariably ends up swallowing Mujaki's devious fabrications. Hence, even when the dreams he dispenses are initially good, they inexorably deteriorate into exasperating nightmares. However, even this final realization — felicitously accompanied by the reassuring discovery that the characters can return to reality with the aid of Baku — does not dissipate totally the film's pervasive atmosphere of unresolved ambiguity. This is because what governs the cast of *Beautiful Dreamer*— and arguably the human species itself—

is ultimately neither the commonsense logic of reality nor the carnivalesque logic of fantasy but rather desire, and desire knows no end.

On the purely visual level, the movie reinforces its ubiquitous sense of ambiguity through the juxtaposition of typical postapocalyptic images such as blasted landscapes and pleasant summertime activities. At the same time, it mixes elements characteristic of noir science fiction that would be instantly recognizable for most Western spectators (labyrinthian streets, abandoned lots, forsaken vehicles and omnipresent shadows) with specifically Eastern motifs, such as the aforementioned references to legendary creatures, and its allusion to the ancient anecdote in which the Chinese philosopher Chuang Tzu dreams he is a butterfly and wakes up wondering whether he might indeed be a butterfly dreaming it were a man.

The opening of *Beautiful Dreamer* encapsulates the entire film's unresolved ambiguity by means of a characteristically Oshiian montage that dexterously juxtaposes conflicting images: a flock of seagulls typical of a summery atmosphere, yet hovering over a mound of barren soil that evokes a sense of environmental depletion, and a partially submerged tank devoid of any obvious function in its context. An old clocktower — the same building which one of Lum's electric onslaughts had caused to nearly collapse in *Only You*—also features prominently, symbolically anticipating the axial role to be played by concepts of time and history, as well as images of both development and stagnation, throughout the filmic narrative to follow. The ensuing images focus on the preparations for the Tomobiki annual High School Festival. *Beautiful Dreamer* here indulges in its most overtly playful flirtation with the spirit of the carnival. Though emphatically instructed *not* to wear costumes by the educational authorities, the pupils blatantly disregard the rules and several of them adopt a science-fiction cosplay motif with veritably carnivalesque zeal. Pupils dressed up as Godzilla (Japan's prototypical giant monster from cinema and hence an especially fitting cameo in this context), Darth Vader and Ultraman can be quite easily spotted.

Ataru's mates are busy setting up a tea-house based — in rather dubious taste — on the theme of the fall of the Third Reich, complete with a real tank the weight of which occasions the edifice's partial demolition. An atmosphere of potentially subversive randomness and disorder is evidently beginning to insinuate itself into the diegetic fabric. This is intensified to preposterous extremes as, the next morning, the pupils *begin* to prepare the festival due to commence the *following* day ... and realize that they are living the same day through and through. A rampant sense of confusion and disorientation escalates as the principal characters attempt to return to their homes only to discover that these are nowhere to be found, and that the town's whole space appears to have morphed into a disconsolately gloomy and perversely liminal wasteland, eerily punctuated by the sporadic appearance of a little girl and a chiming *tindon-ya* (special-sale band).

One of the teachers, Onsen-Mark, does manage to reach his flat. When Sakura visits him there, she finds it infested with mushrooms and covered in a thick layer of dust — which indicates that a substantial period of time has uncannily elapsed since their last visits to the apartment. However, when they return to the school after discussing at some length the possible causes for the phenomenon they are witnessing, Onsen-Mark and Sakura find that the preparations for the festival are *still* under way. The "truth" becomes evident: whereas several years have passed in the world of the town and its buildings, the school is anchored to a perpetual yesterday. As the movie overtly indicates, this idea is inspired by the ancient legend of Urashima Tarou, a fisherman who rides a giant tortoise to the Palace of the Dragon and finds his own village unaccountably altered upon his return. The same tale is echoed by a later sequence in which the characters attempt to flee the town aboard a private aeroplane owned by Mendou and see that Tomobiki-cho has been severed from the Earth and is drifting in space atop a giant tortoise. This turns out to be supported by mighty pillars, four of which assume the appearance of characters from the *Urusei Yatsura* world that have vanished in the course of the story: namely, Onsen-Mark, Cherry, Shinobu and Ryuunosuke.

The time loop now seems to have come to an end as the entire population of Tomobiki-cho has disappeared and most edifices have crumbled, leaving inexplicably functional a convenience store that goes on supplying ostensibly inexhaustible amounts of food, while the daily paper — likewise unfathomably — continues being delivered at the Moroboshi residence, wherein gas, electricity and water supplies also persevere unabated. Everyone deals with the new world in their own fashion: Sakura opens a beef-bowl joint; Mendou drives the tank around all day long; the would-be speculative scholar Megane writes lengthy perorations about the rebirth of humanity; and the others just enjoy themselves rollerskating, watching movies, organizing picnics and fireworks displays and taking trips to the enigmatic lake that has surfaced from nowhere and into which the school gradually sinks.

Cinematographically speaking, *Beautiful Dreamer* employs a number of camera techniques destined to dominate later Oshii productions. One of these is the use of the camera to orchestrate the action according to the figure of the circle. Most notably, this technique comes into play in the thematically pivotal dialogue involving Sakura and Onsen-Mark regarding the issue of temporal displacement. Here the camera surveys by turns the interlocutors' faces, tracing a circular visual path around the table at which they are sitting. The same scene also includes a further distinctively Oshiian operation: that is to say, the use of close-ups focusing on a character's face — especially the eyes— as this looks directly at the camera, as a means of addressing the audience and physically drawing them into the debate without, apparently, the regulatory interference of the director's eye and hand.

The figure of the labyrinth, mentioned earlier, complements that of the circle, since both images point to patterns of motion — and, by metaphorical extension, thought — that preclude either a point of origin or a final destination. The Tomobiki High School and ultimately the town in its entirety are configured precisely as maze-like spaces whose unsettling import is persistently exacerbated by their infusion with a plethora of specular images, spectral shadows, doublings and prismatic reflections in pools, in puddles, in shop windows and — most bafflingly — in the mysterious lake.

Beautiful Dreamer constitutes, amid the comedy and the antics, a thoughtful commentary on the tension between escapism and responsibility, desire and reality, an atmosphere of freedom fueled by the excitement of carnivalesque anarchy and a sense of sorrow intimating that any freedom is ultimately illusory. Thus, while the characters may indulge in a fantasy of self-emancipation from the nightmare of history, treasuring the proposition that time is redeemable and that its injuries may be disavowed, their latent anxieties and feelings of frustration underscore the inevitability of loss and the eventual necessity of coming to terms with its legacy. In psychoanalytical parlance, the polarities thus posited by *Beautiful Dreamer* correspond to the affective modalities of *melancholia* (i.e., the repudiation of loss) and *mourning* (i.e., the acceptance of loss and of its ineluctability). The action indulges in melancholia by somewhat refusing to acknowledge the *no-longerness* of an old, familiar and cherished world, yet alludes to the ultimate inexorability of mourning as an acceptance of change and disillusionment.

Julia Kristeva's views on this subject are especially relevant insofar as she explicitly associates melancholia with a person's inability to sever himself or herself from the preadult domain. If pushed to pathological extremes, melancholia becomes an acute recognition of disinheritance unrelieved by any faith in restoration or compensation. Growing up is always, to some degree, unwelcome for it is predicated upon loss: the loss of innocence, of the freedom to imaginatively inhabit the most fantastical realms, and also of the prerogative to savor the experience of being scared as a delight rather than an ordeal. Nevertheless, there is a crucial difference between the subject that accepts loss and the one that disavows it. The subject that accomplishes a successful entry into the grown-up realm is enabled by a shared language and by accepted rules and norms to identify what she or he has lost and hence to mourn the lost object. In melancholia, by contrast, one pines over a lack that cannot be either expressed or symbolized.

In other words, the subject that comes to terms with the traumatic reality of loss may at least name (symbolically) the object of which she or he feels deprived and find it again in signs (transformed, translated, edited). Such a person is well aware that the object of desire has been irretrievably lost but precisely insofar as she or he is capable of suffering the loss, may bring the object back in images, representations and words. The melancholic subject, conversely, feels bereft without quite knowing what of. Thus, while mourning could be seen as an attempt to resuscitate the lost object in symbolic form, melancholia ultimately defines the predicament engendered by a sense of deficiency that cannot be named: the subject labors under the sign of a lack with no adequate comprehension of what has been lost or how to grieve it (Kristeva).

The characters depicted in *Beautiful Dreamer* have not actually descended into an undilutedly somber state of melancholia but actually manage to hold on to a relatively ludic and vestigially carnivalesque mood. Yet, their anxieties, uncertainties and fears repeatedly come across as not merely real but grievously so. This is largely attributable to Oshii's inclination to consistently foreground a ubiquitous sense of isolation and impending darkness—a psychological climate rendered all the more poignant by the dramatization of loneliness, disconnection and emotional atomization in the very midst of an ostensibly closely knit community. Through this ploy, the film ironically exposes its cast's ultimate solitude as a bleak upshot of friendship and gregariousness, not its adversarial counterpart.

Beautiful Dreamer is most definitely the first film through which Oshii started asserting his unique approach to animation, dramatizing the logic of the carnival through an emphasis on its psychologically dislocating elements rather than on its playfulness. Accordingly, in *Beautiful Dreamer* Oshii appropriates the characters originally brought to life by Takahashi's pencil and deploys them as cinematic puppets capable of articulating his most inveterate preoccupation: the unerasable nebulousness of the boundary separating the empirical from the imagined. Though reasonably well received at the time of its theatrical release, *Beautiful Dreamer* was not adequately noticed by critics until the following year, upon the appearance of *Angel's Egg*—an Original Video Animation that could indeed be regarded as the New Age version of the second Urusei Yatsura feature. This constitutes in itself telling corroboration for *Beautiful Dreamer*'s standing as an eminently surrealist experiment and, relatedly, a baffling visual experience for many viewers accustomed to regarding animation as the dispenser of relatively unproblematic messages. Cumulatively, the movie met with controversial — and often quite acrimonious— responses, and in their wake, the director decided to abandon the world of *Urusei Yatsura* and to develop fresh territories.

As noted earlier, *Beautiful Dreamer*'s legacy can be palpably felt in *Lum the Forever*, the fourth *Urusei Yatsura* feature, and it is for this reason that even though Oshii did not direct this film, the work is here examined in some detail in the next segment of this study.

9

Urusei Yatsura Movie 4: Lum the Forever

When Oshii left the show, Kazuo Yamazaki took over and endeavored to restore *Urusei Yatsura*'s fundamentally comedic nature, thus rectifying Oshii's tendency to problematize the narrative by delving deep into the areas of existential speculation and social commentary. The last TV episode was aired on 19 March 1986. To mark the end of the show, Yamazaki co-wrote (with Toshiki Inoue) and directed the fourth *Urusei Yatsura* movie, namely *Lum the Forever*, an artistically ambitious production dominated throughout by an atmosphere of intensely melancholy lyricism that plays enigmatically with the tangled language of dreams. In dramatizing the oneiric dimension, Yamazaki's movie articulates all of the key ingredients which Steve Johnson evocatively itemizes as characteristic facets of the cinematic representation of oneiric displacement. According to the critic, it is quite customary for such depictions to orchestrate the surfacing of "buried psychological issues" and to have these eruptions

> heralded by a war, party, pageant ... or in the form of subterranean or ambiguous creatures—"things that won't stay dead"; half-human "missing links"; mutations; or masculine-women/feminine men — to demonstrate their "borderline," unresolved nature, often revealed in flashbacks. As in dreams, where other people tend to stand in for people we already know ... characters frequently become doubled, not-themselves ... and must be eliminated, or reconciled with — reincorporated into the self.... When this begins happening to an absurd degree, the mind has totally regressed into itself and begun cannibalizing its own contents [Johnson].

The carnivalesque disruption of the familiar *Urusei Yatsura* world proposed by *Lum the Forever* is indeed ushered in by a lavish *hanami* (blossom-viewing party), held on Mendou's estate to honor the about-to-be-felled gigantic tree Tarouzakura, and, shortly after, by the visionary evocation of an ancient pageant replete with mythical allusions. The film's climax and dénouement, on the other hand, feature prominently a cataclysmic conflict, paradoxically intended to restore a semblance of order by forcing the town's

68

inhabitants to take on clear roles and responsibilities—though at the cost of further and no less tumultuous devastation — rather than torpidly acquiesce to the increasingly numbing sense of anomie that closes in upon them from all sides, threatening to engulf them altogether. When, in the wake of her incremental marginalization from Tomobiki-cho's daily reality, Lum flees human company and takes refuge in the town's forgotten depths, she encounters an underground, foetus-like entity (symbolic of the town's consciousness). This creature is visually crucial to her confrontation of submerged psychological dilemmas—primarily (and echoing *Beautiful Dreamer*), the mystery of how to negotiate the unsavory imperative to grow up — and hence to her emotional reawakening.

Ambiguous, metamorphic and liminal beings also play an important role, notably in the guise of infantile versions of Lum herself and of her friends, which serve as doppelgangers for the present-day characters while again throwing into relief the theme of development as a physical, no less than affective, phenomenon of potentially crushing magnitude. By agreeing to play with those uncanny doubles, Lum metaphorically incorporates the ineluctability of change which their appearance pathetically evokes. The alternative, it seems, would amount to Lum's eventual and irrevocable inability to re-enter the web of intersubjective relations and obligations for which Tomobiki-cho stands and from which she has already been symbolically ostracized.

At the same time, all the central characters' roles are irreverently inverted and their powers redistributed, as the usually strong Lum is emphatically weakened and the generally helpless Ataru endowed with unexpected resourcefulness. Lum's disempowerment arguably constitutes the film's most vital and yet most puzzling dimension. As the plot first dreamily and then nightmarishly unfolds, images of Lum incrementally vanish from the reality of Tomobiki-cho. Instances of the alien princess's gradual evaporation include Ataru's interference with Megane's attempt to film a shot of the Oni beauty amid drifting cherry blossom and playful birds (as part of the independent movie filmed by the high-school pupils); Ataru's sabotaging of the sequence meant to feature Lum in the part of a mythological figure, as he inadvertently dismantles the set; and Lum's disappearance from Mendou's photo album. Furthermore, Lum's preternatural powers and attributes—specifically, the knack of generating high-voltage electricity, the ability to fly and the possession of horns—also dwindle and eventually vanish one by one. The Oni princess herself is aware that her very consciousness appears to be declining, and whenever she comes anywhere near to establishing why this could conceivably be the case, the town hinders her by recourse to prodigious occurrences: for instance, the appearance of an unseasonal swarm of insects, a massive upheaval in

Tomobiki-cho's foundations, and the emergence of hallucinatory visions of an alternate town. At times, Lum seems to have actually become invisible to her very friends, as seething crowds of unrecognizing faces threaten to swallow her being.

Thus, the action increasingly assumes the shape of a conflict between the town and Lum that may well result in the latter's ultimate defeat. On the allegorical level, the conflict in question could be interpreted as a confrontation between the human and the demonic, self and other, or suburban common sense and the irrational. It is intriguing, in this respect, that the social body supposedly standing for the ordinary, the normal and the everyday should resort to offensive phenomena that are no less preposterous than any of Oni's most outlandish faculties. Equally tantalizing is the fact that Lum retains a modicum of power in the face of the town's progressively vicious onslaughts, insofar as her image spectrally returns at several junctures in the narrative to disrupt the scenes of a life without her. For example, in the sequence dramatizing Mendou's and Shinobu's date, Mendou is suddenly distracted by an unsettling memory of Lum. The alien princess also features in the dream wherein Mendou's honeymoon plans— involving a vast horde of gorgeous wives— are undermined by a nagging vision of Lum. Faithful to the tone of unresolved ambiguity set two years earlier by Oshii's *Beautiful Dreamer*, *Lum the Forever* simply refuses to commit itself conclusively to any definitive interpretations. In fact, harking back to Oshii's earlier interventions in the *Urusei Yatsura* universe, Yamazaki gives us a palimpsest of cryptic visuals and plot twists, deliberately jumbled concepts and characters that appear to have no more control over their world than any audience ever might. The metaphors themselves are intentionally wielded in enigmatic terms and at an unpredictable pace, and therefore invite imaginative decoding at each turn.

Lum the Forever concurrently revisits the elusive psychological territories explored by Oshii in *Beautiful Dreamer* through its treatment of the themes of time and memory. The character of Shinobu voices the film's pivotal preoccupations, in this respect, during the *hanami*, as she sadly wonders whether life may ultimately amount to just a trail of memories. If this is indeed the case, she goes on to reflect, it is arduous to ascertain what constitutes human beings while their actions relentlessly morph into the stuff of reminiscences. Moreover, the film proposes that should memories be given free rein, they would inexorably deteriorate into awful dreams and cease to fulfill their function as recorders of the passage of time, thus becoming an unbearable, stultifying burden. The Shinto priestess Sakura's last words—"dreams that the town has"—allude to the possibility that all the disruptions witnessed in the course of the film may have stemmed from a corruption or blockage in the proper flow of memories which constitute the fabric of the Tomobiki-cho community — and thus, by implication, the town itself — whereby what people remember no longer refers to lived experiences but rather to visionary projections of their anxieties and fears. Where the principal characters are concerned, those problematic emotions would seem to emanate primarily — as hinted at earlier —from the imperative to transcend the relatively carefree realm of childhood in the name of adult responsibilities and duties. Like carnival participants, they may indulge for a while in uninhibited living, but the transition to a societally disciplined existence is a destiny they cannot dodge or eclipse.

A possible reason for couching this drama in the particular terms of a conflict between the town and *Lum*, rather than the teenage population at large, lies with her standing — a reputation emplaced by *Beautiful Dreamer* — as the very champion of the quest for an eternally preadult, full-time carnivalized present. At one point, Lum joylessly remarks that she and her mates are "seventeen already" and that she is no longer able to understand the birds as clearly as she could when she was little. Megane and Mendou are similarly anxious about the passing of time, and their apprehension specifically manifests itself as an obsession with the capturing and preservation of images of Lum — although, as noted, they are repeatedly frustrated in the attempt. References to the ineluctability of change abound throughout the film, poignantly echoed by grim comments on the erosion of tradition, and strike their most affecting chords in Mendou's recognition that the giant cherry tree is rotting and "won't survive the next winter."

A further affinity between *Beautiful Dreamer* and *Lum the Forever* lies with their shared emphasis on the inextricability of productive and destructive energies. In the earlier film, this is attested to by the proposition that even the most pleasant of the dreams granted by the demon Mujaki ineluctably degenerates into a disagreeable nightmare. In Yamazaki's production, the same idea is communicated by intimations that even acts meant to elevate a creature may unleash utter chaos. For example, the giant cherry tree must be felled due to an incurable illness, yet it is agreed that its roots should be saved, for they symbolize not only Mendou's dynasty but also the town as a whole. Indeed, it is suggested that Tarouzakura's roots mirror Tomobiki-cho's memories. Saving the roots to graft a new tree constitutes the creative intent, yet this is brutally shattered by the ancient tree's catastrophic disintegration into foam after Ataru has attacked it with a salted axe in keeping with the requirements of an old ritual. What should have been a cleansing and regenerative act turns out to be an outburst of sheer destructiveness.

Pursuing the aforementioned symbolism, moreover, the action proposes that the destruction of the tree entails a debasement of the town itself:

as the roots are sunken in a lake "like plankton drifting to the bottom of the ocean," so are the town's memories. However, what we are presented with is no stark binary opposition between productivity and destructiveness, since the collapse of the little that is left of the tree's roots to the bottom of the eerie basin is not an unequivocal death insofar as it is in this secluded location that the conflict between Lum and Tomobiki-cho is eventually negotiated and a return to some kind of normality made possible. The narrative curve here proposed mirrors the carnival's function as a temporary subversion of order from which a group may resurface in possession of novel strength. Disruption, in this perspective, is deemed to hold eminently regenerative powers.

Impregnated through and through with a keen sense of the absurd and the grotesque, with delirious visions and apocalyptic upsets, both *Beautiful Dreamer* and *Lum the Forever* potently attest to the quintessentially carnivalesque mood of the *Urusei Yatsura* universe as a possibly unmatched blend of the ludic and the macabre, buffoonery and reflectiveness. Oshii's own opus at its most distinctive bears the tantalizing marks of this unholy, yet immensely fruitful, conceptual union. The two films' diegetic trajectories are, accordingly, elusively sinuous—whenever a fantastic occurrence unfolds, hints at a rational explanation thereof are supplied but only to be superseded, in just a matter of minutes if not seconds, by a further deluge of arcane complications. Hence, conclusive interpretations are unattainable: the movies ultimately remain as intractably unresolved as the equivocal liaison between Lum and her "Darling" Ataru.

Plunging the characters—and, by extension, the audience—into bewildering spatial and temporal coordinates, Oshii's contributions to the generation of the *Urusei Yatsura* world (both explicit and tangential) force us to ponder the concurrently liberating and binding nature of the carnival as a temporary release which, ironically, requires a critical assumption of responsibility even as it appears to exonerate the reveler from any conventional notions of duty or commitment. Indeed, even at their most flamboyant, the situations portrayed in both *Beautiful Dreamer* and *Lum the Forever* never allow their characters to shelve totally a whole range of interpersonal obligations among which the injunction to enter a dour adult world reigns supreme.

Beside *Lum the Forever*, the post–Oshii features include *Urusei Yatsura Movie 3: Remember My Love* (dir. Kazuo Yamazaki, 1985), where Ataru is metamorphosed into a pink hippopotamus and Lum pursues the magician responsible for the transformation with catastrophic consequences; *Urusei Yatsura Movie 5: The Final Chapter* (dir. Satoshi Dezaki, 1988), where Ataru and Lum must play once more the game of tag to prevent the Earth's annihilation; and *Urusei Yatsura Movie 6: Always My Darling* (dir. Katsuhisa Yamada, 1991), in which Ataru is kidnapped by the alien princess Lupika and Lum must come to the rescue.

Urusei Yatsura constitutes one of the earliest and most sensationally profitable forays into the relentlessly expanding territory of ancillary merchandise. The plethora of tie-ins and spin-offs which both the TV series and feature-length productions proved capable of spawning indeed represent an important chapter in the history of animé at large in exhaustively documenting the medium's openness to the cultural phenomenon which Jay David Bolter and Richard Grusin have designated as "remediation" (Bolter and Grusin). The veritable explosion in the design, manufacture and marketing of peripheral goods inaugurated by *Urusei Yatsura* pivots on the adventurous translation of an existing medium — namely animé— into an ever-proliferating cluster of satellites. These may consist of toys, garments, or stationery sets— alongside legion other options. What is paramount is the fact that by paying homage to and refashioning an established medium, such products achieve a distinct cultural significance and hence attain the status of new visual media in their own right.

While the value of a T-shirt, doll or calendar inspired by a cherished visual precedent may initially result exclusively from its association with a worthy antecedent, their increasing circulation as widely vendible and exchangeable icons by and by invests them with autonomous signifying powers. Thus, they participate in a process of "remediation," in much the same way as photography once "remediated" painting, film "remediated" stage production, and television "remediated" radio and vaudeville.[1]

Ultimately, the world of *Urusei Yatsura*—and especially Oshii's contributions to its building— yields a tantalizing fusion of science fiction and elements of Japanese mythology and lore that bears witness to the distinctive character of traditional Japanese fantasy as a realm already imbued with that taste for the aberrant that is characteristic of much contemporary science fiction. The animations contain farce, melodrama and fairly barmy erotic exploits, yet also evince serious preoccupations. One such concern pertains to cultural and racial Otherness. This is dramatized through the use of characters that varyingly come across as irrecuperably alien, as societally integrated fixtures of a semi-realistic and seemingly stable Japanese environment, and as ironical commentaries on the actual precariousness and partial disreality thereof.

Furthermore, while both the series and the features employ characters that may, at first sight, appear stereotypical due to their derivation from conventional narrative morphologies (including the categories of the hero, the antihero, the villain, the helper, the questor, the object of the quest), these dramatis personae also constitute a means of engaging in mature reflections upon real attitudes towards concepts of authority, hierarchy and legitimacy, as well as towards gender roles and relations, that offer valuable insights both into traditional Japanese beliefs and into the country's experience of Westernization and globalization.

10

Angel's Egg

Angel's Egg is characterized by an oneirically sinister atmosphere, strongly redolent of Surrealist painting and particularly of the works of Giorgio de Chirico and Salvador Dalí. The OVA's eerie qualities are persistently enhanced by the presence of liquid effects, using reflection and refraction as potently distorting tools. As Richard Suchenski observes in his survey of Oshii's career published in *Senses of Cinema*, *Angel's Egg* constitutes a "steadfastly uncommercial personal project that could only have been made at the height of the Bubble economy" and "remains obscure even in Japan" although "there are many critics and fans of Oshii who would call it his masterpiece." Furthermore, "*Patlabor 2* is more sophisticated, *Ghost in the Shell* is more important, and *Avalon* is more mythically complex, but the low-tech, hand-drawn *Angel's Egg* remains Oshii's most personal film" (Suchenski).

A 71-minute piece containing minimal dialogue and hence relying almost exclusively on visual images to develop its cryptic narrative, *Angel's Egg* eludes definitive explanations: Oshii himself has professed not to know what the film is finally about. The viewer is therefore encouraged to draw his or her own conclusions and, having done so, to be prepared to revisit, reconsider and very possibly subvert their import. Focusing on allusive understatements rather than revelatory epiphanies, and on symbolic presentation rather than action, the OVA persistently invites speculation by simultaneous recourse to an elliptical concatenation of jarring impressions and to a majestically moody integration of graphic, chromatic and aural effects. The plot itself may only be tentatively inferred on the basis of the responses elicited by the depictions. On the surface, the sole ascertainable factor would seem to be that the action centers on a young girl (the titular "Angel") in possession of a gigantic egg and a wandering warrior, roaming through a postapocalyptic city of hallucinatory illusions, transcendental magic and achingly depressing beauty. Indeed, the animation's bleak mood is magnified rather than relieved by its interpenetration with an element of ethereal grace, insofar as the latter serves to throw the former into sharper relief by ironic contrast.

In the opening sequence, a young soldier is seen standing in a paradigmatically dreamlike environment, as a giant orb filled with myriad stone statues descends from the sky and then lands, triggering off sirens. Awakened by the noise, a little girl climbs to the top of a massive staircase, leaving behind a large egg. She looks at the city in the distance, returns downstairs, picks up the egg and sets out on a journey. After traversing a desolate land and a gloomy forest, she eventually comes to a pond, where she fills a flask, observes the world through the fluid, and then drinks from it. A feather floats on the surface of the pond, and the girl has a vision of herself and her egg sinking to its bottom. She next reaches a derelict city of approximately European style, and contemplates pensively its decaying balconies and staircases. Countless tanks suddenly materialize ostensibly out of nowhere and the young soldier seen at the beginning climbs out of one of them. The two characters find themselves facing each other for the first time, at which point the girl runs away and takes refuge in a narrow alleyway. She then visits a forsaken room, picks up another flask, empties it of its red contents and refills it at a monumental fountain — having once more left the egg behind.

As she perceives ominous figures sitting by the fountain and hears a clock chiming fourteen times, the child fearfully drops the flask and runs away once more. Having sheltered in the sunken remains of a formerly grand edifice, she sees the soldier again. Referring to the egg, he tells her that she should look after precious things more carefully but also states that in order to know what the object truly means, it should be opened. Unsurprisingly, the girl instantly flees the man's company. However, he tenaciously goes on following her. As the two characters move through the city, fishermen equipped with spears spill out onto the melancholy streets and the girl comments that the men still pursue their intended prey even though there are no fish left. Shadowy images of colossal fish take form on the sides of the city's abandoned buildings while the hunters foolishly sling their harpoons at them. The girl then takes the warrior into a mansion that houses the fossilized remnants of ancient creatures.

A picture of a tree on a wall reminds the young man of another tree he once saw, containing a dreaming bird in possession of a giant egg. Rows of flasks similar to the ones previously shown can be seen lined along a wall. The soldier asks the girl how long she has been living in the building but she has no idea what the answer might be. He admits that he does not know who he is or where he comes from either and then proceeds to recount the Biblical tale of Noah and the Ark with an altered ending, in which the survivors of the Flood go on drifting purposelessly for eternity, and gradually forget their previous existence altogether. He reckons— an axial moment in the story — that perhaps everybody belongs to somebody else's dream, that nothing genuinely exists as a tangibly independent entity and that even the dreaming bird he so vividly recalls may never have actually obtained. The little girl, however, adamantly declares that the bird in question does exist, and leads the warrior to another part of the building, where the fossilized skeleton of a mammoth bird is indeed located. Coming closer than anywhere else in the film to disclosing her personal reasons for treasuring the mysterious egg, she then states that she intends to hatch a new bird — presumably akin to the ancient one — from her precious possession.

The two characters proceed to sit by a fire on the floor of the child's chamber. The warrior asks if any noise can be heard inside the egg and the girl smiles warmly, saying that she can hear breathing sounds. The young man somewhat cynically opines that what she hears is probably *her own* breathing. She staunchly defends her theory regarding the presence of life inside the egg by claiming that she can also hear the noise of fluttering wings, yet the soldier dismisses her perceptions once more, arguing that what she is hearing is merely the wind blowing outside. Heavy rain beats relentlessly the desolate city as the girl falls asleep and her companion lays her on the bed. She suddenly wakes up and asks him who he is: he replies by merely returning the same question to her. The girl falls asleep again clutching the egg and the soldier sits in silence, gazing at the smoldering fire. He then takes the egg from the slumbering child and uses his cross-shaped weapon to smash it.

Reverberating with memories of the aforementioned Noah tale, the sequence that follows shows rising waters threatening to flood the city, as the crazed fishermen wait for their shadow prey to reappear. When the girl wakes up, she discovers that both the egg and the warrior have gone. She finds a fragment of the cracked shell and is hence forced to consider — in what could be regarded as the film's most inconsolably sad, and yet most revealing, moment — that there is no clear proof that her cherished possession ever contained *anything*. Finally, the child leaves her refuge, sees the soldier in the distance and starts chasing him. In a sequence that vividly echoes the oneiric vision presented earlier in the narrative, we next see her precipitate into a water-filled crevice and sluggishly sink to its dusky depths. In the closing scene, the soldier stands on the beach in a deluge of feathers as the orb introduced in the opening segment of the OVA rises from the sea. One of its statues now exhibits the countenance of the little girl, clasping her egg: the young man impassively watches it ascend. The final sequence of the OVA consists of a protracted reverse zoom that vividly recalls the closing frames of Andrei Tarkovsky's *Solaris* (1972) in its gradual revelation that the island upon which the action turns out to have taken place is a puny and lonely dot in the midst of an overwhelmingly empty ocean.

The animation style used by Oshii in *Angel's Egg* is very distinctive and, though marginally dated, capable nonetheless of yielding exquisite elegance. This impression, bolstered by the haunting tonal tapestry of Yoshi-hiro Kanno's soundtrack, emanates to a significant degree from the use of harmonic oscillation in the manipulation of frames, achieved through a studious rendition of rippling and waving patterns of motion. On the whole, the combination of visual and acoustic effects, simultaneously reminiscent of productions as diverse as Ingmar Bergman's *The Seventh Seal* (1957), Terry Gilliam's *Brazil* (1985) and Stanley Kubrick's *2001: A Space Odyssey* (1968), aptly magnifies the animation's deeply enigmatic character.

The visual identity of *Angel's Egg* is defined throughout by Yoshitaka Amano's distinctive aesthetics, and particularly his unmistakable fusion of the lyrically mellow and the dramatically uncanny, gentleness and menace. Among the most salient traits of Amano's work to be also found in *Angel's Egg* are the juxtaposition of minimalistic forms whereby priority is accorded to simplified and even stark lines— in the rendition of settings and in the evocation of movement — and intricately detailed frames in which the eye is sucked into a kaleidoscopic proliferation of architectural and ornamental minutiae worthy of the most exuberantly adorned Gothic cathedral. Amano's passion for detail also extends to character design, the female protagonist's pictorial distinctiveness emanating from the unobtrusive inclusion of a solitary braid among a mane of unruly locks, tiny jewelry, and meticulously executed fabrics and patterns, no less than from her overall mien as a blend of the waif and the fairytale princess, the unfathomable imp and the innocent angel. The depiction of the setting also features Escheresquely disorienting perspectives wherein seemingly endless staircases, shadowy archways, steep walls and cobbled alleys mock the eye into the vain pursuit of an unreachable sensory destination.

This technique reaches its crowning achievement in the representation of the goliath eye seen in the opening and closing sequences, as an apparently minimalistic icon of power when apprehended from a distance, and a dizzyingly intricate assortment of stone sculptures as the camera gradually picks up the minutiae of its textural configuration. In the representation of the story's environment, the storyboards also capitalize on graphic contrasts between shapes that tend to utilize severely straight lines: a chessboard-like expanse of wasteland, the town's regularly hewn flagstones, the tanks, the spears, and soft forms: the flasks, the protagonist's flowing garments, the conch-like stairwells, recurring bubbles, droplets and ripples, candyfloss clouds and — of course — the eponymous egg.

The characters of the little girl and of the warrior are perfectly at home in Amano's populous gallery of imaginary soldiers, elves, maidens, awesome deities, aliens and vampires. In *Angel's Egg*— as in many other projects through which the artist has asserted his unique signature — Amano is able to engineer mesmerizing encounters of Celtic and Eastern mythologies, and concurrently bring to life a uniquely atmospheric environment. The OVA prioritizes nocturnal settings, chiaroscuro effects, stagnant water, light rays filtering through stained-glass panes, indistinct and amorphous figures, hazy outlines, alternately Baroque and Gothic ornamentation, and the taste of antiquity mingled with anticipations of a latently cyberpunk-ish future.

The Christian imagery utilized throughout *Angel's Egg* has invited much speculation, and the symbolic motifs of the gigantic shadow fish,[1] the Tree of Life, the dove, the cathedral's stained-glass windows, the cross-shaped weapon carried by the character of the warrior and the references to Noah's Ark and to the Flood, in particular, have been read by diverse critics and commentators as laden with multi-accentual connotations. Thus, the OVA has been interpreted as a parable about the corruption of innocence (personified by the "Angel") by organized religion and overzealous dogmatism; as a deconstruction of both Old Testament and New Testament narratives according to which the Flood results not in redemption and a fresh beginning but in a dispiriting scenario of utter hopelessness (epitomized by the people waiting in vain for the dove's return), and the Christ figure is likewise associated not with salvation but with eternal damnation; a stylized account of Oshii's own loss of faith. The relevant extract from the OVA's minimalist script — namely, the only protracted monologue in the entire piece — is worth quoting extensively, in this context, as an emblematic illustration of Oshii's take on Biblical mythology as a whole:

WARRIOR: too have forgotten where I'm from.... Maybe I didn't know from the beginning where I am going ... [starts quoting] "I will blot out man whom I have created from the face of the ground, man and beast and creeping things and birds of the air, for I am sorry that I have made them. I will send rain upon the earth forty days and forty nights, and every living thing that I have made I will blot out from the face of the ground. And after seven days the waters of the flood came upon the earth. On that day all the fountains of the great deep burst forth, and the windows of the heavens were opened. And rain fell upon the earth forty days and forty nights. The ark floated on the face of the waters, and all flesh died that moved upon the earth. Birds, cattle, beasts, all swarming creatures that swarm upon the earth, and every man. Only Noah was left, and those that were with him in the Ark. Then he sent forth a dove from him, to see if the waters had subsided from the face of the ground. Then he waited another seven days ... and she did not return to him any more."

Where did the bird land? Or maybe it weakened and was swallowed by the waters, no one could know. So the people waited for her return, and waited and grew tired of waiting. They forgot they had released the bird, even forgot there was a bird and a world sunken under water. They forgot where they had come from, how long they had been there, and where they were going so long ago that the animals have turned to stone. The bird I saw, I can't even remember where or when, it was so long ago. Perhaps it was a dream. Maybe you and I and the fish exist only in the memory of a person who is gone. Maybe no one really exists and it is only raining outside. Maybe the bird never existed at all [*Angel's Egg* Script].

The religious symbolism is consistently communicated by means not only of objects but also of postures and gestures. This is evident in the statuesque poses, redolent of traditional Christian sculpture, adopted by the protagonists at several junctures in the story, in the seemingly ritualistic breaking of the egg, and in the girl's quasi-baptismal, cathartic immersion into water at two pivotal points in the film.

In assessing the religious symbolism that courses through *Angel's Egg*, it should be noted that in the Christian tradition, the image of the egg is regarded as a symbol of renewal—hence, its ritual role at Easter. In this tradition, breaking the egg is a symbolically crucial act insofar as it is the very fracture of the protective shell that enables the release of the purifying and regenerating energies the symbol supposedly holds. Thus, while the destruction of the egg in Oshii's OVA may constitute a denial of innocence and hope on one level, the act could also be interpreted as a positive choice.

This hypothesis may be substantiated with reference to the Buddhist notion of emptiness, according to which the annihilation of comforting prosthetic adjuncts does not unequivocally represent a descent into tenebrous nihilism but may also stand for an assertion of self-reliance and autonomy, and a mature recognition of the necessity of dismantling all manner of deceptive idols in the quest for knowledge. In this light, the warrior's smashing of the egg could be said to symbolize a deliberate embracing of emptiness as a salutary removal of pseudo-consolatory delusions rather than a callous denial of meaning and promise. The image of the egg, moreover, is central to the creation legend contained in the *Nihongi*, a largely mythological record of Japan's ancient history, according to which the world was initially an egg-shaped mass evincing no distinction between heaven and earth and hosting the germs capable of bringing forth new life.

While constituting Oshii's most elusive dramatization of the inextricability of actuality from dreams and the alternation between reality and its shadow, *Angel's Egg* could also be approached as an environmentally conscious warning about the evils of overfishing, an extremely serious economic and ideological issue in modern and contemporary Japan. The ecomessage gains poignancy by its coupling with another concern close to Oshii's heart, namely the ultimate perversity of all forms of blind fanaticism and, by implication, of all institutionalized creeds. Indeed, the fishermen's zealous pursuit of a non-existent prey could be said to symbolize the unreflectively fatuous worship of unscrutinized icons and beliefs.

No less implausible are appraisals of *Angel's Egg* as a coming-of-age tale or as an existentialist meditation. The sheer recurrence of the question "Who are you?" in the script succinctly encapsulates these philosophical dimensions. In its virtually plotless, stream-of-consciousness approach to narration, *Angel's Egg* both echoes *Beautiful Dreamer*'s surrealism and looks forward to *Ghost in the Shell*. Where the latter is concerned, the OVA could be specifically said to anticipate the feature film's penchant for a seamless amalgamation of disparate narrative strands, open to diverse readings and a correspondingly prismatic range of speculations about the ontological and epistemological status of identity.

Cinematographically, *Angel's Egg* features several of Oshii's favorite stylistic trademarks, and especially the methodical inclusion of numerous uninterrupted long takes, as well as the tendency to concentrate on languidly slow patterns of motion across dusky townscapes furnished with decaying architectural tableaux, spectral presences and skeletally attenuated shapes. The film makes abundant use of fixed frames and horizontally scrolling pans in which full frame-to-frame animation is relegated to just a handful of relatively brief, albeit highly elegant, scenes. Hence, mood and atmosphere are insistently prioritized over movement. The film indeed reaches towards the audacious extremes of *non-animation*, of an aesthetic realm wherein the classic animated cartoon gives way to the concept of *animated painting*. Moreover, as emphasized by Suchenski, the OVA also incorporates "sustained lateral tracks, the slowing down of human motion, a rhythmic alternation between long takes and montage-style cross-cutting, and a tendency to frame objects so as to maximise their contrast with the light sources on the edges of the screen" (Suchenski).

The film's most representative sequence — where both camera operations and symbolic images are concerned — is arguably the one which shows the little girl walking through a murkily lit forest, falling into a pit and flashing in and out of the gloom in the process, and then cuts back to a long shot of the same character as she sits by the lake and fills a bottle with water. This consists of a series of cut-ins, followed by a close-up of the bottom of the bottle capturing a distorted reflection of the forest. A lateral pan over the lake then ensues, tailed by a montage that includes a downward floating feather, a tree's mirror-image on the water's surface, a wave of weeds seething beneath it, and finally a succession of amorphous dark masses seemingly moving over it. Their shadow eventually travels over the girl's face and we next see her underwater, sinking and pathetically clutching the egg one last time.

Angel's Egg was used as the skeleton for the live-action film *In the Aftermath* (dir. Carl Colpaert, 1987), a postapocalyptic tale in which a pair of brother and sister angels (Colpaert's reincarnations of the little girl and the warrior) are meant to find a group of human survivors and rescue them with the help of an egg. The movie's action occasionally intercuts with footage from Oshii's OVA, heavily dubbed over with dialogue that does not appear in *Angel's Egg* and integrated into the action mainly by means of superimpositions of images of the child from the *animé* onto images of the live-action child (who is strongly and somewhat incongruously reminiscent, incidentally, of Disney's Alice from *Alice in Wonderland*). *In the Aftermath* is hardly a memorable production and, perhaps even more disturbingly for Oshii's most loyal fans, a strange attempt at synergetic remediation that arbitrarily suppresses the original's studiously formalist refinement.

In the overall trajectory of Oshii's engagement with the carnivalesque, *Angel's Egg* demonstrates how — having already moved from the fundamentally comedic tone of *Only You* to the hauntingly surreal, yet still liminally ludic, spirit of *Beautiful Dreamer* — the director strove to shift gears in the direction of a decidedly somber tone, stripped of even the scantiest vestige of levity. Thus, the 1985 OVA is definitely *not* carnivalesque in the sense that it provides jocular distortions of the everyday but in the sense that it alchemically rarefies the comic formula to the point that it depicts an upside-down world consonant with the logic of the carnival and yet precludes any consolatory outcomes. This makes *Angel's Egg* an expression of the carnivalesque at its most baleful, supplying several incursions into the carnival's favorite playgrounds — the grotesque, the bizarre, the uncanny — yet removing all traces of the jolly din one might customarily expect to be exuded by a playground. The heart-warming echoes of young voices are, in fact, unsentimentally displaced by daunting choral melodies, the shouts of blood-thirsty predators and the cheerless moan of an ancestral wind that knows no peace.

11

Twilight Q2: Labyrinth Objects File 538

The second and final episode of the *Twilight Q2* OVA series, *Twilight Q2: Labyrinth Objects File 538*, revisits the equivocal ambience conveyed with equal intensity, albeit in vastly different ways, by the *Urusei Yatsura* films and *Angel's Egg* by once more blurring the boundary between the real and the imaginary. Initially designed to provide an arena wherein budding directors could exhibit their skills through a collection of unrelated narratives, the project did not develop beyond its second installment. The title echoes two popular black-and-white television programs of the 1960s, *The Twilight Zone*[1] and *Ultra Q*,[2] with which it shares a penchant for the *noir* and for grotesque distortion.

The first episode was directed by Tomomi Mochizuki (*Kimagure Orange Road*, 1988, and *Ocean Waves*, 1993) and revolves around the character of a girl who finds a camera on the beach which turns out to contain images of herself in the company of a stranger, and then starts journeying back and forth in time. The episode written and directed by Oshii elaborates Mochizuki's conception of time as a markedly elastic dimension, concurrently bringing into play generic and graphic motifs characteristic of classic science-fiction cinema and literature, as well as autobiographical elements. The portrayal of the film's detective, in particular, is based largely on Oshii's memories of his father as a frequently unemployed private investigator.

It is also worth stressing, in this regard, that the *investigation* topos is rarely absent from Oshii's work, and indeed features almost as persistently as the dream dimension. The investigation motif will become pivotal in the *Patlabor* features in the late 1980s and early 1990s— to be revisited in the post-Oshii sequel *Patlabor WXIII: Movie 3*— and will be dealt with again through the lenses of cybertechnology and cyberterrorism in the *Ghost in the Shell* films. *Blood: The Last Vampire* is also a detective story of sorts, though filtered through the codes and conventions of the gothic tale, on the one hand, and political allegory, on the other. *Avalon*, too, is ultimately an investigation, seeking to penetrate the Chinese-box domain of a multi-zone virtual-reality environment to establish whether or not any empirical reality obtains beyond the synthetic surfaces supplied by technology.

The plot of *Twilight Q2: Labyrinth Objects File 538* pivots on a young girl who shares a dilapidated flat in the Tokyo suburbs with a man who appears to be her caretaker (and possibly father). Intrigued with fish and aeroplanes—which she often mixes up as though they were interchangeable or even indistinguishable entities—she dons throughout the story an oversized T-shirt bearing the caption "fish" and an army helmet. In the opening segment, the Japan Air Lines passenger flight 538 begins to disintegrate in mid-flight, the plunging scraps of metal gradually take on the semblance of giant scales and the plane itself incrementally morphs into a colossal *koi*.[3]

In a small and cluttered apartment, a large and sweaty man (the girl's guardian) listens to the news concerning the disappearance of flight 538 and the analogous vanishing of an Air Zimbabwe flight the previous day. Meanwhile, the child stands staring at a tank housing a bulky *koi* and mimicking its mouth movements. The two characters proceed to eat a frugal meal of plain noodles, which the girl interrupts when she hears a plane flying overhead and hurries to the window shrieking "Fish! Fish!" In the next scene, a man garbed in a trenchcoat and dark glasses is seen gazing at the city from across the bay, as the radio reports the disappearance of yet another JAL aircraft and announces that seventeen jets are deemed to have vanished over the past month. The man walks to the flat inhabited by the girl and her guardian and finds the child asleep on the floor with the *koi* tank by her side. His attention then turns to a computer, which he instructs to "execute." As a result, the machine types out the content of its memory: a message from the large man intended for his "successor." The man in dark glasses turns out to be a detective supposed to be investigating the private lives of the large man and the girl and contractually bound *not* to enter their property—a rule he has now patently violated. The investigator finally resolves to peruse the message, thus narrating his predecessor's story.

We thus learn that the large man was also a detective once, and that after countless days spent waiting in vain for a client he had eventually been given a case identical to the one received by the present-day PI—namely, to investigate the lives of a man and a little girl sharing an apartment. In the course of the case, the former detective had been unable to garner any helpful clues about the objects of his probing, neither the post office nor the family register, nor the providers of gas, electricity, water and TV connection holding any record of the two characters' existence. This quest had taken place in an atmosphere not unlike the one pertaining to the present-day narrative: a stiflingly hot summer in the course of which the passing of time appeared to have become indiscernible and several aircrafts had likewise mysteriously evaporated. Having observed the pair through a hole in the wall and found that they did precious little other than eat or sleep, the fat man had eventually taken advantage of their leaving the residence to visit a public bath and discovered that the place bore no sign of recent occupation and indeed looked quite different from the way it had looked when inspected from the outside.

Twilight Q2: Labyrinth Objects File 538 echoes *Beautiful Dreamer*, in this respect, and specifically the scene in which Sakura visits Onsen-Mark's flat and finds it in a state of utter decrepitude and neglect. Parallels with the second *Urusei Yatsura* movie continue to reveal themselves as the large man discovers that the land on which the dwelling is supposed to be situated is a non-existent area, according to the city map, having once been marked as due for reclamation but still — in terms of the official records— part of the sea. It should also be noted that the area as seen by the detective is infested with goldenrod (*seitaka*), a plant that traditionally symbolizes desolation, infertility and Nature at its least benign.

Moreover, the character finds that the aeronautical mishaps have all occurred in the flight zone above the phantom domicile. By and by, the fat man loses all sense of his original identity, becoming totally engrossed in the fate of the enigmatic pair and unable to ascertain the ultimate reality of either the apartment or the world beyond it. The puzzle at the heart of *Beautiful Dreamer* is here again invoked, as the empirical validity of the factual and the hypothetical alike is drastically brought to trial and found irremediably wanting. Having eventually entered the abode while it was occupied, the large man had become further engulfed in the conundrum and powerless to transcend it.

It is the present-day investigator's destiny to follow in his tracks: having also entered the couple's residence, he is now bound to it — and to act as the girl's guardian, as well as write a similar missive for his own successor. The bottom line is that the large man was appointed as a detective by the very man he was supposed to investigate and then had *become* that man. The next detective, in turn, has been appointed by the large man to probe into his own and his charge's lives. Just as the large man had turned into his client, so the present-day PI must turn into his own client — namely, the large man. This is dramatically confirmed by the fact that after he has read the letter, the detective removes his dark glasses and is openly revealed to be the same large man we saw in the initial sequence.

However, the episode's real climax does not occur until the very end, where the circularly self-reflexive character of the entire experience is fully disclosed. It here transpires that the events presented in *Twilight Q2: Labyrinth Objects File 538* are actually part of a yarn constructed by an aspiring artist, that his idea is met with puzzled skepticism by his editor, and that it is in the wake of the rejection that a portentous incident occurs. This ending makes it feasible to interpret the story as something of a disgruntled-author parable taken to ludicrously absurdist extremes. Indeed, the large man could even symbolize Oshii himself, as a director nagged by the awareness that his films are often befuddling and hence hard to accept into the mainstream. This element of self-parody adds a further carnivalesque dimension to the Oshiian repertoire.

On the graphic level, *Twilight Q2: Labyrinth Objects File 538* proposes an effectively disconcerting contrast between the humorous and even, occasionally, clownish appearance of the little girl and the fat man, whose depiction prioritizes soft, round shapes and bright colors, and the architectural setting's forbiddingly realistic gloom. The oversized fish provides a visual link between these two conflicting pictorial registers, coming across as concurrently caricatural and strangely uncomely. Thus, the particular stylistic approach to the carnivalesque exhibited by *Twilight Q2: Labyrinth Objects File 538* could be said to constitute a meeting point between the ludic modality proposed by the *Urusei Yatsura* productions at their most flamboyantly comedic and the uncompromisingly disorientating surrealism of *Angel's Egg*. As far as animation techniques are specifically concerned, the episode's studiously detailed opening sequence with its bizarrely morphing plane probably offers the most enduring memories. Also noteworthy is the pseudo-documentary style evinced by the bulk of the production, with its extensive use of still photographs and accompanying voiceover.

The ultimate investigators depicted by *Twilight Q2: Labyrinth Objects File 538* are the author seeking to engage with a narrative about the limitations of empirical verification, and the camera endeavoring to fathom even the most prosaic nooks of filmed — and filmable — territory in order to assess their own latent lure and distinctiveness.

Part Three
OSHII'S TECHNOPOLITICS

The future is unwritten. There are best-case scenarios. There are worst-case scenarios. Both of them are great fun to write about if you're a science fiction novelist, but neither of them ever happens in the real world. What happens in the real world is always a sideways-case scenario. World-changing marvels to us, are only wallpaper to our children.

— Bruce Sterling, 1993

I think it's difficult for us to know what we lose. We are constantly losing things, and often, as we lose them, we can't remember what they were. They go, they really do; we lose them totally as we move forward in this increasingly mediated existence. I think that's probably one of the tasks of the contemporary poet: to try to capture that sense of constant loss.

— William Gibson, 1995b, p. 21

12

Visions of Power in Live-Action and Animé

The films covered in this section of the book constitute the opening chapter, within the prismatic history of Oshii's creative trajectory, of the director's rise to his current status as one of the most exceptional personalities in modern Japanese filmmaking. They demonstrate Oshii's knack of amalgamating broad political preoccupations regarding economic exploitation and the abuse of power with speculations about the future of technology and introspective philosophical reflection.

Fans of animé across the globe are keen on stressing that in Japan, animated films are not just for kids, and this assertion is undoubtedly valid to a considerable degree. However, the volume of animated films that explicitly target critically thinking adults and actually use animation as a vehicle for sociopolitical and philosophical analysis is rather slim. Approached from this perspective, the atmospherically sophisticated movies here examined are of singular importance in their provision of a unique, profoundly personal and topically cogent meditation on mutating configurations of individual, national and global identities in the late twentieth century and in the early twenty-first century.

As a piece of science fiction imbued with serious political preoccupations, *Dallos* constitutes a thematic prelude to the *Patlabor* universe, though many animé viewers and critics will feasibly remember it more as an epoch-making technical innovation inaugurating single-handedly the fertile field of Original Video Animation than as a particularly inspiring visual narrative. Both the *Patlabor* productions and the movies centered on the "Kerberos" motif — namely, the live-action features *The Red Spectacles* and *Stray Dog* and the animation *Jin-Roh: The Wolf Brigade*—focus on issues of law and order, painstakingly examining the precariousness of the dividing line between a fair commitment to justice and a fanatical excess of zeal.

Both sets of films, moreover, interweave these issues with reflections on the impact of technology on ethical values, while also sharing a concern with the unresolved tension between individual ambitions and collective

agendas, isolation and belonging, personal principles and socially sanctioned norms and regulations, emphasizing the proclivity of virtually any
rule-bound form of stability to degenerate into peremptory dogmatism.
Oshii's engagement with the exploration of political issues via the medium
of animé persists in the live-action productions *Talking Head* (a feature-
length movie) and *Killers: .50 Woman* (a short film included in a five-part
omnibus venture), with a shift of emphasis on the economic and aesthetic
priorities of the film and fashion industries and related attention to the
crimes that pervade them.

Oshii's technopolitical productions bring to life a vast array of human-
machine hybrids: automata that are humanized by their anthropomorphic
traits and investment with quasi-human affects, on the one hand; and
human beings that are mechanized by their encasement in or enhancement
by automated armors and gear, on the other. These two typologies, taken
in tandem, could be seen as embodiments of the concept of "robotic fantasy" as theorized by J.P. Telotte. This phrase designates the cinematic
implementation of techniques that foster the representation of a "seductive
view of the self as fantasy, able to be shaped and reshaped, defined and
redefined at our will" (Telotte, p. 51). Oshii's films vividly capture this
vision, concurrently proposing a challenging perspective on the self as a
mutable product of culture, language and ideology rather than the putatively stable and sealed entity glorified by Western anthropocentrism.

In stylistic and technical terms, the animated productions examined
in the present section encompass practically all of the defining facets of
Oshii's cinematographical signature assessed in the introductory segment
of this book. Indeed, it could be safely maintained that the *Patlabor* features and *Jin-Roh* mark Oshii's attainment of arguably unprecedented levels of sophistication in the capacities of director and script writer
respectively. The evaluation of Oshii's live-action cinema in which this section also engages, for its part, requires some consideration of the ways in
which Oshii's non-animé productions relate, technically and stylistically,
to the animations for which the director is better known on both domestic grounds and abroad.

First of all, it should be noted that Oshii's career has not been informed
by some kind of tectonic shift from animation to live-action cinema or vice
versa, entailing the relinquishing of one medium to the advantage of the
other. In fact, Oshii has recurrently and fluidly traversed the boundary conventionally presumed to separate the two representational modes, seemingly
applying the lessons learnt from his involvement in animé to live-action
filmmaking and simultaneously experimenting with the codes and conventions of live-action cinema within the animated realm, as though to assess
how far and how adventurously these could be stretched.

While, as noted, the animations and the live-action works discussed in this section in order to document Oshii's technopolitical vision share thematic preoccupations, more intriguing still are their dramatic and rhetorical affinities. In looking at the live-action "Kerberos" features, one detects a studious integration of the principal formulae of the animated medium with those of live-action film that gives rise to an utterly novel and visually tantalizing cinematic synthesis. The movies in question imaginatively appropriate several of the traits commonly associated with animé, including the alternation of hyperactive slapstick comedy with brooding moments of inaction, of ludic explosions of wit and passion with suavely lyrical pillow sequences, as well as a proclivity for stylized visuals, graphic intensity and exaggerated patterns of motion. This also applies to a considerable degree to the short live-action film *Killers: .50 Woman* despite the relatively minimalist breadth of the piece.

Of the various element of *animé* mentioned above, exaggeration is plausibly the most distinctive. Indeed Japanese animation proverbially (or notoriously, as some would argue) relishes exaggeration, and diverse subgenres of animé have capitalized in specific ways on the performative value of this notion. At times, the penchant for graphic overstatement takes the guise of hyperbolically gory fight sequences of the kind that punctuate Yoshiaki Kawajiri's period piece *Ninja Scroll* (1993) and, though far less prominently, make a cameo appearance in Hayao Miyazaki's *Princess Mononoke* (1997). At other times, it manifests itself in awe-inspiring sets of postapocalyptic drama such as those repeatedly encountered in the *Neon Genesis Evangelion* TV series and features (dir. Hideaki Anno, 1995, 1997). At others still, it emerges in substantially more prosaic forms by means of a plot's deliberate (and even tongue-in-cheek) concessions to the absurdly overinflated crises of the soap opera genre — as evinced, for instance, by the TV feature *Ocean Waves* (dir. Tomomi Mochizuki, 1993).

Animé is obviously not alone in treasuring the aesthetic of exaggeration, since this is also undoubtedly a marker of Western animation. Instances abound throughout the history of the medium, from the irreverent capers of Otto Messmer's Felix the Cat, through the aquatic exertions of Disney's Magician's Apprentice and the balletic exploits of the (also Disneyan) Beast's dynamic tableware, to the deployment of Wallace and Gromit's contraptions in Nick Park's animations, and the *danse-macabre* set pieces of Tim Burton's Goth puppets. No less representative are Western animations in which the character designs are in themselves so gloriously overextended as to be capable of conveying a sense of disproportionateness by merely being what they are and, most crucially, looking the way they do. The lineage of characters so versed is long and honorable: a selective gallery likely to spring to mind, were animation lovers invited to take part in a brainstorming exercise, would almost certainly include personas as exuberantly varied — both temporally and pictorially — as Betty Boop, Bugs Bunny, Tom and Jerry, Cinderella's Fairy Godmother, Simba the Lion, Shrek, the Grinch, and Woody.

Oshii's animation does not seem inclined to follow this stylistic trend uniformly — or indeed predominantly — and this is fully attested to by the animé titles discussed in this section of the book. With the exception of the three parodic shorts included in *Minipato*, which adopt overtly caricatural graphics and deliberately overinflated rhetoric, the animated films here examined eschew theatricality and glamor, opting instead for a markedly subdued acting style corroborated by suitably discreet palettes and soundtracks.

The live-action films delivered by Oshii's camera, conversely, embrace to the fullest the exaggeration-based ethos. This point will be elaborated later in this segment. It should first be noted that while exaggeration undeniably constitutes a key ingredient of both Eastern and Western types of animation, there is nonetheless one aspect of animé's own imbrication with the twin discourses of action-oriented and character-centered hyperbole that is distinctive to this form instead of being common to animation at large. This has to do with a specifically Eastern — and not exclusively Japanese — legacy tied up with traditional theatre and modern live-action cinema. Especially worthy of notice, in this regard, are the Japanese theatrical traditions of Kabuki and Noh, the samurai movie, and the martial-arts film of quintessentially Chinese provenance.

Kabuki, a popular form that burgeoned in the seventeenth century, thrives on exaggeration, as evinced by a markedly stylized approach to acting wherein an overly spectacular repertoire of postures and gestures — complemented by rhythmic dialogue, music and dance — is routinely employed to individuate the superhuman heroes and the villains on which the stories hinge. Magnificent flowing costumes — at times so heavy as to require the onstage presence of black-clad assistants (*kurogo*) to manipulate the robes while the actual performers play their parts — are possibly Kabuki's most memorable component for many (especially Western) spectators. Comparably elaborate makeup serves to heighten the overall mood of dramatic excess — a mood, importantly, that eludes the danger of degenerating into the undilutedly ludicrous thanks to a punctilious dedication to the perpetuation of time-honored formulae, and to correspondingly exacting performance patterns. Kabuki, therefore, is dominated by the principle of hyperbolic stylization in ways barely known to Western drama since Aeschylus.

Noh theatre, in contradistinction to Kabuki, is a classical (rather than popular) form developed in the fourteenth century that pursues the aesthetic of exaggeration in the opposite direction — that is to say, not gaudy excess but stark minimalism. Stylization plays no less crucial a role, however, within Noh drama's criteria, impacting crucially on its use of dance, eerie flute-and-drum music, poetry, mime and, perhaps most famously, laboriously designed masks. The expressions evinced by several of Oshii's personas in both the animated and the live-action works here studied often recall, in their penchant for stylization, the traditional masks of Noh theatre. As John Twelve Hawks has observed, these illustrious cultural artifacts are above all characterized by an aura of impassivity:

> Ghosts, demons, and crazy people had garish masks that showed one strong emotion, but most actors wore a mask with a deliberately neutral expression. Even the middle-aged men acting without masks tried not to move their faces. Each gesture on the stage, each statement and reaction was a conscious choice [Twelve Hawks, p. 98].

In Oshii's cinema, this impassivity is most pronounced at times of uncertainty and doubt, where it does not denote a self-confident transcendence of one's troubled affects but actually operates as a powerful correlative for a character's epistemological unanchoring and for the cognate suspension of any dependable referents.

As shown in some detail in the relevant portions of this section, Oshii's live-action productions partake of both excess and minimalism, alternating between hyperbolically enhanced body language and formalized restraint, lavishly polychromatic and somberly monochromatic palettes, intentionally flamboyant overacting and meditative languor. Music, mime and dance are also incorporated into the action in fashions redolent of Japanese theatre, while costumes and makeup varyingly serve to intensify the action's commitment to baroque intricacy and rarefied simplicity by turns.

Several of the dramatic conventions commonly associated with the far more recent genres of the samurai movie and the martial-arts movie also come into play. In their handling of body language and visual effects, the films frequently allude to the tradition of the *chanbara* (or sword-fight film), the action-oriented subgenre within the tradition of Japanese samurai cinema that is normally regarded as the action-movie counterpart to the period drama (*jidai-geki*). Technically, the films also partake of this legacy in the use of the *chanbara* movie's most salient technical attributes. As Nicholas Rucka has noted, these encompass "hyperreal sound effects, dynamic (and funky) musical scores, inter-titles, lens flares, slow/fast motion, whip pans and snap zooms, special optical effects." Moreover, the live-action productions included in the trilogy echo "the more pessimistic *chanbara* film" in their dramatization of violence not merely as a pretext for action-packed sequences but rather as a stylized correlative for "the existential state of the world" (Rucka).

The martial-arts movie, generally deemed to have originated in Shanghai in the 1920s and therefore to be almost as old as the Chinese cinema industry itself, is an especially noteworthy instance of the preference for exaggeration evinced by various aspects of Eastern performance arts which Oshii's live-action films appropriate to their own ends. While martial-arts films have time and again celebrated the prowess of supernatural heroes and indulged in a profusion of magical feats, established plots have incrementally gained charisma from the fusion of the explicitly imaginary with allusions to contemporary facts.

Furthermore, as Robert Garcia has observed, "[k]ung fu films were successfully revitalized — after Bruce Lee's death — by the introduction of humor that seemed more appropriate to contemporary comedy than period epics.... In martial-arts films, audiences like to identify with chivalrous knights, swordsmen, or heroic fighters of the past — but only if their values and wisecracks are tuned to the modern world" (Garcia). This proposition is substantiated by an assessment of the martial-arts film supplied in the context of an extensive fan site dedicated to Zhang Ziyi: the "*wuxia pian*, or film of martial chivalry, is rooted in a mythical China, but it has always reinvented itself for each age. Like the American Western, the genre has been reworked to keep in touch with audiences' changing tastes and to take advantage of new filmmaking technology. Yet at the center it retains common themes and visceral appeals" ("Hong Kong Martial Arts Cinema").

As noted, Oshii's live-action movies partake of the hearty appetite for dramatic excess characteristically evinced by Kabuki theatre while also cultivating a graphic minimalism redolent of Noh. In so doing, they concurrently appropriate some of the most salient cinematographical, performative and diegetic traits of various forms of action-oriented modern Eastern cinema. Above all, in their elliptical references both to traditional Japanese drama and to the samurai and the kung-fu cinematic genres, Oshii's live-action films bear witness to precisely the kind of stylistic and thematic adaptability highlighted in the evaluation of the *wuxia pian* offered above. The director's apparent concessions to established generic codes ultimately explode a number of esteemed cultural tenets, boldly refusing to pay homage to lofty myths of superhuman valor and choosing instead to focus on all-too-human — and, occasionally, even subhuman — appetites and foibles.

13

Dallos

Oshii's first foray into the realm of overtly serious science fiction, *Dallos* also holds an important position as a pioneering intervention in the *animé* industry, insofar as it constitutes the first made-for-video animated production in Japan. The series consisted of four half-hour episodes, later compiled into a single feature. As Patrick Drazen has observed, the invention of the OVA format authentically revolutionized the realm of Japanese animation:

> [T]he videocassette ... revived some old favorites, and relieved some studios from the burden of having to think in terms of shaping their animation for broadcast.... The ability to create direct-to-viewer animation [via OVAs] not only stretched the content envelope, but stretched the fan base literally around the world. As soon as unedited, unadulterated Japanese animation became just another offering on the American videostore shelf, word began to spread [Drazen, pp. 10–11].

The OVA format undeniably allows for degrees of stylistic and thematic freedom unavailable to animé divulged in more conventional packages. According to Christopher Panzner, moreover, its emergence was a direct corollary of a crucial shift in the domestic entertainment industry and, by extension, Japanese lifestyle in the early 1980s:

> OVA originally appeared in Japan in the 1980s ... as the VCR became a ubiquitous appliance in Japanese households. Such was the demand for animé that people short-circuited conventional television and the boom was on. Freed from the constraints of time limits, commercials, sponsor obligations, episode formats, identical openings and closings and, well, just about all the *rules*, OVA took on a life of its own. Creators could make shows as long or as short as they pleased, a series (*Bubblegum Crisis*), a one-shot (*Black Magic M-66, Riding Bean*), a film (*The Heroic Legend of Arislan*) or anything in between, although most OVA series episodes are normally between a half hour or an hour long — and about half the amount of the original TV series episodes (*Record of Lodoss War*) — and an hour at the shortest for movies (*Welcome to Lodoss Island*, the film version) [Panzner].

It should also be noted, as shown in the next section with reference to the *Patlabor* franchise, that OVAs are by no means fixed cultural products, since OVAs can become television series and television series, in turn, can become OVAs; likewise, OVAs may beget feature films and feature films may give rise to OVAs. Nor is it uncommon for an OVA to result from a popular TV run during or after its broadcasting.

The narrative offered by *Dallos* revolves around a community of colonists who have moved from a severely resource-depleted and dramatically overpopulated Earth to a Moon replete with bountiful assets and as yet untapped ores. However, as the generations go by, the Moon-based miners begin to grow resentful towards the Earth-based administration that benefits from the newly found prosperity — and from their sweat and toil — and engage in acts of terrorism to which the exploitative governors respond with ruthless countermeasures.

Furthermore, the colonists face a generational rift within their own ranks, for those born on Earth remember the days when the Moon was a far more perilous and inhospitable place and even a seemingly minor error could annihilate entire communities — and are therefore more accepting of the current state of affairs — whereas the newer, Moon-born generations feel more secure in their environment and accordingly less well-disposed towards the autocratic Earth-bound commanders who claim control of the satellite on behalf of their planet.

Neither the movement nor the repressive leaders appears conclusively able to vanquish the opponent, and it gradually transpires that the insurgents' only hope rests with the "Dallos" of the title: a colossal and mysterious artifact discovered on the Moon by the first landers, the origins and function of which are unclear even though it has been adopted among the older beleaguered colonists as the hub of a religious sect. To the modern lunar citizens, however, Dallos is more of a weird relic than a god. There are intimations that Dallos might be a sentient entity, and when, in a climactic sequence, it goes haywire and fires off laser beams at the combatants trapped in its interior, it actually seems to be protecting the Moon colonists. However, as is customarily the case with Oshii, the issue is left intentionally open-ended.

Vital to the plot is the segment wherein the police unleash their cyber-hounds in order to capture the rebel leader Doug McCoy. When the protagonist, a young man named Shun, is assaulted by such a beast and kills it in self-defence with an old piece of mining gear, and is hence jailed, he comes to be roped into the rebellion by McCoy and his associates. The sheriff of Monopolis, Alex Riger, is simply eager to clean up the place and restore a modicum of order, but his icily calculating mask of authority cracks when his girlfriend, an angelic woman from Earth named Melinda, is kidnapped by McCoy's forces. To complicate matters further, Melinda turns out to be not totally unsympathetic to the dissidents' cause. Shun, who is now a member of McCoy's band, feels rather divided about the entire Moon-versus-Earth issue, having been swept up somewhat unexpectedly in the revolutionary movement, and his ideological dilemma is exacerbated by personal feelings. Indeed, there is evidence for mutual romantic attraction between the ethereal Earthling and the strapping Shun — much to the chagrin of the latter's longsuffering sweetheart Rachel. The ending of the OVA arguably provides its most memorable sequence, as Shun takes his dying grandfather to the Moon's near side where the young man gazes, awestruck, at the planet that spawned his species in the first place but now betrays it so callously and vows he will do his best to oppose the colonists' exploitation by the arrogant Earth.

The sequences that dramatize terrorist acts and the siege of a hideout by the police are reminiscent of Gillo Pontecorvo's *The Battle of Algiers* (1965). However, the major influence behind Oshii's *Dallos* is undoubtedly Robert Heinlein's novel *The Moon Is a Harsh Mistress* (1966), a story set in 2074 in Luna City, a prosperous community based on the Moon that also happens to be a penal colony operated by the United Nations Lunar Authority. For the unfortunate convicts, the journey to Luna City is ineluctably a one-way trip since, sooner or later, they will become unable to handle the uncongenial gravitational conditions of Earth. Furthermore, the colony's resources are limited and the Authority knows full well — though it strives to conceal this knowledge from the prisoners— that the settlement's survival prospects are therefore inauspicious. Although many feel that the time for a revolution has come, the novel's hero, computer engineer Manuel Garcia O'Kelly, does not believe that there is the slightest chance of a successful rebellion against the Earth's intransigent power structures, and would rather fill his days in conversation with his thinking computer and in the pleasurable company of his wives and co-husbands. However, the passionate activists Wyoming Knott and Bernardo De La Paz manage to enlist his support and technical brilliance to their side and Manuel eventually agrees to channel his entire being into the conspiracy and the resulting no-holds-barred war against the Earth's iniquitous authorities.

Oshii's simultaneous concerns with economic exploitation, the dangers inherent in religious fanaticism, and the complexity of both communal and personal relationships anticipate some of his later productions. So do the lengthy dialogical sequences devoted to the evaluation of thorny ideological issues, the deliberate avoidance of a neat resolution, and an eager graphic sensitivity to the minutest facets of densely atmospheric and chromatically graduated combat scenes. Thus, it could be argued that beside vaunting epoch-making credentials as the first OVA ever made, *Dallos* is also interesting, from a historical point of view, as an anticipation of later Oshii productions. While it looks forward to the mechanical apparatuses and chromatic palette (dominated by blue and brown hues) of the *Patlabor* features, it also foreshadows the *Ghost in the Shell* films in its depiction of futuristic urban settings and representation of advanced computer technology. The latter arguably constitutes one of the OVA's most original visual aspects, and pivots on the recurrent use of putatively digital scannings that render their subjects in the guise of quasi-Impressionist assortments of specks, blots and smudges of mellow pastel hues.

Dallos concurrently heralds Oshii's dedication to the accurate rendition of animal movement — a trait destined to develop steadily throughout his subsequent output and to reach its crowning achievements in *Avalon*, within the domain of live-action cinema, and in *Ghost in the Shell 2: Innocence*, within that of animé. An especially remarkable illustration of the animation's handling of animal body language can be found in the representation of the stately hound belonging to the character of Alex Riger. At one point, for example, the action focuses on the animal's amusing transition from a ferocious urge to attack his opponents to a yawn followed by a peaceful nap the moment he is instructed by his master simply to "stay." Any viewer with some experience of (or indeed sympathy towards) the quotidian "drama" of human-dog interaction across the twin coordinates of Pavlovian determinism and instinct-based randomness will be quick to warm to this scene's appeal. An exemplary instance of the OVA's flair for realism in the depiction of animal motion, the scene just described contrasts starkly with the deliberately non-naturalistic and preposterously rapid patterns of movement adopted in the animation of the cybernetically enhanced police dogs— who, incidentally, don red goggles and cable-equipped reinforcement suits analogous to those worn by the "Kerberos" agents in later productions.

The character design pivots on a fusion of typically Japanese elements traditionally associated with the visual discourse of the *kawaii* ("cute") and a sense of elegantly urbane restraint, especially in the rendition of the principal female characters. The robot designs, for their part, are varied and dramatically effective in the portrayal of both humanoid and overtly mechanical automata. Even though the design and the overall animation style are not, on the whole, as meticulously detailed as they would be in subsequent Oshii films, the architectural design is unremittingly remarkable and often downright spectacular. The sprawling conurbation of Monopolis, the laborers' cramped quarters, the tunnels, mines, subways and Dallos's own mechanical infrastructure (exhibiting patterns redolent of gigantic computer chips) recall at once science fiction classics as varied as *Metropolis* (dir. Fritz Lang,

1927), *Forbidden Planet* (dir. Fred M. Wilcox, 1956), *2001: A Space Odyssey* (dir. Stanley Kubrick, 1968), *Castle in the Sky* (dir. Hayao Miyazaki, 1986) and the *Matrix* trilogy (dirs. Andy and Larry Wachowski, 1999–2003).

Most notable, where setting is concerned, is the OVA's handling of oppositions. For example, the sublime grandeur of star-studded cosmic infinity is consistently contrasted with the Moon's utter desolation outside the oxygenated dome that encloses the capital. At the same time, *Dallos* plays with the visual discordance between the opulence of the wealthy areas—with their swan ponds, waterfalls, imposing bridges and arches, polished flagstones and pervasive atmosphere of luminosity—and the hive-like workers' quarters, consisting of seemingly endless rows of cubicle-shaped dwellings organized into descending concentric circles, where a sense of entrapment, conversely, tends to dominate. It is from this aesthetic vision of architectural incongruities, and from the dispassionate contemplation of the ideological and psychological conflicts to which they are germane, that the deeply divided technopolitical realms explored in the *Patlabor* and "Kerberos" movies pertinently emanate.

Mobile Police Patlabor
OVA 1

Mobile Police Patlabor started out as a manga written and drawn by Masami Yuuki in 1988. Its narrative premise was that by the year 1999 heavy construction projects—of which there would be an ever-mushrooming number—would be undertaken by automata tagged "Labors," and that the Tokyo Police Force would use robots known as "*Patlabors*" (i.e., "Patrol Labors") to deal with crimes and accidents involving the construction Labors and abusive deployment thereof by unscrupulous individuals and organizations. The manga's story arcs tended to pivot on the Tokyo Metropolitan Police Special Vehicle Division 2 (SV2), Section 2, frequently with the timid but highly dedicated female pilot Noa Izumi as the protagonist.

The franchise created by Oshii with the animé team "Headgear" encompasses the first OVA series (7 episodes), directed by Oshii in 1988–89; the two feature films *Patlabor 1: The Mobile Police* and *Patlabor 2: The Movie*, also directed by Oshii and released in 1989 and 1993 respectively; a TV series aired in 1989–1990 (47 episodes); and a second OVA series (16 episodes), released between 1990 and 1992. Oshii provided the script for a number of episodes included in the TV series and for parts of the second OVA. The first and second segments of this section of the book assess the OVA and TV series. Case studies of the two feature-length productions directed by Oshii are next supplied. Further developments in the *Patlabor* universe, namely the feature film *Patlabor WXIII: Movie 3* (dir. Fumihiko Takayama, 2002) and the short animations included in the *Minipato* collection (dir. Kenji Kamiyama, 2001) are examined next.

Yuuki had involved his friends—most of whom would go on to become part of the "Headgear" team—in informal discussions about possible ideas for a robot-based television animation in the early 1980s. At the time, the most popular show of the kind was *Mobile Suit Gundam* (1979), created by Yoshiyuki Tomino. The original *Gundam* TV series, now quite unanimously regarded as a cornerstone of sci-fi animé, pivoted on a scenario of interplanetary conflict akin to the type of cosmic drama proposed by Oshii in

Patlabor 1: The Mobile Police (1989). Alphonse is one of the Ingrams deployed by the Special Vehicles Division 2 (SV2) of the Tokyo Police. Shielded by these towering humanoid automata, the SV2 endeavor to protect the city against offenses perpetrated by rogue Labors—giant robots (both manned and self-piloting) initially designed for construction projects but increasingly hijacked by profit-driven crime rings and, in the enigmatic case on which *Patlabor 1* hinges, by one mad scientist. ©HEADGEAR/EMOTION/TFC.

the OVA *Dallos. Gundam* sees the Earth and its space colonies divided between the democratic "Federation" and the "Principality of Zeon," with humanoid piloted "suits" as key weapons in the struggle. The first concept elaborated by Yuuki and his associates, never fully developed, was the story of an intergalactic war and was provisionally titled *Jeilazard* (c. 1981). This was followed, about a year later, by *Lightning Garrakres*: a narrative which, though still set in space, partially anticipates the *Patlabor* universe through its incorporation of various giant machines occasionally endowed with humanoid attributes. *Lightning Garrakres* was never brought to fruition either.

The preliminary concepts ideated by Yuuki and his collaborators began to approximate the actual world and atmosphere destined to distinguish the *Patlabor* productions with *Vidor* (1982–83), something of a *Patlabor* set in space—specifically, on a colonized planet where large humanoid robots named Labors are employed for heavy work but soon degenerate into weapons for fraudulent entrepreneurs and their criminal ventures. Hence, a special police division is established to deal with Labor-connected offences. The character designs for the young policewoman Aldy Rime, pivotal to the entire story arc, exhibit striking similarities to those later produced for *Patlabor*'s Noa.[1]

One of the most evocatively succinct, yet comprehensive, assessments of the *Patlabor* universe available to date is provided by a highly informative Web site devoted to the franchise, named *Schaft Enterprises* after the imaginary Labor-manufacturing company cited in the films:

> *Patlabor* is an amazing series with excellent characters, plots which range from absurd comedies to political drama, wonderfully designed *mecha*, and a sense of realism which you don't find in most robot animé. It is often described as the *Hill Street Blues* of animé. The stories usually focus on the characters and character development rather than the robots as most robot animé does. In fact some of the stories don't feature any robots at all. Unlike most robot animé, *Patlabor* is set in a near future world ... where robots are just everyday vehicles ... All of the main cast are adults who have adult problems. There are no teenagers full of angst or heroes piloting large robots against an alien enemy. It's just a refreshing slice of life, a comedy/drama set in a Tokyo police division — they just happen to use robots in their line of work [Whitley].

Bearing this background information in mind, it could realistically be maintained that the world of *Patlabor* represents Oshii's first incursion into the realm of *mecha*— the subgenre of animé that pivots on giant robots and mechanical suits— and, relatedly, his first opportunity to instill his utterly personal and refreshing vision into an increasingly formulaic and occasionally rather stilted narrative mode. The *mecha* tradition can be traced back to *Tetsujin 28-go* (*Iron Man No. 28*), a popular manga created by the artist Mitsuteru Yokoyama in 1958 and adapted for Japanese television as a 96-episode series, aired from 1963 to 1965, imported to the U.S. in 1966 as *Gigantor*. This show could be said to mirror, albeit tangentially, some of Oshii's own political concerns and their articulation in the *Patlabor* films, insofar as it alludes to real historical forces, if not actual events, by utilizing as its narrative premise the destruction by U.S. bombers of a laboratory wherein Japanese scientists are seeking to develop the ultimate robot weapon to be deployed against the Allies. The main story arc, unfolding a decade after the end of World War Two, encompasses the search for the tremendously powerful giant-robot prototype No. 28 and on plans for its peaceful employment.

Gigantor was the first in a long and prolific line of *mecha* productions. Among them, the most illustrious include the TV series *Mazinger Z* (1972–74), which arguably marked the inception of the animé cult in America; the aforementioned TV series *Mobile Suit Gundam* (1979) and the franchise spawned by this series well into the 1980s and 1990s; the OVA *Bubblegum Crisis* (1987) and its adaptation for television in 1999 with the title of *Bubblegum Crisis: Tokyo 2040*; the 1992 OVA series *Giant Robo* (also based, like *Gigantor*, on a manga designed by Yokoyama); the 26-week TV series *Neon Genesis Evangelion* (1995), commonly regarded as the most successful, most cherished and yet most controversial animé of all times; and the feature films *Appleseed* (1988), *Gunhed* (1989) and *Roujin Z* (1991).

Importantly, some of the most memorable productions featuring *mecha*-based elements also draw inspiration from other sources and traditions—Chinese epic sagas in the case of *Giant Robo*, for instance, and a heady mix of Shinto mythology and Biblical allusions in the case of *Neon Genesis Evangelion*. In this respect, these works provide fitting parallels to Oshii's own assiduous commitment to the integration of science fictional motifs and diverse mythological and religious frames of reference, as famously evinced not solely by the *Patlabor* movies themselves but also by later productions such as *Avalon*, *Ghost in the Shell* and *Ghost in the Shell 2: Innocence*. While acknowledging these similarities, however, it must also be stressed that Oshii's films redefine the customary *mecha* style and mood quite drastically by utilizing the figure of the giant robot as a means of reflecting, allegorically, on the limitations of human vision and of the technological tools resulting from it. Indeed, while denoting technology's seemingly impregnable powers by virtue of their sheer volume and multifarious enhancements, Oshii's Labors are concurrently depicted as somewhat exposed and vulnerable to external forces—most notably, the scientists and technicians responsible for programming their computerized brains.

In an interview given at the *Big Apple Animé Fest—Mecha in Animé—2003*, the producer of the *Mobile Police Patlabor* series, Taro Maki, has stated that while he is interested in making "cool *mecha*" that are capable of attracting both lay spectators and toy companies, he is not solely concerned with the effectiveness of the robotic element: "[i]n *Patlabor* a robot is dealt with as a machine, but I wanted the machine to be interesting.... The show also shows the comic everyday life of the police. While I wanted the machines to look cool, I wanted them to reflect the comic overall level of the story." *Patlabor*'s robots are endowed with individual personalities that replicate both their specific functions and purposes and the proclivities of their owners. "It is possible to design a robot with no personality," Maki states, "but I think when people see that portrayal the robot is going to come off as stupid.... It's not about the robot, it's the way that people react to it. Tetsujin 28 is a machine and people pilot it, but there are scenes where it rains and water pools in the eyes of the robot—no matter what you do, it looks like the robot is crying" (*Big Apple Animé Fest—Mecha in Animé—2003*).

The manga itself had sought to represent pictorially intriguing robots that could, nonetheless, be believed to feature in the everyday life of a world set in the imminent future. Yuuki was undoubtedly successful in his endeavor, the sale of over 19 million copies of the manga in the course of its six-year run indicating that the work was admired not just as yet another instance of tantalizing action adventure but also, more importantly, for its unsentimental sensitivity to human psychology and dramas.

Moreover, Oshii pushes the *mecha* subgenre well beyond its customary remit by engaging with complex historical and political issues, and aspects of Japanese history and politics in the post–WW2 era. Especially important, in the context of the *Patlabor* universe, are the controversies surrounding Japan's military status. The 9th article of the Japanese Constitution, drafted in 1947, prohibits the country from having an army. Yet, the Self Defence Forces (SDF) were created in 1950 (under the name of National Safety Forces) at the behest of Douglas MacArthur, the commander of the U.S. Occupation Forces, to replace Allied troops to be sent to Korea. Many believed — and still believe — that the very existence of the SDF is unconstitutional. The *Patlabor* productions engage explicitly with this awkward issue. At the same time, they hark back to another military question close to Oshii's heart at the time of his involvement in the student protest movement — namely, the ideological and ethical propriety of Japan's participation in a security pact with the U.S. on the basis of which Japan would be required to host American troops to be deployed in Korea and in Vietnam. If Japan is forbidden from subscribing to warfare of any sort, it is hard to see why it should abet military exploits conducted by other nations anywhere else in the world. *Blood: The Last Vampire*, a film directed by Hiroyuki Kitakubo for which Oshii and his team supplied the original concept, would revisit this thorny issue about a decade later in the deeply defamiliarizing context of the horror genre.

The first *Patlabor* OVA (April–December 1988 with one additional episode in June 1989) focuses on the Tokyo Metropolitan Police Special Vehicle Division 2 in their confrontations with villains as diverse as rogue military officers, ecoterrorists and disaffected construction workers. While Labors are being most profitably employed to cope with a phase of massive urban development and land reclamation — while also being used for military purposes, undersea exploration and even recreation — their abuse by all manner of mighty felons, corrupt politicians and petty crooks comes to constitute an escalating threat for the Tokyo Metropolitan Police, and it is up to Special Vehicles Section 2 to use their own Patrol Labors, giant mechanical suits known as "Ingrams," to restore order. Section 2 comprises two branches: Unit 1, commanded by Captain Nagumo, and Unit 2, led by Captain Gotoh. Throughout the series, and again in the features, it is not hard to sense that the latter is regarded as somewhat second-rate in comparison with the former, not least due to its members' alternately hilarious and pathetic idiosyncrasies.

However, there are indications that the Section in its entirety lacks both trust and support. This is vividly conveyed by its physical relegation to a hanger situated on a rather desolate plot of reclaimed land, and provision with mechanical equipment that is frequently less than up to scratch. It is from the Section's underprivileged status, from the graphic (and often humorous) depiction of its members' quotidian exertions, and from the prudently optimistic celebration of their knack of making the best of a poor deal that the *Patlabor* universe ultimately derives its narrative vitality and dramatic intensity. Firstly, it should be noted that the various characters appear to have ended up in the SV2 for somewhat spurious reasons and, in some cases, even against their personal predilections. This very factor endows the situation with a poignant sense of verisimilitude. Secondly, as Chris Beveridge has pointed out in his review of the series, their everyday interactions come across as eminently authentic for the simple reason that they

> have to work with each other, but there isn't the usual egging on of opposites you get in *mecha* series over who has to work with who. They're realistic in the sense that they're there to do a job and sometimes the job can suck. They love getting some down time and they occasionally disagree with their boss.... Captain Gotoh ... is the classic deadpan commander that simply rattles off what must be done and often looks bored by what he's been given to do.... Through their attempts to learn ... we see the interactions of the characters come to life as well as the bonding with the Labors [Beveridge].

The plots included in the first OVA series run the full gamut from thriller to farce, police procedural to science fiction, social satire to monster movie parody, political drama to ghost story. Yet, an element of realism courses consistently through its filmic veins. This is attested to by the characters' tenacious—though not unequivocally successful—efforts to work together as a proper team, on the one hand, and by a highly credible portrayal of the urban setting, on the other. Alongside glimpses of a futuristic megalopolis, we are supplied with realistic pictures of the actual Tokyo of today, with its intimidating high-rises abutting dilapidated edifices, shrines and playgrounds.

One of the most memorable segments in the *Patlabor* franchise as a whole is the opening episode of the first OVA series, "Second Unit, Move Out!" (released on 25 April 1988), where the team are introduced on the very day of the Division's formation, with their quirks, foibles and endearing traits instantly emerging. Thus, we get to meet Noa, a girl who has been inspired to join the section by the fact that she quite simply loves Labors; the seemingly laid-back but extremely shrewd captain Gotoh; the weapon-obsessed Ota; the gentle-giant type Hiromi; Shinshi the hen-pecked husband; and Asuma the reluctant cadet. Episode 1 sets the tone for what is to come in more ways than one. It offers comedy as the team are delayed in the collection of their Labors as a result, rather prosaically, of appalling traffic congestion, as well as serious references to the general state of Tokyo and to related environmental issues. It concurrently emphasizes the poor reputation enjoyed by the Tokyo Metropolitan Police Special Vehicle Division 2 among both the general public and the rest of the police, while also hinting at the complexity of group dynamics.

The series engages with the topic of terrorism in the second episode, "Longshot" (released on 25 June 1988), where the mayor of New York visits the Babylon Project, a colossal off-shore landfill in the middle of Tokyo Bay created for reclamation purposes, and has to be protected by the SV2 against dire threats. In its handling of the theme of terrorist menace, this episode foreshadows the second *Patlabor* feature. The giant monster genre, destined to play a pivotal role in the third *Patlabor* movie, is introduced in the third OVA episode, "The 450 Million-Year-Old Trap" (released on 25 July 1988), as the SV2 investigate a series of accidents in Tokyo Bay that are overtly echoed , more than a decade later, by Kamiyama's feature. Another favorite genre in Japanese pop culture, the ghost story, is invoked in Episode 4, "The Tragedy of L" (released on 25 September 1988), where the police academy appears to be haunted by the specter of a young woman reputedly killed by a paint bullet from a Labor gun as she was watching a mock battle.

Episodes 5 and 6, "The SV2's Longest Day, Part I and Part II" (released on 10 November 1988 and 10 December 1998 respectively) are arguably among the most noteworthy insofar as they constitute the prototype behind *Patlabor 2: The Movie*. The threats of a military coup and a civil war, combined with precarious diplomatic relations involving Japan and the U.S., are brought to the fore in ways that incontrovertibly foreshadow Oshii's second *Patlabor* feature. The first OVA was originally intended to be a six-part series, but a seventh episode — "Go North, SV2!" — was added (and released on 25 June 1989) in order to promote *Patlabor 1: The Mobile Police*. Its focus is once more on the theme of terrorism, and specifically on the nefarious activities of a group known as "Beach House."

While endeavoring to infuse the cumulatively convincing tone of the episodes with an energizing element of humor, Oshii nonetheless aims to draw attention to the doubts and difficulties experienced by its protagonists and supporting cast. In so doing, he proffers an elliptical commentary on the particular chapter of Japan's history with which the production of the *Patlabor* universe as a whole is chronologically associated. Indeed, the destabilization of the characters' empirical certainties points to a dissolution of cognitive and ethical tenets which pithily hints at the ephemerality of the "Bubble" era and to the bursting of its economic promises. 2 Cinematographically, this sense of social and existential insecurity is communicated by camera moves that often cut away from the characters themselves to highlight the imprisoning nature of their world as a stifling bell-jar. At the same time, Oshii frequently resorts to shots that throw into relief a character's reflection on a window pane, as though to allude to the replacement of reality as such by a framed simulacrum thereof. While the OVA series is the harbinger of these techniques, which can indeed be detected across its episodes in embryonic form, Oshii's distinctive directorial signature — of which such camera operations are emblematic — will become more markedly obvious in the feature films to come.

15

Mobile Police Patlabor
TV Series and OVA 2

The *Mobile Police Patlabor* TV series, directed by Naoyuki Yoshinori, encompassed 47 episodes and was aired from 11 October 1989 to 26 September 1990. At the beginning of the series, the SV2 are recruiting new pilots and expecting a new Labor. As this is suddenly hijacked, Noa Izumi takes off after it and her efforts gain her a permanent position within the Division. As elsewhere in the *Patlabor* franchise, in the TV series there are frequent allusions to the dubious reputation enjoyed by Captain Gotoh's unit as a result of its presumed incompetence and eccentricity, as well as an excess of zeal bordering, in the least felicitous circumstances, on plain brutality. These themes are also axial, as argued later in this study, to the Kerberos productions.

The TV series is as varied, generically speaking, as the first OVA series was seen to be. Its episodes include forays into the realms of suspenseful drama, the sci-fi spoof, the monster show, and *Hill-Street-Blues*-like tales revolving around the quotidian chores of the often exhausted and grumpy — yet remarkably resilient — members of the SV2. It should also be noted, however, that despite these generic affinities with the first OVA, the TV series works with a different timeline and cast of characters, frequently bringing into play personas from the original manga not used in either the OVA series or the features.

Oshii contributed the screenplays for five of the episodes: Episode 3, "We're Special Vehicles Section 2"; Episode 9, "Red Labor Landing"; Episode 14, "You Win!"; Episode 29, "The Destruction of the SV2"; and Episode 38, "The Underground Mystery Tour." Episode 3 (originally broadcast on 1 November 1989) follows Noa's initiation into the lifestyle of the SV2. We learn that the unit's location on a vacant lot virtually in the middle of nowhere compels its members to improvise when it comes to food, and hence spend virtually all of their scarce off-duty hours fishing, raising chickens and growing tomatoes. The episode focuses on a fishing expedition in which the crew somehow manage to run the police speed-boat aground, and Ota's attempt to rescue it results in the sinking of his Labor. Noa saves the day, admirably confirming the timely appositeness of her recent addition to the team.

In Episode 9 (originally broadcast on 13 December 1989), Oshii returns once more to the topic of terrorism, this time with a focus on the character of Itchoku Inubashiri, an ex-military Labor pilot now associated with the militant anti–Babylon Project organization "Home of the Sea." At the same time, the episode intimates that terrorists are not Japan's sole — or indeed principal — cause for concern, since government officials such as the Public Safety Agents involved in the plot are themselves motivated by hidden agendas with rather questionable credentials.[1]

Episode 14 (originally broadcast on 24 January 1990) is undoubtedly one of the most overtly comical pieces in the entire series, joyously indulging in a rapid sequence of gags that revolve around Division 2's abysmal performance in a Police Judo Tournament, and a fierce disagreement between the characters of Noa and Kanuka resulting in the further deterioration of their already tense relationship. The plot culminates in a drinking competition of truly herculean proportions.

In Episode 29 (originally broadcast on 23 May 1990), Oshii revisits the type of surreal territory previously explored in the context of *Beautiful Dreamer* and *Twilight Q2: Labyrinth Objects File 538* by recourse to a simple but playfully troubling tale in which what should have been the unproblematic delivery of a take-away food order absurdly mutates into a case of multiple disappearances. When the food fails to reach the SV2 hangar, it transpires that the delivery boy has disappeared with the order. Ota's trip to the restaurant to solve the conundrum results in his own vanishing and when, a few hours later, other members of the crew take off to find him, they too seemingly dissolve into thin air.

Oshii's taste for the surreal manifests itself again in Episode 38 (originally broadcast on 25 July 1990), where the mysterious disappearance of victuals from the SV2 hangar eventually leads to the discovery of a labyrinth of tunnels situated just beneath the landfill upon which the unit's quarters have been erected. (Like the labyrinth, the tunnel constitutes a favorite visual trope in Oshii's cinema, as eloquently borne out by productions as generically diverse and chronologically distant as *Dallos*, *Angel's Egg* and *Ghost in the Shell 2: Innocence*.) As members of the SV2 team resolve to explore the maze in search of an answer to their initial dilemma, they find that cats, rats and utter disorientation are not their only woes. Lurking in the depths of the sewage system is also a most unexpected guest: none other than an albino alligator.

Mike Crandol's review of the *Mobile Police Patlabor* TV series (DVD Vol. 1) for Animé News Network has tersely described it as "one of the crowning achievements of the giant robot genre ... presented in a plausible, realistic manner, with an emphasis on character-driven humor as opposed to superheroic *mecha* battles." The series, as a result, is capable of reaching beyond the scope of adolescent viewers, who constitute the bulk of the audience for conventional *mecha* animations: "everyone's personality and motivations are clearly delineated. Even the smaller players have been imbued with defining character traits." No less remarkable, however, is the narrative use of the robots themselves in a realistic fashion, whereby the Labors' formidable assets are endearingly dwarfed by their deployment in the handling of what often turn out to be jocularly trivial incidents and paltry offences:

> The *Patlabor* team is more likely to encounter a drunken Labor pilot accidentally stepping on buildings than an evil warlord with an army of robotic followers. And while *Patlabor*'s Ingrams may not be the most realistic way to deal with a rogue Labor, the manner in which they are used is entirely logical: instead of launching out of a hidden underground base the Ingrams are loaded on a truck and driven to the scene of the crime, where the Ingram pilot is then guided by another officer in a patrol car [Crandol 2002].

In his later review of the fourth volume of the series on DVD, Crandol has further defined *Patlabor: The Mobile Police*, in affectionately apposite terms as "the little animé series that could. From humble beginnings it launched the careers of many of the industry's top talents and has gone on to become one of the most respected titles in the medium's history" (Crandol 2003).

Tasha Robinson's review of the TV series for *Science Fiction Weekly* has commented along similar lines on its distinctive tone — and, relatedly, on its stylistic, thematic and aesthetic distance from much habitual fare in the animé universe: "The *Patlabor* franchise has gotten high marks from fans simply because the series wastes little time on its eponymous, ubiquitous *mecha*. The Labors do have a sharply detailed, high-tech design.... But the machines spend relatively little time in combat ... as Division 2 farms, fishes, chatters about baffling cases and often only rolls into battle at the end of an episode, if at all. As a result, *Patlabor* comes off more as a good-natured cop comedy than an action series. It moves at a placid, even pace compared to ... any of animé's other similarly hyperkinetic personality-intensive police shows ... most of *Patlabor*'s characters seem as subdued as the flat blue-and-brown color palette that constrains much of the animation" (Robinson 1998).

The second *Patlabor* OVA comprised 16 episodes and was released between 22 November 1990 and 23 April 1992. The second OVA follows directly from the TV series, its first four episodes serving to resolve the "Griffin" saga developed in the TV series. In these episodes, the SV2 has to deal with a powerful but mischievous Labor created by the Schaft Corporation—the "Griffin" in question—and repeated confrontations between Captain Gotoh's forces and the Griffin allow for more *mecha* action than aficionados of Oshii's *Patlabor* features may be accustomed to or even prepared for. The core of the Griffin episodes consists of the conflict between Noa Izumi and the pilot of the rogue Labor, Bud, a highly competitive videogame prodigy who appears to have lost (or possibly deliberately suppressed) any sense of the boundary separating reality from virtuality and, as a result, treats his contests with Noa as inherently ludic events. (Oshii will revisit this topos in the live-action and CGI hybrid *Avalon* in 2001 in a drastically more ominous and metaphysically resonant vein.)

While the red-tressed heroine's courage, skills and enthusiasm are often foregrounded, the Griffin episodes remain faithful to the franchise's seminal conception of the SV2 as an ensemble of complementary—though frequently discordant—personalities. The collaborative spirit is accordingly stressed as both a key theme in the *Patlabor* universe in its entirety and, self-reflexively, as a metaphor for the eminently team-based modus operandi underlying the very notion of animé as an art form. Simultaneously, the series commodiously allows for a jubilant exposure of the SV2's blunders and quirks, portraying its members sympathetically and unsentimentally at once as a bunch of oddballs, misfits and loose cannons.

Oshii's contributions to the second OVA consist of the scripts for Episode 7, "Black Trinary"; Episode 8, "The Seven Days of Fire"; Episode 10, "It's Called Amnesia"; and Episode 13, "The Dungeon—Again." Episode 7 (released on 23 May 1991; dir. Yasunao Aoki) evinces overt links with both *Patlabor 1: The Mobile Police* and *Patlabor 2: The Movie* in its treatment of the topic of terrorism, which here pivots on a series of bombings targeted at business organizations that vaunt connections with the Babylon Project.

Episode 8 (released on 25 July 1991; dir. Yasunori Urata) engages with the issue of intersubjective dynamics, focusing on unresolved tensions between the individual and the group. The discovery of large amounts of pornographic materials among the SV2 mechanics leads to the enforcement of strict rules that leaves these characters with almost no private life. Incensed by their bosses' adoption of such draconian measures, the mechanics revolt, splinter groups rapidly form, and beatings and kidnappings ensue. The episode's overall tone is comedic, yet its narrative concomitantly offers a potentially serious commentary on the ephemerality of harmony and consensus even within the most closely knit of communities.

In Episode 10 (released on 26 September 1991; dir. Nana Harada), the theme closest to Oshii's heart comes to full — and consummately surreal — life as Ota is placed at the center of disturbing oneiric experiences that once more echo *Beautiful Dreamer*. Ota dreams that he is responsible for killing his colleagues, who have turned out to be criminals after all. He wakes up and finds himself in Shinshi's house with Hiromi, Asuma, Shige and Shinshi himself — all of them dead as a result of gun wounds — holding a gun in his hand. Unable to remember who he is, he checks his wallet but this now seems to actually belong to Shinshi. The SV2 must find Ota — whom Gotoh deems the victim of an especially severe case of amnesia — before any *real* harm may come to pass.

Episode 13 (released on 23 January 1992; dir. Nana Harada) is the least explicitly related to the rest of Oshii's oeuvre in thematic terms insofar as neither the political nor the dream dimensions so central to his signature make any obvious appearance. It is, however, distinctively Oshiian at the philosophical level in that it places considerable emphasis on the topos of the *quest*: a motif that traverses Oshii's creative career from the OVA *Angel's Egg* through to the *Ghost in the Shell* features. In this case, the object of the quest is an extremely valuable pearl excreted by the albino alligator that was found in the labyrinth underneath the SV2 hangar in Episode 38 of the TV series and now turns out to have been accommodated in the Tokyo Zoo. Some SV2 mechanics revisit the tunnels in greedy search of more alligators who might, ideally, also prove to be treasure trunks. When they fail to return, other members of the team are forced to embark — albeit rather reluctantly — on a rescue mission.

Although Oshii's contributions to the *Patlabor* TV series and to the second OVA could hardly be described as the most outstanding moments in his creative parable as a director, graphic artist, author and script writer, they undeniably bear witness in their own unobtrusive and unpretentious fashion to his unique filmmaking style and tantalizing knack of intermingling the most ethereal perceptions with the wildest rides into the bizarre.

16

Patlabor 1:
The Mobile Police

The narrative of *Patlabor 1* is triggered by the collusion of two at first seemingly unrelated events: a man's spectacular plunge to his death from the heights of a manufacturing facility located on Tokyo Bay (and capable of servicing all kinds of Labors) known as the "Ark," and the hunting down by the Japanese Self Defence Forces of a rogue Labor which, after its eventual vanquishing, turns out to be pilotless. It is up to Captain Gotoh and to his SV2 associates Noa Izumi and Asuma Shinohara to figure out whether the two occurrences are somehow related and, if so, what the connection amounts to.

It gradually transpires that the suicide presented in the opening sequence was the designer of the Hyper Operating System (HOS) installed in the most recent type of Labor, the software genius Eiichi Hoba working for Shinohara Heavy Industries, and that his self-annihilation had been motivated by guilt resulting from his deliberate insertion into the program of a flaw bound to render the Labors tumultuously destructive. The mutinous robot presented in the early sequence is an instance of precisely a Labor thus infected. As several more automata upgraded with the new Hyper Operating System inexplicably run amok, it is feared that the Ingrams deployed by the Tokyo Metropolitan Police Special Vehicle Division 2 — also, supposedly, upgraded — will likewise go on the rampage.

Captain Gotoh turns out to have been aware all along of the suspicious nature of the new HOS and to have deliberately kept his knowledge from the SV2 agents. This behavior on the boss's part may well be seen as a detestable form of behind-the-scenes puppeteering, and Asuma is understandably angry when he finds out that Gotoh had secretly put a stop to the upgrading procedure by specifically instructing the team's technowizard, Shige, not to install the novel software into the Ingrams. Having devoted a lot of time and energy to the investigation that eventually led him to the discovery of the infected HOS masterdisk, the young man feels, quite simply, used.

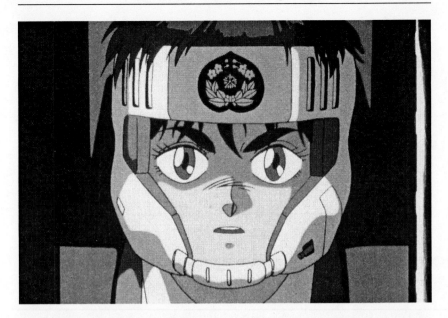

Patlabor 1: The Mobile Police (1989). Young and sensitive yet dauntless, Noa Izumi of SV2 bravely embarks upon the herculean task of deactivating an infected computer with the potential for triggering a cataclysmic Labor rampage. The character's facial features epitomize some of the most distinctive graphic conventions that have come to be associated with animé across the globe. ©HEADGEAR/EMOTION/TFC.

It should also be noted, in this respect, that Asuma is an especially problematic character within the overall milieu of the SV2. As we have seen, the Section in its entirety has to cope with the often unpalatable repercussions of its isolated status—a state of affairs resulting from the fact that in spite of its key role in addressing Labor-induced crimes under the direction of its captivatingly shrewd commander, neither the government nor the general public are automatically willing to lend it their support. However, in Asuma's case matters are further complicated by his divided social standing as both a member of the SV2 and the disaffected son of the president of Shinohara Heavy Industries. This split is exacerbated, in the specific context of *Patlabor 1*, by the suspicion that Asuma's unflinching commitment to the unraveling of Hoba's grand plot may be — at least partly — motivated by personal acrimony towards his father. Oshii's inveterate preoccupation with the difficulty, and perhaps even the impossibility, of reconciling private and collective aspirations finds resonant and affecting formulation in this particular dimension of the first *Patlabor* feature. Tangential allusions to the topics of class-related conflict and cross-generational tension are simultaneously evident.

While Gotoh's strategy undeniably is, on one level, manipulative, it could also be argued that it ensues from a well-intentioned commitment to his subordinates' self-development and that the captain's priority, in this regard, is to enable them to learn by their own efforts rather than merely expect them to follow someone else's orders. Hence, Gotoh's circuitous route may ultimately constitute an at least partially benevolent white lie. It is worth observing that the character's inclination to withhold information as a means of prompting his corps to engage in personal investigative undertakings is not a totally new development in the *Patlabor* world, for it was actually already evident in the seventh episode of the first OVA series, where Gotoh was eventually found to have staged the "haunting" case around which the plot revolves solely for the purpose of sharpening the SV2 members' wits.

Asuma comes gradually to realize that the goal of the virus embedded in the new program is to make the Labors sensitive to certain high-pitched sounds and go berserk as a result. Helped by Shige, he also finds out that sounds of such a kind may be produced by architectural structures situated in particular locations, especially if these were caused to resonate together by a major atmospheric commotion such as a typhoon — one of which, alas, is due to strike Tokyo in no more than a couple of days. There is little doubt that the outcome would be nothing short of cataclysmic. Insofar as the principal trigger would be the noise produced by the Ark, its destruction would certainly mean that no sufficiently high-pitched resonances could be emitted to stimulate the Labors and give free rein to their frenzy. The SV2 are hence charged with the formidable task of demolishing the mighty edifice — a mission they accomplish with indubitably spectacular effects.

In the film's climax, the reflective police procedural concedes way to the countdown-thriller modality. This, however, is unconventionally handled — arguably, well in accordance with Oshii's iconoclastic flair: the heroes and heroines are just about able to stem the impending catastrophe but are powerless to attenuate its impact and repercussions. Gotoh recognizes that, in the circumstances, the end justifies the means and, embodying the anarchic spirit of which he has already shown himself capable at its boldest, does not hesitate to bend the rules. Nevertheless, he has no faith in politicians and is well aware that once the SV2's mission is over, should he be unable to warrant his decision, the entire team would go down in history as a bunch not of champions of law and order but as archcriminals. Furthermore, a foreboding aura of dire ineluctability appears to surround the whole operation: as the captain at one point observes, the very moment Hoba jumped to his death, the game was in a sense already over, and it has therefore all along been a case of opting for the lesser of two evils, not of seeking salvation or redemption.

When, in the action's crowning moments, the typhoon from China hits Tokyo and Noa triggers the self-destruction of the Ark, thus preventing the spread of lethal resonances across the city, we are given a partly consolatory finale. Yet, the damage done is irreparable, and the deep sense of social and political disruption unleashed by the concatenation of events which the computer genius unleashed can hardly be eradicated by the closing shots of smiling and cheering SV2 agents.

Patlabor 1 offers a dexterously orchestrated and discreetly cerebral detective yarn. One of its most enticing aspects consists precisely of its gradual unraveling of the riddle set in motion by Hoba, a process which we are encouraged to participate in by identifying with the character of Asuma as he resolutely pursues his initially flimsy leads, while Captain Gotoh and his lifelong and loyal friend Detective Matsui retrace the scientist's steps along twenty-six different residences in the most derelict nooks of Tokyo. This particular component of the SV2's collaborative unearthing of Hoba's nefarious scheme contributes some of the most somberly memorable scenes to the movie as a whole.

While playing an instrumental role in the advancement of the filmic plot, these scenes concomitantly constitute tastefully restrained pieces of social commentary in exhibiting the two older characters' peregrinations through Tokyo as this is quotidianly transformed by seemingly endless construction projects, and yet uncannily manages to preserve elusive pockets of traditional architecture and related lifestyles. Furthermore, Oshii's recurrent use of slow tracking shots that minutely capture Tokyo's ever-mutating architecture afford him scope for documenting the hybrid character of the contemporary Japanese megalopolis—and, by extension, for contemplating metaphorically that of contemporary Japanese culture at large—as an admixture of the old and the new, the indigenous and the global, the shiny spectacle of glass and chrome and the murky underbelly of trash-infested slums.

The shift from the serial format to a feature-length production inaugurated by *Patlabor 1: The Mobile Police* enabled Oshii not only to articulate a more complex narrative than had previously been feasible but also to slow down the overall pace of the action and incorporate elaborate long takes and brooding moments of introspection most consonant with his aesthetic preferences. Rapid action is actually confined to four sequences: the intensely moody opening battle in the forest, involving a platoon of military Labors and human soldiers, in which a malfunctioning automaton is first apprehended; the SV2's relatively comical fight against a deranged construction Labor that has alarmingly managed to restart by its own initiative in the aftermath of an accident; the SV2's assault upon the Ark; and the final duel engaging Noa Izumi's Labor "Alphonse" and an enraged HOS-equipped specimen. On the whole, however, Oshii typically favors a markedly deliberate, meticulously timed and methodically paced rhythm. A classic example of this stylistic predilection is supplied by the early sequence in which a helicopter surveys Tokyo Bay while a reporter comments on the Babylon Project and on Labor-related developments. So judiciously unhasty is its capture that the image of the helicopter appears to be glued to the background picture of the sky for quite some time, and the spectator does not actually become aware of its motion until a small portion of a building which was not originally incorporated in the scene becomes evident at the edge of the frame, signaling dynamic change.

A subtly varied and generally subdued soundtrack, characterized by the alternation of simple single-instrument pieces with faster themes for the action sequences— articulated in conjunction with an analogous chromatic oscillation between dusky and vivacious palettes—fittingly complements the film's distinctive rhythm. The character designs created by Akemi Takada yield attractively well-rounded personas— largely by recourse to fastidiously detailed and suggestively shadowed graphics— without pandering to the ethos of cuteness fostered by the same artist in animations such as *Maison Ikkoku*, the hugely popular 1986 TV series directed by Kazuo Yamazaki (*et alia*).

Patlabor 1 was the first animé in the franchise to be released to the Anglophone world. The English dub is arguably marred by some rather bizarre changes which at times alter the mood of a scene. On the whole, the language is more graphic and the dialogue is more explicitly intended to bolster the action than in the original, where — as also indicated by the relatively literal and unadorned English subtitles in contrast with the dub — a more reflective tone tends to be adopted. A particularly amusing instance of utterly unnecessary adjustment is provided by the scene where in the original the airport official asks the SV2 associate Kanuka Clancy— in English —"Sightseeing?" and she replies— also in English —"No, combat." This brief exchange has a crisply humorous impact that is very much in keeping with the terse and generally laconic disposition evinced by Kanuka, and it is hard to imagine what could possibly have inspired the producers of the Anglophone version to amend the exchange so that the airport official's line becomes "Occupation?" and Kanuka's reply "Labor pilot"— thereby yielding a purely and uninspiringly factual piece of language.

Among the recurring traits of Oshii's signature that feature most prominently in the movie are bird-related symbolic images evocative of both freedom and entrapment — most memorably, in the profusion of empty and decrepit cages associated with the numerous apartments inhabited by Hoba prior to his suicide — and religious allusions. As observed in Part One, Oshii tends to utilize bird-related tropes in order to conjure up

metaphorically notions of freedom and transcendence. The association of
the deranged computer scientist in *Patlabor 1* with ornithological imagery
in general is underscored from the start, the last living creature with which
Hoba interacts being either a raven or a crow (depending on the individual critic's choice).[1] When, at the end, Noa reaches the top level of the Ark
wherein its disactivation may be effected, she encounters myriad birds. One
of these is especially noticeable insofar as it flaunts Hoba's own ID tag,
bearing the number 666 upon it — namely, a traditional symbol for the
"Antichrist" or the "Beast." On one level, Hoba could indeed be regarded
as a free spirit capable of pursuing to the bitter end a wholly personal dream,
unshackled by societally validated mores. On another level, however, the
dream in question proves utterly poisonous, and its pursuit inexorably
becomes a path to self-hatred and, finally, self-erasure. The recurrent use
of empty cages alludes precisely to the vacuously delusory character of the
genius's vision, exposing a trap that may ultimately only open out onto a
disconsolate void.

Where religious references are concerned, Biblical imagery is especially prominent, and consistently translated into technological correlatives. Thus, the Ark becomes a gigantic factory, while the Tower of Babel
comes to be equated with Tokyo's skyscrapers and, more specifically, with
their diabolical connotations as perceived by Hoba (whose very name, incidentally, could be read as a deliberate distortion of the Hebrew word for
God, "Heova," or "Jeova"). Oshii's film makes subtle use of the Babel myth
as a quintessential indictment of human arrogance, causing God's wrath
and eliciting punishment. In the Bible, this takes the form of a proliferation of languages conducive to a total breakdown in human communication and hence chaos. In *Patlabor 1*, Hoba plays God by recourse to the virus
implanted into the new HOS — and indeed tagged "Babel" — as a means of
engineering an apocalyptic collapse of any options of constructive interaction among humans and Labors. The name assigned to the Babylon Project is itself worthy of notice, "Babylon" being the designation given to Babel
after God's unleashing of linguistic diversity and usually taken to mean
"confusion," even though — strictly speaking — it is actually the Greek adaptation of the Semitic word "Bab-Illu," which literally means "The Gate of
God."

Given the scientist's destructive aspirations, Hoba's conduct clearly
does not contribute to the investment of the notion of divinity with an
especially impeccable reputation. Furthermore, he comes across as a divided
and psychologically vulnerable personality, as evinced by the fact that he
concomitantly seeks to delete all traces of his existence and provenance by
moving repeatedly from one dilapidated apartment to the next, and yet
appears to yearn to have his path retraced after his death by fastidiously

caring to communicate his multiple changes of address to the relevant authorities. Even the words found by Gotoh and by Detective Matsui on the wall of the last Hoba residence could be interpreted as a cryptic attempt on the scientist's part to make contact with a future which he clearly could not envisage but to which he nonetheless felt mysteriously drawn. These read: "He bowed the heavens also, and came down: and darkness was under his feet." Gotoh opines that the citation comes from the Old Testament but cannot remember its exact source. As it happens, its origin resides with Psalm 18:9 and its context is that of a song intended to praise God for releasing David's soul from his enemies.

Taken in conjunction, the textual and visual references discussed above are used to suggest that technology holds lethal potentialities in some of its both actual and hypothetical configurations. Hence, the film could be read as a dispassionate commentary on the perennial human fear of technological advancement, conducted through the articulation of the birth-gone-wrong topos traceable back to the Frankenstein story (and very possibly beyond). Nevertheless, *Patlabor 1* also emphasizes that organized religion is ultimately no less deleterious an instrument for oppression and misinformation than technological development. The evils of ideological dogmatism, as argued in the next section of this study, continue playing a pivotal part in the second *Patlabor* feature.

17

Patlabor 2: The Movie

The second *Patlabor* feature is set in early 2002, three years after the adventure depicted in *Patlabor 1* took place. Since the events presented in Oshii's first feature, most of the SV2 members have either retired or moved to subordinate duty. Only Captains Gotoh and Nagumo have retained permanent official positions in their original capacities.

The first film was indubitably a politically engaged work tackling the iniquitous prioritization of financial interests over the safety of the people, the nefarious effects of rampant and endless construction projects and concomitant sleaze, the evolution of technology well beyond the boundaries of common sense, and the physical and psychological exhaustion of the very forces presumed to bolster law and order. *Patlabor 2*, however, reaches new heights and a greater level of both thematic and technical refinement. Central to its narrative is the theme of war as a concurrently collective and personal aberration, involving governmental and international issues at the macrolevel, and personal disappointments and grudges at the microlevel.

This point is brought home right from the start by the sequence in which the character of Yukihito Tsuge, the commander of a Japanese *mecha* force who asks headquarters for permission to fire while under severe attack by enemy troops in a Cambodian forest, is denied consent, and ends up losing all his subordinates in the operation. Beset by resentment towards his superiors, by the sheer horror of his recollections of warfare and by a latent sense of guilt brought about by his being the sole survivor, Tsuge decides to take revenge by staging his own personal war and throwing Tokyo into utter chaos. He hence engineers a series of terrorist attacks on the city, the graphic rendition of which eerily anticipates a set of images now imprinted in global consciousness in connection with 9/11—especially in the sequence dramatizing the disintegration of a bridge in metropolitan Tokyo meant to stand out as one of the city's most prominent landmarks. Tsuge thus aims at forcing ordinary citizens to experience a taste of the atrocities he himself has witnessed on the battlefield.

In the wake of the explosion, an amateur video of the event is shown on the news reports. This flaunts the image of a Japanese Self Defence Force fighter jet flying overhead moments after the explosion, intimating that this plane was responsible for firing a live missile into the car parked on Yokohama Bay Bridge that contained the fatal bomb. However, when the enigmatic character of Arakawa Shigeki — who claims to work for an organization named Ground Defence Force — visits Captains Gotoh and Nagumo and shows them another video of the bridge taken from a different camera, quite a different plane comes into view that is patently *not* of the type owned by the JSDF. According to Arakawa, the jet displayed by the putatively undoctored footage of which he is in possession was an American plane coming from a Japanese base. He also maintains that behind the attack lie the machinations of the National Defence Family, a group of military contractors eager to stimulate Japan's interest in arms to expand their business network. This organization's aim would be to foster a pervasive psychology of anxiety and fear but not to actually trigger a catastrophic accident. The twin facts that the missile fired by the plane was, however, seriously armed and that the firing fighter jet did not return to base leads to the assumption that some other force driven by quite a separate agenda must also be involved.

It is this speculative trail that throws Tsuge into relief as the primary suspect. As Arakawa explains to the somewhat bewildered SV2 chiefs, the likely offender is a founding member of the National Defence Family who has gone on to elaborate a personal plan beyond the original aims and objectives of that organization. Tsuge is said to have coordinated a UN peacekeeping mission[1] in Southeast Asia involving military Labors that resulted in calamitous failure in 1999. The incident in question is clearly the one dramatized in the early sequence mentioned above. Tsuge then vanished and no record of his moves beyond that fatal event seems available. We later discover that the suspect had also been the founder of one of the pioneering Labor schools — the very institution at which Shinobu Nagumo had trained and gained a sterling reputation as a top student. Unfortunately for her career, Captain Nagumo had also had an affair with Tsuge, which was considered rather unpropitious in light of his status at the time as a married man.

The National Defence Family is quick to strike again while the Bay Bridge attack is still the object of anxious speculation among politicians and the general public alike. In their second assault, the Japanese Self Defence Force radar system is hacked into, making it possible for the transgressor to stage a fake attack on Tokyo. Oshii's acerbic critique of the specious alliances quotidianly forged, dismantled and renovated afresh among economic, political and military forces strikes its distinctive chords: the Air Force computers, we are told, had been supposed to constitute a perfectly sealed and therefore impregnable network, but the security system had been crippled by political priorities and even indirectly sabotaged by them as a result of inadequate financing. As a result, the JSDF had ended up linking their mainframes to U.S. bases, which inevitably increased the possibility of the system being infiltrated and of phony attacks being thereby staged.

It should also be noted that this portion of the movie echoes actual occurrences. In 1978, a Russian MIG-25 pilot defected and flew into Japanese airspace, thus panicking the whole nation. Moreover, there is the notorious case of a botched-up computerized simulation intended for training purposes which accidentally sent the U.S. to Defcon 3, posing the threat of nuclear confrontation with what was then the Soviet Union.

The action rapidly accelerates towards irreversible crisis as the Tokyo Metropolitan Police endeavors to gain dominance over the JSDF, planting the seeds for a deleterious conflict of interests between the police and the military. The government, in turn, appears keen on emplacing the police forces themselves in the role of a convenient scapegoat. The entire country is thus recklessly forced onto a dismal path, the logical destinations of which can only be anarchy and, potentially, a civil war. Arakawa at one point proposes that this is a "drama" in which nobody is willing or prepared to "play the lead."

To exemplify the state of pernicious disunity resulting from human beings' sectarian defensiveness, *Patlabor 2* makes use of Biblical references and imagery in much the same way as the first feature did. The film captures this theme in markedly foreboding terms by recourse to the following passage from the New Testament:

> Suppose ye that I am come to give peace on earth? I tell you, Nay; but rather division:
> For from henceforth there shall be five in one house divided, three against two, and two against three.
> The father shall be divided against the son, and the son against the father; the mother against the daughter, and the daughter against the mother; the mother in law against her daughter in law, and the daughter in law against her mother in law [Luke 12:51–53].

The situation precipitates as the military occupy Tokyo, while mysterious blimps disable the city's communication networks throwing its population into total mayhem even as gently cascading snowflakes incongruously mantle the blighted metropolis in fairytale charm. The SV2 agents, eventually reunited by Captain Gotoh to stop Tsuge, once again save the day, though they cannot be certain until the very end whether Shinobu is unequivocally dependable or whether there is still a danger that her personal feelings towards the terrorist will hamper the mission.

Patlabor 2 is arguably the most overtly political animé ever produced, striking as it does right at the heart of Japan's myths of peace and stability laboriously constructed and furbished since the Second World War and the ensuing Occupation. In elliptically commenting on Japan's post-WW2 history, the movie alludes to the hypothesis that Japanese democracy is actually, as cultural critic Masao Murayama has suggested, a "sham of democracy" (Murayama). It could even be maintained, in this regard, that *Patlabor 2* constitutes a politically deconstructive film, insofar as it is eager to contemplate conflicting attitudes to the concepts of peace and war, social stability and transgression, justice and iniquity, and ultimately points to an insoluble conundrum whereby no one particular attitude may be unproblematically upheld as more defensible or demonstrably more legitimate.

The pivotal enigma at the core of the movie is the question of whether an "unjust peace" is finally to be preferred to a "just war." The thesis examined by Oshii is the notion that wars can never be just insofar as they are ineluctably motivated by dogmatism, self-interest and mindless pugnacity — as attested to by Japan's cooperation with the Nazis in WW2. However, peace itself can only be preserved by unjust means, namely at the expense of other countries having to suffer for the benefit of the privileged. As Arakawa observes in the course of a philosophical exchange with Captain Gotoh, "Japan's prosperity is built on the corpses of racial violence and civil wars. Our peace comes from ignoring the misery of the world." He later adds: "Perhaps some day we'll realize that peace is more than the absence of war." Nevertheless, the film reflects, it would hardly be equitable, in recognition of this state of affairs, to allow terrorism to gain the upper hand. It is on this front that *Patlabor 2*'s central characters find themselves contending with a concurrently ethical and ideological aporia.

Whereas Hoba's malevolent intent in the first *Patlabor* movie was quite overt and relatively easy to grasp, Tsuge's evil is more complex, potentially deserving of a certain degree of sympathy and, accordingly, more intricately constellated. Furthermore, the narrative's ethical ambiguity is heightened by the psychological and affective conflicts experienced by the upholders of justice themselves — particularly, by Captain Nagumo who, while endeavoring to apprehend those responsible for the acts of terrorism, also has to negotiate the legacy of her romantic past with Tsuge.

Cinematographically, both *Patlabor* features evince Oshii's distinctive penchant for slow and deliberate pacing. *Patlabor 1* may disappoint fans of wall-to-wall action, whereas *Patlabor 2* contains plenty of extremely dynamic activity. Yet, this difference is almost negligible if one approaches the two films as companion pieces, subtly bound by complementary preoccupations. The second *Patlabor* feature marks Oshii's first foray into a sustained integration of traditional cel animation and computer-generated graphics — a technique destined to reach its apotheosis in the *Ghost in the*

Shell movies. As CGI expert Seiichi Tanaka has emphasized, digital techniques were brought into play very discriminately, on the basis of Oshii's genuine conviction that they would benefit a sequence in ways which traditional animation could not aspire to equal, and never for their own sake. An especially telling example of this judicious approach to CGI is supplied by the early sequence in which Tsuge's troops are ambushed and annihilated. The execution of this sequence gained considerably from the implementation of digital technology but this was the result of considered and incremental experimentation and not a foregone conclusion. As Tanaka explains,

> at the time the Southeast Asia scenes were being composed, the soldiers were only represented as flat silhouettes. To express the nervous feeling before a battle, the director ... came up with the idea of using shadows.... To cut the time needed for the calculations to render the images, the outlines of the soldiers were highlighted and traced, then rendered in 2D images [Tanaka].

However, the film's technical distinctiveness is due not solely to its adventurous manipulation of disparate animational styles and corresponding methodologies but also, no less crucially, to Oshii's steadfast commitment to camera-based operations. In the filming of *Patlabor 2*, Oshii maintains, particular attention was devoted to the choreography of conversation scenes. The "basic approach" here employed "was to make the characters face the same way. I didn't want to give the impression of humans confronting humans, but more of humans facing a monitor. I wanted the idea of 'interface' to permeate the overall composition of the film. The film is about people who look at monitors and the information on them" (Oshii 2003). This criterion was sustained throughout the execution of *Patlabor 2*: not merely in sequences where characters are literally gazing at television or computer screens but also in those where the object of attention is an alternative form of visual display in which the characters seem far more interested than in holding eye contact with one another. A paradigmatic instance is provided by the scene in the aquarium where Captain Gotoh and Arakawa voice their respective views (with Arakawa, as elsewhere, engaging in a fair amount of lecturing) regarding the impending crisis. The two characters face a tank unremittingly as they converse, never exchanging even the merest glance, the hypnotizing beauty of the tropical fish therein providing an unsettling contrast with the gruesome political reality ravaging the outside world.

In *Patlabor 2*, Oshii concurrently capitalizes on what may well be considered the most elementary cinematographical concept, namely that of the *frame*, to memorable effect. As the director has observed, a "frame is used to see an object more clearly. Your point of view changes, depending on what kind of framing you use. You need a particular framing mode to express an object accurately." Comparing the second *Patlabor* feature with its predecessor in the franchise, Oshii has also noted: "This time, I used people sitting in a row, scenes composed with opposite frames, and moving viewpoints. Last time, I focused on confrontational eye contact. This time, I focused heavily on vehicles. I wanted to put across the situation from the cockpit of a vehicle, *seeing the town from a moving point of view*. And what the people are thinking about from that viewpoint"—hence, the sustained deployment of long shooting as a means of allowing the audience to garner and assimilate the often profuse details of a scene slowly and gradually (Oshii 2003; emphasis added).

As hinted at in the above citation, the cinematographical distinctiveness of *Patlabor 2* largely stems from its potent dramatization of both the actual space and the speculative notion of the city as a living organism, whereby Tokyo ultimately asserts itself as its true protagonist. *Patlabor 1*, as we have seen, already pointed in this direction by consistently engaging in studiously orchestrated surveys of urban architecture by means of some of the most unforgettable pillow sequences ever offered by an animated film. The sequel develops the trend inaugurated by the first movie, gaining considerably from the director's hands-on involvement in the exploration of the actual urban spaces from which the semi-fictional Tokyo portrayed in the film would emanate.

To this effect, Oshii undertook carefully planned fieldwork and instead of simply relying on the photographs obtained by location scouts (though hundreds of these were indeed taken), he took part in helicopter rides over Tokyo which maintained an altitude comparable to that at which a bird would fly and hence enabled the director to conceive of realistic bird's-eye views of the city. Refreshingly, Oshii is perfectly capable of acknowledging the jocular dimension of this enterprise and has indeed stated that exploring places one would not normally visit and riding unfamiliar vehicles are part of the "fun" (Oshii 2003) of making a film and that it is vital to devise ways of communicating this sense of fun to the audience and to enable them to participate in it—even in the context of harrowing visual narratives such as *Patlabor 2*.

Oshii has also commented eloquently on his personal perception of metropolitan experience and urban expansion, thereby shedding light on the social and psychological concerns underlying the representation of Tokyo in the *Patlabor* films:

> I've been living in Tokyo for forty-some years. It's easy to think that this is an uninteresting city, or that you want to destroy it. The most frustrating thing I feel when I watch movies such as *Akira* [dir. Katsuhiro Otomo, 1988] is that they destroy Tokyo so easily. If you depict it as a city which you won't miss even if it were destroyed, as a fake thing made from only steel and concrete from the begin-

ning, destroying it won't accomplish anything. It's far from being a real catharsis. Even in Tokyo, if you look carefully, if you dig up your memories, you can
find some scenery which you are very much attracted to. It can be the evening
at the train crossing, or it can be scenery of some vacant land ... in Tokyo Bay
area. We have scenery we love inside of us [Oshii 1993].

Most vitally, in this respect, the *Patlabor* movies suggest that space is never
a uniform reality. In fact, disparate realities meet and merge within its
uncertain boundaries to create a hybrid and composite world. This is
typified by the contemporary city: rationalized by electronic technology as
a neat computational grid, urban reality is nevertheless often messy and
sprawling. The postmodern metropolis stands out as a mixture of sanitized
virtual spaces and loci of physical decay and anarchy: the immaterial geography of computer networks is at all times interwoven with a corporeal
geography of pollution and decay.

At the same time, the city as ideated by Oshii serves to underscore the
significance of the specifically bodily dimension of space, entailing the plausibility of a mutual transformation of architectural and organic bodies. On
the one hand, human beings can be conceived of as artificial structures:
here humanity is *architecturalized*. On the other hand, it is possible to think
about buildings as bodies: here architecture becomes *humanized*. Above all,
it could be argued that cities themselves both *are* and *have* bodies: the city
is born, grows, conceives, reproduces and dies; it has sex, as suggested by
the idea of the city reaching a climax; it follows certain diets; it develops
diseases, neuroses and disabilities, such as congestion, tumorous over-
growth, hyperactivity and the fear of alien infractions; it exhibits anabolic
and catabolic processes, corresponding to its creative and destructive
moments; it has both naked and clothed facets, both sealed and leaky elements, and adorns itself, either uniformly or eclectically; it contains ideal-
ized and monumental body parts to be proudly flaunted, and secret,
intimate parts to be cautious or ashamed of; finally, it bears the signs of the
passing of time as so many indentations, folds, lines and wrinkles in the
tissue of its architectural make-up. Oshii's urban settings also constitute
markedly *textual* bodies since they are persistently posited as networks of
narratives that people weave as they move through them, constantly remapping space by creating ever new (evanescent, ghostly) routes.

Oshii undeniably foregrounds the negative repercussions of unre-
strained metropolization by subtly implying a transition from a model of
the city based on the principle of implosion, namely the mobilization of
disparate activities in the service of the human community, to a cultural
scenario dominated by rhythms of explosion, whereby the city bursts open
and disperses its vital organs over a broad landscape. However, one should
also acknowledge the positive potentialities of explosion: namely, those ele-

ments of plurality and difference—central to postmodern versions of the deterritorialized city—that serve to unsettle rigidly hierarchical configurations of order and, by extension, to call into question the ultimate value of thoroughly routinized urban lives.

Ultimately, whichever way one looks at it, Oshii's cinema does not for a moment allow us to ignore that the contemporary megalopolis has problematized conventional notions of both space and time by positing a diffuse geography wherein space engulfs time and motion, and by underscoring the vital part played by memory in the apprehension of space. Memory represents not so much a personal attribute or possession as the receptacle for a collective imagination in which even the most intimate thoughts are endlessly translatable into public signs. Furthermore, the pervasiveness of electronic systems of signification and communication has fostered a progressive flattening of both spatial and temporal depth by making an astonishing amount of data simultaneously available across the immaterial realm of cyberspace—the sum total of the data produced and disseminated by electronic means. Oshii's engagement with diverse technopolitical preoccupations by means of the *Patlabor* movies and of their rendition of urban hybridity will evolve so as to elect cyberspace itself as the primary arena in *Avalon* and in the *Ghost in the Shell* features.

18

Patlabor WXIII: Movie 3

Patlabor 3 is loosely based on volumes 7 to 10 of the original manga from which the *Patlabor* franchise draws inspiration, known as *Waste Product 13* or just *Wasted 13*, even though it should be noted that in the parent text, the new detectives portrayed in Fumihiko Takayama's film did not feature at all. Work on the movie began in 1994, at which stage it was meant to be an OVA rather than a feature-length production and was not intended to contain the word "*Patlabor*" in its title in consideration of its status as a side story to the main narrative arc, set between *Patlabor 1* and *Patlabor 2*. Indeed, the film only belongs to the *Patlabor* universe in a tangential sense, given that it patently does not focus on the SV2 and their Ingrams: mere cameo appearances, amounting to no more than fifteen minutes of screen-time, are reserved for Captain Gotoh, for Noa Izumi and for Asuma Shinohara, and Labor action, limited to the finale, likewise covers about a quarter of an hour of the film's overall 107-minute duration. The project was eventually promoted to the feature format in 1997 but the production process dragged into 2002 due to protracted financial difficulties.

As R.J. Havis has observed, the third *Patlabor* feature "puts character development before action…. The appeal of the *Patlabor* series largely comes down to the action antics of the Special Vehicle Division Section 2 and their terrific machinery. But *WXIII* takes a different stance, relegating the giant robots to a showcase finale in an abandoned stadium. Instead, the story plays out as a delicate sci-fi." Thus, even though Takayama's film is "not as philosophically complex as its predecessors," it is undeniably "sophisticated enough to attract a select crowd" and therefore represents an undeniably worthy complement to the franchise as a whole (Havis).

Patlabor 3 integrates the usually separate animé subgenres of the giant robot movie and the monster movie. The former, as shown earlier in this section, is part and parcel of the *mecha* tradition, on which the *Patlabor* animations constitute a refreshingly novel variation. The latter represents a distinctively Japanese artifact normally designated by the label "*kaijuu*," a term that could be literally translated as "strange beast" or "mysterious beast." A more accurate denomination, incidentally, would be "*daikaijuu*," the prefix *dai-* specifically indicating the creature's imposing dimensions. The prototype for this indigenous form is quite unanimously associated with *Godzilla.*[1]

In *Patlabor 3*'s opening sequence — eerily reminiscent of Oshii's *Twilight Q2: Labyrinth Objects File 538* in its emphasis on the surreal conjunction of flying vehicles and marine creatures — a fishing boat on Tokyo Bay spots a malfunctioning plane overhead, as large fish and other sea species fall out of the sky, violently rocking the boat. The plane ends up crashing into the ocean. Two months later, Detectives Takashi Kusumi and Shinichiro Hata are called to investigate Labor-related accidents in the harbor: several automata manufactured by "Schaft" have apparently been attacked and their pilots ruthlessly exterminated. The assaults, of which four have thus far been recorded, appear to have started ten days after the plane crash — and attendant fish deluge — seen in the opening scene, and it seems feasible to suspect there may be a link between the two sets of mishaps. Henceforth, the two agents' investigative efforts are subtly intertwined with a parallel plot pivoting on a discreetly understated romantic liaison between Hata and the enigmatic female scientist Saeko Misaki, as the latter struggles to come to terms with the tragedy of a deeply traumatic double bereavement, having lost both her husband and her only child in quick succession.

The culprit behind the Tokyo Bay incidents turns out to be a colossal and eminently adaptive biological mutation worthy of H.R. Giger at his most gruesomely inspired. When a fragment of the fishy beast's living tissue is obtained and subjected to DNA tests, these reveal that its makeup consists of a combination of cancer cells and special "Nishiwaki" cells that have the ability to reproduce at a staggering rate. Hata's investigation leads him to a suspicious medical company where the dejected Saeko is employed in the capacity of researcher. The plot's intensity suddenly escalates, following protracted stretches of methodically paced investigative sequences, when it transpires that Saeko herself has engendered the calamitous mutant with the use of cancerous cells from the body of her dead daughter Hitomi in order to enable the child to live on.[2]

Central to the film's philosophy is the idea that the two detectives find themselves in a position to shift gears from a slowly plodding investigation to the potentially scandalous exposure of a major political drama, and hence to the murky core of the case, quite coincidentally. The plot thus hints at the pervasive incidence of random chance and of unplanned contingencies in human life, tersely reprising Oshii's own persistent emphasis on the unpredictability of existence, on the mythical character of the laws of both logic and physics and on the intractably ephemeral nature of the dreamed and the empirical alike.

Furthermore, even though Oshii was not personally involved in the production of *Patlabor 3*, the movie frequently echoes the thematic concerns, cinematographical approach and cumulative tone characteristic of the first two *Patlabor* features. Like *Patlabor 1*, the third film features faulty Labors as the clue to a broader drama, concurrently incorporating a romantic element redolent of *Patlabor 2*. The film also revisits the quintessentially Frankensteinian birth-gone-wrong topos in quite a literal sense. In *Patlabor 1* and in *Patlabor 2*, the monstrous progeny was featured in the guise of perverse ideological agendas— Hoba's and Tsuge's, respectively — whereas in Takayama's movie, the unruly prodigy is an intensely material and full-fledged genetic aberration. At the same time, however, *Patlabor 3* shares with its predecessors a foreboding message concerning the ultimate inseparability of driven idealism and insanity whereby even initially benevolent and loving intentions may yield nefarious results. Moreover, all three perpetrators of varying deviant acts are eventually doomed to suicidal moves, consisting of graphic jumps to unseemly deaths in the cases of Hoba and Saeko, and a more metaphorical but no less poignantly compulsive journey towards self-annihilation in the case of Tsuge.

From a cinematographical point of view, *Patlabor 3* evinces a marked preference for the same kind of measured and deliberate pace, regularly punctuated by meditative pan shots, to be characteristically found in Oshii's own features. This is especially evident in the pillow sequences dramatizing Detectives Kusumi and Hata's frustrating investigation, following their steps across minutely detailed urban scenery which once again emplaces the city as the true protagonist. Indeed, the director wished to incorporate several "ordinary life" sequences to enable spectators to experience a "feeling of the era, as well as an urban atmosphere." According to Takayama,

> [f]ilm should not pursue the "why" aspects of the story. Rather, its pursuit should be "how to present it." I placed a particularly heavy emphasis on the mood in the air…. While we were working on the story concept of *WXIII*, there were some horrific events in Japan including the catastrophic earthquake in Kobe and Aum Shinrikyo Sarin attack in Tokyo. Everyone … felt the prosperous era of Japan was coming to an end. You could actually feel it in the air. I wanted to recreate this mood in *Patlabor 3* [Takayama].[3]

This aesthetic mission inexorably translated into extremely time-consuming production processes, insofar as authentic backgrounds for all the scenes (and especially those involving cityscapes) had to be executed in the tiniest details. The director remained adamantly faithful throughout the movie's laborious gestation to the importance of investing *Patlabor 3* with a distinctive visual identity by presenting ordinary situations so that they would look authentically commonplace and not merely come across as artificial approximations to the everyday. To achieve this effect, the animators had to devote close attention to those prosaic elements of a setting that most animations—and indeed many live-action productions, too—tend to gloss over. The result is a stunning plethora of painstakingly rendered minutiae that enable even the most obdurately inanimate objects —fences, rails, flagstones and brick walls included—to come exuberantly to life.

As supervisor Yutaka Izubuchi has emphasized, the sense of the ordinary treasured by the director and his animating team was consistently bolstered by the use of particular camera angles: "Takayama's camera angles show each scene from within, as if from the eyes of a person" (Izubuchi), thus conveying a sense of intimacy whereby the spectator is absorbed into the action and encouraged to savor its quotidian flavor.

At the same time, Takayama is capable of evoking a paradoxically haunting sense of tranquility, juxtaposing his visual poetry of glowing sunsets and tenebrous nights, of melancholy rain and dappled shade, with an intricate acoustic design underscored by pregnant pauses and grim silences. Takayama's style also echoes Oshii's in the recursive employment of reflections, refractions, prismatic effects, and the play of light and shadow on transparent and semi-transparent surfaces. In spite of its forays into sensational confrontations by more or less vulnerable humans of the awesome mutant, the overall atmosphere conveyed by the film is lyrically subdued. One can perceive throughout the unfolding of the action a nostalgically palpable sense of the inexorable passing of time, of missed opportunities and of irretrievable losses. R.K. Elder's review of the movie for *The Chicago Tribune* captures most faithfully this distinctive mood, drawing attention to the ubiquitous apprehension of lack under which its varyingly forlorn characters ponderously labor: "while sci-fi conceits still permeate the plot (alien DNA, rogue scientists), attention to personal detail floats world-weary, superbly drawn protagonists in a rare movie—a character-driven animated film" (Elder).

Kenji Kawai's soundtrack complements ideally the cumulative mood conveyed by *Patlabor 3*'s visuals. As the composer has stated, his objective was to generate "a sound which is not melodious, but rather a noise-like sound representing [a] worry waiting deep within the mind" (Kawai, K.). Interestingly, Kawai would use the same approach for Hideo Nakata's *The Ring* (1998) and for Oshii's live-action feature *Avalon* (2001),[4] capitalizing on a relatively discordant synthesis of string and percussion instruments, classical themes and folk tunes to evoke a ubiquitous sense of dislocation and anxiety.

The film's distinctiveness undeniably owes much to script writer Miki Tori's determination to transcend established formulae. "My generation is haunted by monster movies in a way," Tori has stated, "since we grew up surrounded by them.... One of *Patlabor*'s major premises are robots called Labors, which are completely fictitious characters.... If we added another large fictitious monster ... we might end up creating another ridiculous looking 'Robot Versus Monster' kind of movie, of which I was most afraid. Thus, I thought the key was how to make a monster feel like a true creature." The script writer has also usefully contextualized the appearance and role of the creature portrayed in *Patlabor 3* with reference to the principal representational modalities deployed by the conventional *kaijuu* film: "There are four main ways to create monster movies. The first is to follow the stereotypes of traditional Japanese monster films, even if the result lacks a sense of reality.... Second: create a parody of the traditional monster movie. Third: depict the monster as a symbol.... Fourth: depict the monster as an actual living organism. This requires a lot of research in such areas as biotechnology and theoretical cosmic mechanisms" (Tori).

Tori has undeniably succeeded, in this regard, managing to make the mutant appear not only convincingly alive as an organic entity but also capable of eliciting deeply human emotions, including compassion. In the pathos of the finale, in particular, much as we may want to see the beast conclusively defeated, it is hard not to sense Hitomi's vestigial presence behind its hideous countenance, and hence to empathize with its and Saeko's joint predicaments. However, the film's characteristically restrained disposition remains solidly in place through to the end, and any danger of its deteriorating into facile sentimentalism is resolutely avoided by the presentation of the dire inevitability of Saeko's self-annihilation as the only tenable resolution to the story. It is at this level that the otherwise preposterous brute attains to the status of a widely adaptable symbol for the ineradicable and incurable alienation under which the inhabitants of *Patlabor 3* grievously toil — not solely the literal monster but also the constellation of varyingly disillusioned, embittered or downright deranged humans revolving around its balefully charismatic aura.

Like the preceding *Patlabor* features, Takayama's movie tackles its fantastic subject matter in a dramatically somber and judicious fashion, developing Oshii's own inclination to endow the understated and the matter-of-fact with no less value than the overtly spectacular. Nevertheless, as pointed out by "Erick" in his review of the film for *Beyond Hollywood.com*, *Patlabor 3* "presents death and violence in a very visceral manner that's a marked change from previous entries in the franchise. For the first time in a *Patlabor* movie, we see characters die and bleed, though this is still not enough to warrant the R-rating the movie got for its brief theatrical run. Being that the basis of the threat is biological rather than technological, it makes sense for the movie to get down and dirty with the blood and bodies" (Erick). The movie undoubtedly exudes, despite its generally subdued and pensively sullen tone, a strong sense of tactile physicality that makes its take on science fiction close to the ethos promulgated by cyberpunk. Threats to both the individual and the collectivity, this ethos intimates, do not emanate from the squeaky-clean glass-and-chrome apparatuses of a crystallinely refined technology but rather from the eminently — and often also repulsively—corporeal reality of flesh and blood, of sweat and tears.

19

Minipato

Originally conceived and penned by Oshii, and directed by Kenji Kamiyama, *Minipato* consists of a set of three 10-minute shorts that adopt an utterly unique animational style. Its characters are hand-made cardboard cutouts attached to chopsticks, and manipulated by their creators in much the same way as puppeteers would handle their charges in traditional Bunraku theatre, whose movements are digitally captured, scanned into the computer and then applied to computer-generated images of the material characters. The process essentially allows the animators and technicians to transfer a set of mathematical formulae extrapolated from real actions, performed by the puppets by means of their manipulators, onto digital drawings. Intriguingly, the collection derives much of its distinctive flavor and verve not so much from its standing as a technically groundbreaking intervention in the history of animé (since this aspect is unobtrusively handled throughout) but from its intentional retention of elements of childlike energy and artlessness in both the rendition of the characters' appearances and in the deployment of innovative camera angles in order to produce overtly bubbly and bouncy patterns of motion. The overall production process encompasses five key stages:

- preliminary character designs are executed by recourse to brush-pens, in the handling of which the artist Nishio Tetsuya singled out by Oshii for this project is reputed to be the unchallenged champion;
- storyboards delineating the frame-by-frame unfolding of the visual narrative are produced, and the action is provisionally timed by recording the relevant lines of dialogue against each frame;[1]
- cutouts of the various characters in different postures, and of individual body parts in different situations are made, stuck to chopsticks and employed to stage a live-action puppet show against a black background;
- the performance is recorded by means of digital cameras and the data thus obtained are fed to the computer where the subsequent editing moves referred to above will then be effected;
- the computer-generated characters are composited, and clay animation

is also brought into play where appropriate (e.g., to simulate the pattern traced by a bullet as this cuts through a semi-malleable substance): animation clay is here chiseled and filmed frame by frame to convey the impression of its being incrementally penetrated and traversed.

Each short constitutes a mock instructional documentary that shreds apart the *Patlabor* universe with irreverent glee. Captain Gotoh is the protagonist of the first short animation ("Roar Revolver Cannon!"), where the weaponry is discussed in mind-boggling detail. The second short ("Ah, Victorious 98 Model AV") is dominated by the figure of Shige and is devoted to the dissection of robot design. This episode also pokes fun at the universe of ancillary merchandise, proposing that the production of spin-offs may well be the ultimate priority for the animé industry at large, and that the *Patlabor* franchise ought to focus on the creation of endlessly transformable Ingrams in order to spawn a virtually interminable progeny of robot-based toys. In the third ("The Secret of Special Vehicle Unit 2"), Captain Nagumo takes the collection's parodic thrust to absurdist extremes in addressing an essentially fluffy, trivial and inconsequential topic (namely, the SV2 team's addiction to dried *goby*) by recourse to an utterly recondite discourse and a hilariously mock-epic tone. Oshii's script here reveals an amusing flair for self-satire, insofar as the captain's overinflated rhetoric could be seen as a deliberately exaggerated version of the type of philosophical exposé to be often found in the director's own films from *Beautiful Dreamer* onwards.

The key characters are reproposed in all three shorts in the guise of super-deformed puppets. *Super-deformity*—a form of caricatural parody that can undoubtedly be traced back to ancient times—constitutes a very specific convention within the evolution of animé and its inception can be quite exactly dated. As Patrick Drazen has pointed out, the

> spring of 1988 saw two production houses working on "super-deformed" (SD) comedy projects. Sunrise, creators of the *Gundam* series, were working on the movie *Char's Counterattack* when they came up with *SD Gundam*, a series of short episodic OAVs by Gundam director and designer Gen Sato. Both the people and the *mecha* have huge heads, short bodies, childlike appearances, and anarchistic attitudes ... meanwhile, over at Artmic Studios, the creators of the all-woman *Gall Force* crew were working up their own SD project. *Ten Little Gall Force* brings us child-body versions of the crew.... From then on, everything was open to super-deformity [Drazen, p. 24].

Well-known instances of SD animé popular in the West include the *Princess Nine* bumpers, the *Sailor Moon* digressions, and the *Record of Lodoss War* bonus materials. It is also worth noting, in this respect, that the cartoon drawing used as the logo for the official Oshii Web site *Oshii Mamoru*.

com[2] and entitled "Gabriel's Counterattack" features a super-deformed caricature of the director as he is playfully set upon by his pet basset hound. (Elsewhere, Oshii uses an analogous image with inverted roles, supposedly to comment satirically on his relationship with dogs.)

Masamune Shirow's manga version of *Ghost in the Shell*, upon which Oshii's epoch-making 1995 feature film is based, also employs SD versions of its characters at particular junctures. SD child-body versions of Major Kusanagi, specifically, are provided in situations where she is incensed, and distortion becomes a way of humanizing her personality by parodic means so as to throw into relief the fundamentally human nature of her emotions in spite of her cyberorganic constitution. This is patently the case with images presented in the context of Episode 9, "Bye Bye Clay," where the major is evidently angry as a result of Batou not taking her reflections regarding the Puppet Master seriously enough (Shirow, p. 284). The use of child-body images of the heroine gains an extra dimension, retrospectively, insofar as in the finale of Oshii's movie, the major is indeed rehoused within the "shell" of a school-girl—an aspect brought to bear upon the original manga by Oshii himself. On other occasions, SD figures serve the purpose of softening the rather hermetic philosophical tone into which the dialogue frequently heads—this is evident, for example, in Episode 11, "Ghost Coast" (p. 339).

On the whole, *Minipato* constitutes a fitting conclusion to Oshii's personal involvement in the *Patlabor* franchise, bringing together his passion for abstract reflection and theoretical speculation, his commitment to painstakingly conceived characters and settings, and his eagerness to experiment with intrepid camera angles. At the same time, it playfully celebrates Oshii's refreshing ability to approach his cinematographical agenda with a keen eye on the sheer fun it may yield for both his audience and himself despite the overhanging darkness of his recurrent themes and motifs.

20

The Red Spectacles, Stray Dog *and* Talking Head

Oshii has also engaged in the dramatization of political issues related to those brought to the fore by *Dallos* and by the *Patlabor* productions in a range of live-action movies. These films (in the cases of both feature-length and short productions) tend to reflect a political pessimism that emerged during Oshii's days as a student protester — specifically against the renewal of the U.S.-Japan security treaty, which allowed America to maintain troops on Japanese soil, and against Japan's subsequent collusion in the Vietnam war.

The somber mood engendered by the director's ideological disillusionment with the causes he had passionately embraced in his youth finds a potent visual correlative in the particular cinematographical style elaborated by Oshii for these productions. Incorporating many of the conventions and strategies usually associated with manga and animé into the province of live-action cinema — such as farcical humor and moments of disjunctively exaggerated violence juxtaposed with the mellow poetry of long takes and meditative sequences — the films deliver a tantalizingly jarring alternation of cartoonish expressionism and photographic naturalism without indulging in any placid concessions to either fantasy or realism.

The Red Spectacles — unquestioningly the most manic and surreal of the productions included in the trilogy — makes explicit reference to Oshii's political background and involvement in the student protest movement of the late 1960s and early 1970s. As the prologue informs us, the movie is set in the late twentieth century at a time of relentlessly escalating crime of an "increasingly vicious nature," with which the conventional Metropolitan Police are unable to cope, and related establishment of the "Anti Vicious Crime Heavily Armored Mobile Special Investigation Unit" in order to deal with the situation. The unit consists of "[p]olice men and women of superior intellect and physical strength" who harbor an almost fanatical sense of justice and are tagged Kerberos (a Japanese adaptation of the name *Cer-*

137

berus, the Watchdog of Hell). The agents are equipped with special "reinforcement gear" inclusive of body suits and lethal weaponry.

A potentially brave and even noble endeavor to stem the onslaught of crime, the Kerberos operation rapidly spirals out of control, as its immoderately zealous members start employing increasingly energetic, unethical and eventually brutal investigational tactics: "in their fervent hatred of evil, their actions were quite severe. Their almost cruel investigation activities became the target of strong public criticism." When, in the course of a routine mission, a Kerberos agent beats an offender to death, the unit is dissolved. Oshii presents this preliminary information as a putative "excerpt" from "*The Glory and Downfall of the Kerberos*" by one "Hyohe Shiozawa." The adoption of this strategy is worthy of notice, since it implicitly invites reflection upon the generic standing of the film as a whole in relation to so-called historical cinema. *The Red Spectacles* is patently not a historical movie in the sense that it offers a dramatization of officially recorded events. In fact, the history it depicts is essentially a product of Oshii's personal speculations. However, this does not automatically entail that it has nothing to say about lived history. After all, numerous works claiming to represent historical occurrences in a descriptively transparent fashion actually provide varyingly fictional versions of history, not history per se. This becomes instantly obvious if one considers, for example, that the plethora of war movies produced practically across the globe to comment on legion disparate conflicts hardly supply objective accounts of ascertainable facts insofar as they are inevitably colored by local ideological assumptions and prejudices.

The Red Spectacles is no less historical a film, in this respect, than those productions may be deemed to be: although it does not register empirically verifiable occurrences, it does propose a version of history in its own peculiar way — namely, that of history as a series of snapshot-like pieces of evidence for the ubiquitous incidence of repressive, exploitative and ultimately downright inhumane drives within diverse political formations. The contingent society which necessitates both the establishment and the dissolution of the Kerberos Unit may never have obtained as such, yet its cinematic articulation operates as a convincing template for virtually any dispensation governed by such drives. In this perspective, the film could be said to embrace the ethos of historicity rather that historiography. Whereas historiography refers to the discipline that purports to *record* history through texts, historicity constitutes the process that *makes* history through texts — that is to say, brings history into being not by claiming to represent given facts but by encoding diverse *interpretations* of lived experience as discourses. This term, it must be emphasized, is here employed in accordance with the significance imparted upon it by Michel Foucault (Foucault, 1973;

1979).[1] (A cognate argument to the one outlined above is also eminently applicable, as shown in a later chapter, to *Jin-Roh: The Wolf Brigade.*)

In the film's opening segment, three of the Kerberos Unit's erstwhile members refuse to disarm and rebel sanguinely against the system, but only one of them, Koichi Todome, manages to elude capture and flee after promising to his injured companions, Ao and Midori, that he will return. By the time Koichi does go back, three years later, his city has altered beyond recognition and faded into an abstruse blur, and the more the ex-agent struggles to unearth vestiges of his past, the more his environment creepily defies his efforts. As the character of the old man Ginji tells the protagonist, during his absence many things have changed: the "traffic light" itself is said to have "changed to muddy blue. It may never turn back to clear red again. Nobody stops for you." These lines paradigmatically capture the character of the dismal society depicted in the film as a whole: namely, an uncaring and befuddled world ruled by an obdurately atomizing ideology whereby even sitting down to eat in groups at restaurants is considered a heinous crime.[2] The sense of hopelessness that malignantly extends throughout this ragged social fabric is tersely encapsulated by Ao's description of how, in jail, the ex-"Kerberos" agents went gradually from hope to despair, and of how the government defeated him and his unrepentant comrades by destroying their vision to the point that they were rendered utterly spiritless and hence unworthy of incarceration.

As he struggles to locate his old allies, Koichi is relentlessly pursued by government-appointed assassins and torturers and haunted by enigmatic feline figures and by the image of a young woman with cat-like eyes featuring on posters, monitors and the screen of a large and utterly deserted auditorium. The feline symbolism could be read as an indicator of Koichi's alienation: professionally and historically associated with dogs, he evidently does not belong in a society pervaded by cats. As for the image of the girl, Musashi has persuasively described it as denoting "[t]he idea ... of a Big Sister ... a pair of watchful eyes that follow you everywhere" (Musashi).

When the protagonist does manage to get hold of his former co-conspirators, it is by no means clear whether they are on his side or are working in the service of the government-employed persecutors, since their allegiances repeatedly vacillate in keeping with the film's frequent tonal shifts across an extensive generic gamut. Indeed, *The Red Spectacles* draws on visual and performative sources as diverse as kung-fu action cinema, stage drama, vaudeville and *film noir*, consistently bathing its black-and-white or sepia-tinted images in stark lighting reminiscent of Fritz Lang's oeuvre at its most portentous. The overall atmosphere is not merely murky but tenebrized and quite literally night-soaked. Moreover, as we follow Koichi along countless stairways, corridors and tunnels, we can palpably sense the character's paranoia intensifying at each step. The recurrent inclusion of scenes in which the character experiences bouts of volcanically gut-wrenching diarrhea barely alleviates the overarching mood, insofar as the scatological topos never quite delivers a flamboyantly carnivalesque sense of comic relief but only serves, in fact, to exacerbate the sense of Koichi's possession by malignant forces. No less unsettling are the sequences in which the camera suspensefully pans across perfectly anonymous rooms that are nonetheless rendered ominous by the nightmarish vividness of materials and textures: nothing can be taken at face value, as even the blandest door, carpet or basin threaten suddenly to spring to malevolent life.

Despite the nightmarish connotations of its subject matter and its elaboration of a veritably Lynchian cinematic vision of decay, the film's mood often strikes jocularly bizarre notes by virtue of Oshii's ironical use of slapstick and pantomime elements, theatrical facial expressions, tongue-in-cheek non-sequiturs, hilarious musical touches and, on the whole, an irreverent disregard for mimetic verisimilitude. While these traits would not be in the least surprising in the context of an animated film, their deliberate and deft insertion into a piece of live-action cinema makes *The Red Spectacles* quite a unique experience. Its experimental employment of chromatic palettes and textural effects, moreover, contributes crucially to the cumulative experience of this identifiable and yet utterly unfamiliar world.

The spaces depicted in *The Red Spectacles* are especially memorable insofar as they obsessively rely on a chillingly boxy architectural style redolent of Chris Marker's *La Jetée* (1962), one of Oshii's favorite productions.[3] Moreover, these spaces are predicated on the dispersion of the center of vision through the proliferation of errant lines of orientation and on the unbalancing of perspective through unpredictable oscillations and rotations in the distribution of matter, to the point that depth appears to dissolve into a loose, unpunctuated becoming. As walls vanish, collapse or suddenly materialize amid the treacherous play of light and shadow, any conventional sense of natural form is recklessly forsaken. At the heart of the film there lies a spatio-temporal paradox whereby the more things appear to change, the more they stay exactly the same: the protagonist is trapped in an inescapable, intensely claustrophobic nightmare that repeats itself *ad infinitum* as he moves from one scene to the next. An arbitrarily assembled bundle of purely marginal variations seems to have been thrown into the mix just to mock him with the illusion of change.

Koichi increasingly appears to be living within the synthetic space of a film as everything around him takes on the semblance of a set. Often inconsequential lines spoken by disparate personae, moreover, come to sound like portions of a Theatre-of-the-Absurd script intent on parodying hackneyed plots in the traditions of the gangster movie, the psycho-thriller or hard-boiled detective fiction. The eerie attraction of *The Red Spectacles* may ultimately reside with this particular facet of its prismatic cinematographical configuration, to the extent that self-reflexivity enables Oshii to deliver a deliberately barmy pastiche not merely of established genres and styles—which could barely be deemed original—but, more specifically, of expressions of popular filmic and narrative forms at their most torpidly formulaic. Hence, the movie offers (among other things) a darkly comedic critique of the degeneration of all manner of codes and conventions as a result of indiscriminate overuse. Oshii's camera work corroborates this indictment of the emptiness of words by exhibiting characters that scarcely look at one another while they spew out their stilted lines, as though they were subliminally aware that their utterances could never really communicate anything. Eye contact is accordingly deemed redundant, since interaction is quite simply of no consequence. For all they know or care, they could just as well be addressing a hypothetical black hole on the outermost edges of the farthest galaxy.

In *Stray Dog: Kerberos Panzer Cops*, a prequel to *The Red Spectacles* explaining how Koichi spent his exiled years, a younger member of the Kerberos Unit named Inui is released after a protracted period of detention and sets off to find Koichi in order to establish why the latter abandoned his troops and fled. Unsure as to whether what he seeks is merely answers or—more grimly—revenge, Inui embarks upon a journey that leads him to Mei, a young girl formerly attached to the now missing Koichi, and the two decide to trail the elusive man together. At the same time, other mysterious forces also appear to be looking for Koichi in the conviction that, as a fugitive from government and as a latent political foe, he represents an ongoing menace to the system.

As the centerpiece in the live-action triptych also comprising *The Red Spectacles* and *Talking Head*, *Stray Dog* acts as something of a bridge between the sinister and bitingly cold desperation of the preceding film and the technical eccentricity of the next. *Stray Dog* has unequivocally afforded Oshii an unsurpassed means of flaunting his impeccable directorial style, and evinces throughout an organic fluidity in the handling of cuts, long takes, camera positionings and transitions that far surpasses in caliber the film's engaging but somewhat unembroidered storyline. As Inui and Mei travel together in search of Koichi, the action often resembles a documentary, especially in the use of pillow sequences exhibiting elaborate urban scenes replete with shops, adverts, temples, pagodas, fairgrounds, congested avenues, elegant edifices, desolate hovels and vacant lots. In these sequences, the camera subtly emphasizes the two characters' roles as spectators in their own right, thus encouraging us to identify with them and share their point of view.

Oshii's touchingly unpretentious visual poetry, frequently underscored by a poignant lack of dialogue, consistently communicates a disarming sense of mellow, indeed almost whimsical, pleasure. This potentially gratifying, serene mood derives much of its cinematographical intensity from its ironic juxtaposition with the violence that besieges the protagonists' lives and its ominous potential to erupt without warning. On the whole, therefore, even though *Stray Dog* is far sunnier than either its live-action predecessor or its successor, its pivotal concerns are no less somber. This is evinced by the emphasis which Oshii places on the harrowing themes of political strife and existential discontent. Likewise affecting is the film's allegorical reference to the relinquishment of parental responsibility through the cardinal symbol of the abandoned dog.

The opening sequence (situated before the credits), where members of the Kerberos platoon stand still and silent against the aural background of Kenji Kawai's daunting guitar melody, having just heard that their unit has been disbanded, could be described as vintage Oshii. The same is true of the climactic scenes, in which Inui dons for the last time the Kerberos armored suit and nimbly vanquishes a horde of mimes. The opening portion of the movie encapsulates Oshii's preference for methodically paced and meditative sequences which, in this particular case, seems a highly appropriate means of communicating the composite mood of disbelief, anguish and humiliation in which the defeated agents are locked.

The closing section, by contrast, reflects the director's ability to handle no less proficiently rapid-fire action sequences replete with state-of-the-art visual and special effects. Moreover, the film's hyperdynamic climax serves to momentarily revive the darkly humorous tone adopted in *The Red Spectacles* by means of deliberately exaggerated — and hence latently farcical — depictions of legion gory deaths redolent of Quentin Tarantino's cinema, and of elliptical references to the visual formulae of a variety of popular genres ranging from the *yakuza* movie to the spaghetti western. An even more outrageous expression of caricatural humor is supplied by Koichi and Inui's eventual reunion on the beach, a fairly protracted sequence featuring much leaping, grappling, knocking and splashing about — as well as stylized postures reminiscent of Kabuki theatre — which contrast sharply with the lyrical sublimity of the landscape against which the mock battle is enacted.

In spite of such occasional revampings of the earlier live-action film's ubiquitous penchant for the absurd, *Stray Dog* essentially offers a subdued experience even as it engages with the harrowing ethical and ideological issues alluded to earlier. As Tasha Robinson has noted,

[r]ather than tipping his hand, Oshii simply follows the character on his voyage of self-discovery, which includes much silent exploration of local scenery, including one languid ten-minute wordless sequence backed by swelling piano. The film marks Oshii's meditative impulses at their most extreme: it draws its central metaphor clearly enough in a monologue that likens [Inui] to a feral dog, but apart from some tone-breaking slapstick between [Inui and Koichi], *Stray Dog* seems more like an extended Yanni music video than a narrative film [Robinson 2003].

The monologue to which Robinson's review refers is delivered by Hayashi, a shifty character who claims to belong to the "Fugitive Support Group" and has supplied Inui with information about Mei in the first place to help him trace his old comrade. As the film unfolds, it becomes increasingly obvious that Hayashi has his own ulterior motives at heart, and quite distinct reasons for wanting Koichi's location pinpointed. The monologue tangentially harks back to the black-and-white, profoundly affecting stills of abandoned dogs presented under the opening credits, while also symbolically alluding to Koichi's and Inui's affiliation with canine figures (*inu*, incidentally, means "dog" in Japanese). Since this portion of *Stray Dog* doubtlessly represents the film's graphic and thematic core and simultaneously speaks volumes about Oshii's ethical and ideological convictions, it appears worthy of extensive citation in the present context:

They are stray dogs. Someone might have dumped them, or they got lost. There are so many of them around here. They co-exist with humans, but from a careful distance ... they'll never open themselves to humans. They hold a strong grudge against the humans who dumped them but they also miss the smell of their masters so much. They are eternally ambivalent. But they're animals no matter what. They will never know the reason why their master had to dump them.

After a digression citing the "impressive" but "tragic" story of a "dog" who would never succeed in finding the "master" and the "future" he yearned for in spite of his "running continuously on his bloody feet" (an elliptical reference to Koichi's ordeal), Hayashi declares that the dumping of dogs is a "historical necessity":

No matter how unreasonable it may sound the dog has to pay for any misfortune on his own even if he can't understand the reason why. That's the only lesson and the saddest lesson ... [*a sudden change of tone from the almost unctuously suave to the harshly menacing occurs at this juncture*] ... that humans and dogs have to learn.

Hayashi is obviously taunting Inui at this point, brutally reminding him that he, too, is something of a "dumped" dog, forsaken by his former employers and colleagues alike and forced to live with a loss for which nobody will assume or even share any degree of responsibility. The scene as a whole is rendered all the more disturbing by the fact that it is unclear where or when it is supposed to take place. Intriguingly, we have been led to the derelict yard strewn with remnants of Kerberos suits that ostensibly constitutes its setting from a flashback of the aforementioned pre-credits sequence, and this, in turn, was seamlessly introduced as we were following Mei in her exploration of Tainan's back alleys. This suspension of the action's reality status both echoes Oshii's inveterate preoccupation with the interpenetration of the actual and the imaginary (as found in *Beautiful Dreamer* and *Angel's Egg*, for instance) and anticipates the drastically off-kilter assault on the empirical world staged by Oshii's subsequent live-action production, *Talking Head.*

Talking Head departs from the story arc proposed in the two earlier live-action films—thus constituting a sequel in merely the vaguest sense of the term — by engaging in the politics and crimes coursing the film industry. The movie constitutes a parodic intertextual commentary on the world of Japanese animation at large, replete with cameos, inside jokes and behind-the-scenes glances at the secrets of the business, and hence something of a documentary. However, *Talking Head* could also be described as a murder mystery, a confessional narrative, a ghost story and very possibly a zombie-driven horror thriller.

While the entire film is lit as though it were a stage play, some of its images are bathed in lights so sensationally stark as to seem indistinguishable from animé drawings. *Talking Head* employs a single set with sparse decor, minimal backdrops and barely any walls. The characters repeatedly adopt an acting style redolent of vaudeville pantomime, indulging in the most overtly theatrical displays of both verbal rhetoric and body language and frequently addressing the audience with authentically Brechtian alacrity. As Adam Arseneau has pointed out,

> the film seems to exist outside any rational notion of reality; it can safely be said that *Talking Head* does not exist inside the reality of *The Red Spectacles* and *Stray Dog*, because the film exists inside no reality but its own. If you are quick, you can catch a single fleeting reference to the "Kerberos," delivered through the guise of a coffee commercial. Finally, the entire film takes place within a movie theatre (AKA the animation studio) that appears to be identical to the movie theatre in *The Red Spectacles*, with the same washroom, and identical movie playing on constant loop (a young woman's face, on a tight close up, focusing on the eyes).... *Talking Head* completely smash[es] any notion of a "fourth wall" ... in a very unnerving, meaningful, and aggressive way. Characters will be talking,

then stop talking, gaze directly at the camera, as their monologues continue from some unnamed, outside source [Arsenau].

In this respect, *Talking Head* exhibits intriguing affinities with *Dogville* (dir. Lars von Trier, 2003), a film overtly inspired by Bertolt Brecht's Epic Theatre. Echoing the playwright's stylistic agenda, both *Talking Head* and *Dogville* consistently foreground the constructedness and enactedness of their stories, employing nearly bare stages wherein locations are demarcated by purely conventional lines, a handful of props and the performers' miming skills—as well as intrusive narrators—in order to distance the audience from the action. This bold stylistic approach could easily have yielded nothing more than filmed theatre had it not been for Oshii's imaginative use of the camera, and specifically his departure from Hollywood's traditional devotion to the shot-and-reverse-shot formal figure and tendency to sweep instead across scenes with both subtle and perplexing shifts of focus.

This approach delivers a cinematographical style that is ostensibly theatrical, yet achieves visual effects that can only be accomplished cinematically. Not even from the front row of a theatre's stalls would the spectator be in a position to enter quite so intimately, so indiscreetly, the lives of Oshii's exploitative and rapacious personas. Following the camera as it restlessly moves from face to face, posture to posture, gesture to gesture, the audience are incrementally exposed to the reality of a dissolute industry, persistently exposing its iniquity from within.

The surreal plot proposed by *Talking Head* proceeds from the premise that the production of a much anticipated animé has come to a halt even before the script and storyboards have been finalized as a result of the sudden disappearance of its intended director, Rei Maruwa, amid a number of puzzling deaths. In the original director's absence, the production company hires a maverick with a reputation for thriving under pressure and for rescuing doomed projects from certain damnation. A "migrant technical director," the novel appointee is required to mimic the work of his predecessor in completing the film by the stipulated deadline, and thereby bolster a specious illusion of entrepreneurial prosperity on the studio's part.

Oscillating unpredictably between aloof imperturbability and furious agitation, the director hired to salvage the aborted production visits each department and interviews the studio's motley crew, and is thereby graced with a plethora of evasively conjectural lectures—delivered at a staggering pace—about the history, aesthetic significance, ethical import and technical function of a variety of cinematographical concepts and tools. All the various characters, despite their theoretical differences, seem to share the same unfortunate attribute: an inclination to inflate obvious and even fairly pedestrian notions so as to make them sound akin to epiphanic disclosures, and ultimately precipitate into sheer grotesquerie. For example, the script writer grandiosely mourns the "old days" in which people thought of the screen as a form of "magic" and commends the importance of elaborating novel ways of stimulating contemporary audiences but ends up supporting this high-principled argument, alas, by recourse to the most hackneyed circensian tricks: his belly pops open, spilling out a long chain of plump sausages, and his severed head goes on yattering gleefully after being relocated to his lap.

The different characters harbor intricate belief about the most disparate aspects of filmmaking and related distribution practices—from the part played by editing to the production and deployment of trailers, from the politics surrounding the hiring of subcontractors to the artistic implication of the transition from black-and-white to color cinema. The distinctiveness of the art of animation is also addressed in the context of one of the film's most interesting portions—especially for an animation lover. This consists of a series of animated line drawings endowed with both graphic economy and dynamic effervescence, and displaying exquisitely morphing shapes depicted in a phantasmagoric variety of styles—including an explicit homage to Picasso's *Guernica*.

This segment of the film concurrently comments with a lucidity and verve that is signally missing from the other theoretical inferences on some of animation's most salient traits—for example: "there are no characters that cannot exist in animation.... However, because of this unlimited possibility animation characters are forced to shoulder the ideological demands placed upon them. In other words, the preferences and personal feelings of the people involved." These reflections succinctly convey Oshii's own ambivalent feelings about the ethics of animation. As an animation director, his take on the medium's unfettered freedom is indubitably enthusiastic. However, the passion is partially tempered by the intimation that the animated characters that have no choice but to embody the individual predilections and emotions of their creators are not just lifeless puppets but also allegorical incarnations of real people, insofar as breathing humans are also, ultimately, cultural constructs determined by the ideological structures within which they operate and are operated upon.

As he goes about the studio consulting its various employees, the maverick cinematographer rapidly discovers that the crew's pompous ravings and the tight deadline he is expected to meet are the least of his problems: a spectral entity haunts the venue, while the entire production team is being murdered. No less chilling a cause for alarm is the growing realization that the boundary between the director's reality and the movie under production has practically dissolved, which lays the foundations for a metafictional quandary of mind-boggling proportions. Ultimately, therefore, *Talking*

Head is principally a self-referential reflection upon the cinematic art itself, and an experimental investigation of the distinctive structures, registers and rhetoric of filmmaking. This is conducted by means of a radically disconcerting metamovie, a movie about making movies— or, to be more precise, a movie within a movie which, in turn, is feasibly placed within one further movie.

Talking Head appears to end with a shot of the director approaching the foreground as he pushes along a dolly-held camera. The final credits then start scrolling against a black background. However, the actual ending is yet to come. What we see next is an audience exiting a movies theatre, among them a girl carrying a cardboard cut-out of a basset hound to be seen again in *Killers: .50 Woman*. The character of the producer is subsequently seen in the act of congratulating a rather gloomy young woman for completing Rei's work so brilliantly and thereby fully confirming her reputation as the best of his apprentices. It then transpires, through the producer's confession, that Rei had become schizophrenic and had accordingly been hospitalized — hence his disappearance. Pivotal to his pathological behavior had been the creation of an alternative personality intended to compensate for the disintegrating one. This had by and by acquired the guise of an animation ghost director, which indicates that the patient had somewhat uncannily remained anchored to his initial reality despite the mounting pressure exerted upon it by his psychotic brain.

Pursuing exclusively financial interests, the producer had decided to indulge Rei's fantasy — hoping he would eventually recover and resume his role — by appointing a ghost director and inducing the crew to collude in the game. The original director had never recovered but the production had eventually been completed, according to this version of events, by the brilliant apprentice. Although the producer had been satisfied with this outcome, the situation had unexpectedly turned out to be rather more convoluted than initially suspected. Indeed, Rei had developed rather complex feelings towards his crew akin to the urge to kill, and the ghost director had somehow had to fulfill this fantasy as well. This revelation mirrors the ghost director's proposition, put forward in one of the early scenes, that executing a film resembles perpetrating a heinous offence: "Making a movie is the same as committing a crime. No matter how cleverly you hide it, your methodology and process will reveal your motive. Or the production scheme, that is." Asked by the studio's gofer whether, in this scenario, he is expected to take on the role of the "detective," he adamantly asserts that his task is not to expose a "culprit" but to "complete the crime." "I'm a criminal with no personal motive," he adds. "Simply put, sort of a hit man."

The key to *Talking Head*—assuming there is really any such thing — would seem to be that Rei's plan was not just to make a movie. In furthering Rei's plan, the ghost director is supposed to be assisting both a commercial venture and a personal scheme. However, two complicating factors should also be taken into consideration. Firstly, the fact that the character credited with the completion of the filmic product is Rei's assistant and not the ghost director would appear to intimate that the latter is also a pawn in a larger web of nefarious machinations—or even, to pursue the absurdist thread to its most preposterous extremes, a figment of Rei's scrambled psyche. Secondly, the assistant divests herself of any conclusive asset by speculating: "maybe I myself was the third personality conjured up by him [Rei]."

Within this configuration, the original director constitutes, paradoxically, an absent presence (the Japanese word "*Rei*," incidentally, means "zero"):

> a man who is constantly spoken of by others but never shows himself. The existence who rules the situation from outside the frame.... The man who cast a shadow behind every single incident. Everything was done to materialize his intentions and it progressed according to his plan.

Both the ghost director and Rei's apprentice have been brought into play purely in order to "materialize his intentions," to engineer situations wherein they could lend their own performance as actors to the fulfillment of their absentee landlord's vision.

Talking Head may therefore consist of three concentric circles. The largest circle, encompassing the other two, is Oshii's film itself. Within this lies a second circle: the film made by Rei's assistant. Within the latter, lies a third circle: the film consisting of the activities undertaken by the ghost director and his adopted crew and viewed by the assistant. Thus, the ghost director is a character within the assistant's work, just as the assistant is a character in Oshii's work. Where exactly this leaves the spectator of Oshii's film is something of a moot point. The lingering suspicion with which one tends to leave this unsettling visual and diegetic experience is that just as characters in a movie may also be spectators, the spectators of *Talking Head*—we—may also be fictional personae in our own world.

21

Killers: .50 Woman

Killers, an episode within an omnibus production, provides a quasi-absurdist take on a contract killer's mission that pokes fun at the film industry's dubious ethics with impudent gusto while also retaining the surreal components previously foregrounded in *Talking Head*. In his review of *Killers* for *The Japan Times*, Mark Schilling has provided an informatively amusing evaluation of the compilation as a whole and of Oshii's own specific contribution to the project: "Oshii has combined his obsessions with guns, babes and junk food into the strongest and simplest film of the lot, which plays like an erotic daydream-cum-food commercial. It's also an object lesson on how to hold the screen with minimal means. All you really need, Oshii shows us, is a hot babe, a big gun and plenty of fresh *omusubi* [rice balls]" (Schilling).

The direction is typically Oshiian in its emphasis on fastidiously methodical pacing, as the camera follows the protagonist (played by Yui Nino) and the bulky wooden crate she hauls along — treating it with the same nonchalance with which an ordinary businessperson would handle a briefcase or laptop computer — to the place of her assignment. This is a room in a high-rise from where the hit woman is supposed to assassinate a corrupt film producer (played by Studio Ghibli's actual president, Toshio Suzuki) who is said to have embezzled 20 million dollars. The camera's moves are paralleled by Nino's deliberate acting style, whereby meticulous attention is paid to each minute gesture. This is especially notable in the sequence where the character removes her sunglasses and artificial nails (the camera focuses closely on their decorative pattern, which is subtly consonant with the discreetly post-Goth flared-trouser suit), takes off the smart outfit, replaces it with casual clothing and ties back her luxuriant locks as one would upon returning home after a day at the workplace. Ironically, in this instance, the job is yet to begin. Before embarking on her next task, the woman also weighs herself — an act which might appear somewhat irrelevant to the mission in hand but actually proves pivotal to the short piece's ideological message. The same punctiliously measured rhythm characterizes the following sequence, detailing the calculatingly clinical assemblage of the assassin's precision weapon — a monstrous 50-caliber gun capable of blowing massive holes through all kinds of materials with the aid of incongruously elegant-looking shells.

Waiting for her target to emerge, the contract killer whiles the hours away by satisfying the demands of an appetite the size of Mount Fuji through the diligent ingestion of preposterous amounts of pasties, rice balls, sandwiches, buns, wraps, hot dogs and various other snacks of multigastronomic derivation, which she no less systematically flushes down with bottled water. As Nino chomps diligently along with a dedication and sense of duty suggesting that the gargantuan consumption of convenience-store junk is her authentic assignment, and that the assassination is something of an ancillary task casually coinciding with it, we are supplied with the name of each of the products being eaten and with details regarding brands, prices and caloric value. These are accompanied by the recurring *ping* sound characteristic of old-fashioned tills, which comes to serve as something of a refrain or acoustic punctuation.

This protracted and wordless sequence comes across, cumulatively, as a darkly humorous one. Yet, it is also furtively titillating insofar as the protagonist's diligent staging of her interaction with food simultaneously carries the visual connotations of an exhibitionist ploy, translating what would otherwise be an eminently private ritual into a public spectacle for voyeuristic consumption by the audience. Moreover, the *mise-en-scène* allows us to penetrate Nino's space by means of a key-hole perspective analogous to the hit woman's take on her prospective victim via her lethal gear, thus making us marginally complicitous with her nefarious intent. The element of scopophilia inherent in Nino's food consumption could thus be read as a metaphorical form of foreplay aptly prefacing the short film's climactic blast.

Killers: .50 Woman resembles an animé production in its use of predominantly silent action. Indeed, the only available sounds (beside the aforementioned *ping*) are those emanating from the monitor through which the protagonist keeps an eye on the hospital building whence the intended victim is supposed to materialize. One of the background characters seen on the screen wears a T-shirt emblazoned with one of the most assiduously recurrent images in Oshii's cinema, namely the picture of a basset hound. (A further canine reference, incidentally, is offered by the logo on the crate wherein the killing machinery is stored: a pawprint crowned by the simple caption "dog.")

The character in question is promoting some new slimming equipment in a program that is being broadcast while news reporters await the fraudulent producer's exit from the hospital. This apparently peripheral aspect of the film turns out to be quite axial to its diegetic logic, insofar as

Killers: .50 Woman ultimately constitutes a deconstructive exposure of the fashion system: when the assassin weighs herself at the very end, it appears that she has not gained a single pound despite the amount of food and water she has been voraciously swallowing since the start of the action.[1] Oshii thus intimates that the hit woman's ultimate mission consists of assassinating *two* equally infamous sectors of the entertainment industry: the film world's pockets of depravity, in a literal sense, and the health-and-beauty circus, in a metaphorical one.

At the end, the killer is just about to shoot the Suzuki character as he stands outside the hospital with a nurse, smoking a cigarette, when a young girl carrying a large cardboard cut-out of a basset hound (redolent of the one seen in *Talking Head*) walks past just behind him. The protagonist therefore shoots the bodyguards' vehicle instead, creating panic and causing the nurse to flee — despite the producer's slapstick struggle to use her as a shield. Finally, the hit woman manages to shoot her target: as the producer's head explodes in a fashion reminiscent of manga gore, realism is patently suspended in favor of cartoonish exuberance.

For financial reasons, the production of cinematic anthologies has increased significantly in Japan over recent years, allowing budding filmmakers to benefit from the coexistence within the same collaborative work of their own films with those of established directors. *Killers*, specifically, was prompted by the "Gun Action Short Movie Competition," a biannual contest sponsored by *Gun* magazine. Schilling has explained the genesis and evolution of the project in the review cited earlier: "Three contest judges— Oshii, manga artist and director Kazuhiro Kiuchi and script writer and director Shundo Okawa — proposed a cinematic battle royal between them and recent contest winners. In other words, amateurs vs. pros, with the results to be screened on satellite television and released on video. For various reasons, the project has since morphed into a five-part omnibus film, with the contest aspect eliminated." As this same review later suggests, the "other four directors are equally in love of firepower, but are more conventional [than Oshii] in their approach to both action and comedy" (Schilling).

The first segment, Kazuhiro Kiuchi's "Pay-Off," pivots on the character of a swaggering contract assassin pretending to be an arms dealer and his semi-farcical efforts to withstand the lethal onslaught of a bunch of classic babes well versed in all manner of martial skills. The second, Shundo Okawa's "Candy," introduces us to the charismatic figure of Megumi, a former office secretary who, seeking employment at a cabaret, realizes rather late in the day that she has been hired as a contract killer and not a cabaret performer as originally hoped. The action sequences in which Megumi is consequently involved are among the most exciting portions of the anthology from a strictly cinematographical viewpoint, especially in virtue of their deft intermingling of several of the classic formulae associated with both kung-fu movies and the Western, and felicitous anticipations of the *Kill Bill* and the *Matrix* productions.

The third segment, Takanori Tsujimoto's "Perfect Partner," is closer in tone to *Pulp Fiction*, as it follows two hit men who miraculously manage to retain an enthusiastic partiality for vaporous rhetoric and foolish gags even as they are hounded down by increasingly blood-thirsty gangsters. The fourth segment, Shuji Kawata's "Killer Idol," is possibly the closest, in thematic terms, to Oshii's own contribution to the project, dealing as it does with the crimes of the entertainment industry. The short film indeed supplies a dispassionately acerbic critique of the *idoru* (idol singer or star) system and of so-called reality television through a comedically macabre exposure of media sensationalism centered on a cowboy-hatted idol contract killer.

Throughout the collection, one detects the influence of Quentin Tarantino and John Woo, and of classics such as *Nikita* (dir. Luc Besson, 1991) and the *Gun Crazy* series. The amalgamation of dark humor, a taste for the absurd and a deliberately melodramatic exaggeration in the acting style is arguably the most memorable attribute of the production in its entirety.

Killers: .50 Woman, specifically, is indubitably an unusual production, yet it will not come as a total surprise to viewers acquainted with Oshii's animated cinema, insofar as it derives visual personality and verve from the very elements that have made the director's animé instantly recognizable. Indeed, the short movie's overall mood paradigmatically captures Oshii's distinctive preference for a paradoxical fusion of the ominous and the farcical, the somber and the bizarre, restraint and excess, in an ebulliently satiric treatment of violence.

22

Jin-Roh: The Wolf Brigade

The films personally directed by Oshii in which the Kerberos world, with its distinctive iconography and mores, features prominently are, as we have seen, live-action productions. Nonetheless, it is arguably in the animated feature *Jin-Roh*, which Hiroyuki Okiura[1] directed and for which Oshii wrote the script, that such a universe comes most elaborately and portentously to life. For this reason, the film deserves detailed attention in the context of the present study. At the levels of narrative complexity and aesthetic specificity, moreover, *Jin-Roh* is especially central to Oshii's oeuvre due to its dispassionate elaboration of a rhetoric and a style that had found inception in the *Patlabor* features and in the first *Ghost in the Shell* movie and would reach something of an aesthetic apotheosis in *Ghost in the Shell 2: Innocence* in the following millennium.[2]

Jin-Roh's inception can be traced back to the production company Bandai Visual's plan to make an OVA based on Oshii's comic book *Kenrou Densetsu* that would comprise six episodes, one for each of the original manga installments. However, *Ghost in the Shell* was their priority at the time. In the wake of that film's sensational success, Manga Entertainment — who were familiar with the *Kenrou Densetsu* story as a result of its publication in English by Dark Horse Comics in 1994 as *Hellhounds: Panzer Cops* — asked Oshii to create an animated version of the story but would not settle for anything other than a feature-length production. All the various parties involved believed firmly in Okiura's suitability as a director, and Oshii himself was fully supportive of that choice even though his path to accepting involvement in the sole capacity of script writer was not exactly smooth: "I begged [them] to let me do the script at least and everybody at Bandai made a wry face," he has stated in an interview conducted by Kenji Kamiyama for the Production I.G Web site. "Yeah, they'd already appointed Itoh to do the script. Itoh didn't want to do it so he refused. I knew he was going to refuse it because he once told me that he didn't want to write a story that had dogs in it, especially after he wrote *Akai Megane* [*The Red Spectacles*]. Well, so they asked me to do the script after Itoh refused it.... Since I was the original author, nobody needed to argue with anybody else.

Jin-Roh: The Wolf Brigade (1998). A valiant but tormented member of the Kerberos — the elite unit formed to combat escalating crime rates — Fuse has to choose between his allegiance to the force and his attraction to ex-terrorist Kei. In the film's alternate-history postwar Japan — a country defeated and occupied not by the U.S. but by Nazi Germany — political concerns are interwoven with ominous allegorical references to the tale of "Little Red Riding-Hood," here alluded to by Kei's attire. ©1999 Mamoru Oshii/BANDAI VISUAL • Production I.G.

The script always turns out the best if it's written by the original author."

Asked specifically if he would also have wished to direct the movie himself, Oshii passionately replied:

> Very much so, especially when I wrote the script. Honestly speaking, I still think that I should've done it myself. I didn't want to give it away to anyone else.... The moment you write, you want to direct.... I will have no control over the final product that is definitely going to be different, so I only hope that they will try to do their best. I'm talking about the pictures here. After all, the final product only comes out as the director wants it. No one knows what's inside until you open the lid. Directing is nothing but to find your ideas and identities in the already-existing script, and you just use them in what you create [Oshii 1997].

In what is plausibly the most concisely apposite assessment of *Jin-Roh* published to date, Fred Patten has described the film as "a taut and suspenseful political thriller" (Patten 2000). The movie undeniably exhibits an exceptionally adult sensibility in its approach to animé but not in the usual "X-rated" sense of the term. Indeed, instead of gratuitously indulging in lurid depictions of violence, sex and gore, it assiduously engages in the deeply ethical ramifications of a society riven by civil unrest, sectarian antagonism, intricate personal connections and the sinister intrigues that unrelentingly brew in the murky depths of the governmental maze.

The premise upon which the Kerberos world as presented in *Jin-Roh* is erected is that at the end of the Second World War, Japan was defeated and occupied not by the U.S. but by Nazi Germany, and that the country's struggle to recover from the economic crisis and psychological disarray caused by the conflict was severely hampered by ever-escalating crime rates and by the disruptive activities of anti-Fascist revolutionaries known as the "Sect." As already proposed in the live-action features *The Red Spectacles* and *Stray Dog: Kerberos Panzer Cops*, the government is supposed to have reacted to this menacing situation by establishing the Capital Police. An armored, helmeted and red-goggled elite force dubbed Kerberos are specifically responsible for curbing the Sect's operations. Laudable in terms of their unflinching commitment to their mission, the shock-troops are nevertheless notorious for trespassing the boundary of legitimate law enforcement, and for thus allowing strength of purpose to degenerate into corporal bestiality. As a consequence, they are admired and loathed in equal proportions. Matters are rendered murkier still by rumors regarding the existence of a rogue element within the Special Unit, which trouble deeply the government's upper echelons, and eventually provide them with a pretext for disbanding the Kerberos altogether — thus attenuating the humiliating legacy of military defeat and occupation. As we shall see, *Jin-Roh*'s principal characters are victims of precisely such a scheme, and especially of the political determination to move away from armed activity in favor of diplomatic philandering.

The diegetic premise outlined above makes *Jin-Roh* a provocative variation on the classic sci-fi trope of temporal displacement, capitalizing on the notion of an alternate history. Hence, it could be realistically described as a historical movie in much the same way as *The Red Spectacles*, as argued in Chapter 20, could also be accorded this generic designation. Even though it does not presume to provide either documentary information about an identifiable era or a reportorial reconstruction of lived events (and nor does it pander to the conventions of costume drama), *Jin-Roh* does offer a searingly resonant evaluation of the very *concepts* of history and historiography. In this respect, the film would seem to fully validate Robert A. Rosenstone's propositions regarding cinematic options for refashioning the past. While acknowledging film's imbrication with history by means of visual narratives that purport to document actual facts, Rosenstone notes: "another kind of contribution to our understanding of the past ... depends less upon data than upon what we might call vision, upon how we look at and think about and remember and make meaningful what remains of people and events" (Rosenstone, p. 6). In specifically assessing the significance of alternate perspectives on the past of precisely the type one encounters in *Jin-Roh*, the critic ushers in the concept of the "New History film" as a cinematic construct that

> tests the boundaries of what we can say about the past and how we can say it, points to the limitations of conventional historical form, suggests new ways to envision the past, and alters our sense of what it is.... [T]his past ... is somehow different from both fiction and academic history, this past ... does not depend entirely on data for the way it asserts truths or engages the ongoing discourse of history [pp. 12–13].

Jin-Roh embraces a revisionary disposition towards history that closely echoes the stance proposed by Rosenstone, in positing the passage of time as a process of fluid becoming rather than a frozen object for classical historiographers to contemplate — and damn or idealize by turns in keeping with the whims and requirements of their age. In so doing, the film forbears the passive absorption of data and accordingly encourages the exercise of the faculties of reflection and speculation at their keenest. Concomitantly, it throws into relief the virtual inseparability of fact and fiction by interweaving the grim realities of despotism, oppression and corruption with fantastic elements derived from traditional lore, and editing both sets of materials by recourse to a parallel history that is disturbingly real even as it verges on the utterly hypothetical. Stylistically, the interpenetration of actual and imagined histories is crisply communicated by the sequence preceding the opening credits, where the concatenation of events leading to the state of affairs portrayed in *Jin-Roh* is visualized by recourse to drawings that simulate the quality of black-and-white newspaper photographs (with the occasional addition of unobtrusive touches of blue and brown for extra pathos). As the account reaches its climax, the initially slow transition from one picture to the next gives way to the jump-cut modality, and incrementally unsettling evidence of bloody unrest accordingly accumulates.

Jin-Roh's opening sequence immediately introduces the film's central themes by dramatizing a fierce confrontation between protesters and the police on the streets of an eminently Europeanized Tokyo at night. In the course of the battle, a young girl named Nanami, who is responsible for conveying munitions from one set of guerrilla fighters to another, hides in the sewers to elude the pursuing Kerberos agents and unexpectedly finds herself face to face with a lone cop. In an act of self-sacrifice, Nanami detonates the bomb in her satchel. The Kerberos member who witnesses this desperate act, Kazuki Fuse, is deeply affected by the experience and, in reflecting upon its implications, is thrown into a vortex of guilt, remorse and self-doubt.

So alarmed are his superiors by the impact of the accident on Fuse's psychological balance that they require him to retrain. However, the agent is unable to relinquish his vivid recollections of the young suicide and, having obtained information about Nanami from Atsushi Henmi (an old friend employed in the government's Public Security Section), he decides to visit the mausoleum wherein her ashes are stored. Here he meets Nanami's elder sister and lookalike, Kei, who gives him a copy of *Rotkappchen*— one of the German-language versions of the popular *Little Red Riding Hood* tale — and urges him to accept the young insurgent's death as an inevitable corollary of both her and Fuse's respective duties.

Nonetheless, Fuse remains unrelentingly haunted by images of Nanami — which gradually appear to coalesce with more recent memories of Kei — and his concentration is hence impaired to the point that in the course of a training session simulating a battle, he manages to get himself "killed." Fuse and Kei begin to meet regularly, their perambulations through the city disclosing a scenario that recalls the *Patlabor* features: namely, an urbanscape in the grips of ceaseless demolition and rebuilding fueled by the imperatives of a ruthless construction state. During a visit to an amusement park, the Kerberos policeman experiences a vision that could be regarded as the entire film's symbolic core. He sees Nanami fleeing through the sewers, and as he runs after her, a pack of wolves materializes behind him. When Fuse reaches Nanami, she bafflingly morphs into Kei and is mercilessly ravaged by the beasts, whom Fuse is powerless to keep at bay despite his efforts.

Abiding by the peculiar logic of dream discourse, the scene seamlessly gives way to two quite different, though symbolically related, images: one displays Fuse emptying a machine-gun into Kei, and the other focuses on the protagonist surrounded by a pack of wolves in the context of a forbidding snow-swept setting. The sequence brings together in a poetically poignant form some of the movie's pivotal preoccupations, its graphic vigor deriving much of its intensity from the suspension of meaning and aversion to conclusive decodings of the cryptic language on which it thrives. The symbolic analogy introduced in the sequence mentioned above is recursively sustained by the key scenes set in the Natural History Museum where Fuse's figure is tantalizingly projected against the display cases housing stuffed specimens of numerous mammals and, most importantly, of the protagonist's lupine avatar.

The events that are meanwhile unfolding behind the scenes— and in Fuse's total ignorance of his part therein — turn out to be even more sinister than the Kerberos agent's darkest hallucinations. Indeed, various strata of the police hierarchy have resolved to suspend all forms of armed confrontation and rely instead on counterintelligence strategies, and a central component of the plan consists of the dismantling of the Kerberos Special

Unit — as a branch of the Capital Police felt to damage the latter's overall credentials due to its notoriety in the deployment of overly physical measures. Fuse, in the interim, is being exploited as an unwitting puppet in the game. His so-called friend Henmi, it transpires, has cunningly engineered Fuse's meeting with Kei — a former terrorist who now works for the police and was never actually related to Nanami — in order to get the cop involved in a disreputable attachment bound to lead to a scandal and hence to tarnish irrevocably the Special Unit's name.

However, the Kerberos Unit know about Henmi's betrayal and are even in possession of photographic evidence for his rendezvous with Kei, which they disclose to Fuse. Thus, when the young woman contacts the agent and asks him to meet her at the Natural History Museum, he anticipates an ambush and goes there armed with a pistol which, evocatively, he has been concealing in a hollowed-out copy of *Tristan und Isolde*. Having eluded his pursuers, Fuse revisits the infamous sewers with Kei, who has resolved to stand by him out of genuine affection. Here they are met by Fuse's former training instructor, Tobe, and his men, and it is at last revealed that Fuse belongs to an underground splinter group — a sort of inner cabal within the police ranks — known indeed as the Wolf Brigade.

When Henmi and his forces track their prey down to the subterranean labyrinth thanks to a detector planted on Kei, they are spectacularly exterminated in a series of incrementally graphic skirmishes. Once the battle is over, Tobe tersely informs Fuse that he is now left with no alternative but to kill Kei and hide her body so as to induce the Public Security Section to think that she is truly in the Brigade's hands and alive. Kei desperately holds onto Fuse while reciting the closing segment of *Little Red Riding Hood*, until a gunshot is heard and the young woman slides out of the ill-fated embrace. The final image is that of Fuse's copy of the tale abandoned in a desolate junkyard. Although there is evidence that the lethal bullet emanated from the gun of one of Tobe's associates, the scene's graphic composition and sheer drama allegorically allude to Fuse's own inherent culpability. A creature like Fuse, it is implied, cannot allow himself to harbor tender emotions for even the flimsiest of moments.

Fuse epitomizes the dramatic figure of a man engulfed in a whirlpool of uncontrollable events, desperate to fathom the mystery of his personal identity and to ascertain the legitimacy of his mission as a law-enforcer. The film's central predator on one level, Fuse is simultaneously its most intractably pathetic prey on another. Not only is he tormented by guilt following the young terrorist's suicide, he is at the same time powerless to protect the one person about whom he is tentatively disposed to care, and hideously humiliated by the obligation to watch her die in his very arms like a sacrificial lamb of old. This ethical perspective is pithily intensified by Oshii's retelling of the *Little Red Riding Hood* tale from the wolf's point of view. This serves to underscore the proposition that the rapacious pursuer is not a free agent but rather a pawn in a power game engaging superior — and far more ominously acquisitive — powers.[3]

This dismal finale dispassionately proclaims that Fuse was committed from the start to the enactment of a pre-established script and was never, therefore, at liberty to steer the course of events in accordance with individual predilections or desires. The film is thus dominated throughout by the ghastly specter of a sealed destiny that allows no leeway whatever for consolatory escape routes. This mood is succinctly conveyed by the temporal framing of the climax. In the course of just one night, a tangled skein of deceptions, betrayals and conspiracies harrowingly unravels, to culminate in a cold dawn utterly devoid of hope. In dramatizing Fuse's personal ordeal, *Jin-Roh* concurrently intimates that the very concept of friendship amounts to little more than a specious myth: Fuse is betrayed by his putative best friend, pretends to play the game as though he had not penetrated the deception and eventually kills him without proffering a single word of either accusation or regret, let alone forgiveness.

Each of the personae woven into *Jin-Roh*'s narrative tapestry is, ultimately, portrayed as lupinely predatory: the special agents due to their unscrupulous brutality; the members of the Wolf Brigade in their adoption of the incontrovertibly Hobbesian dictum "*homo homini lupus*" ("each man is a wolf to the other man"); the government in its callously conspiratorial, circuitous and even overtly mendacious tactics; and even the ostensibly innocent characters of Kei —for playing a duplicitous role — and of Nanami —for abetting the insurgents' own ferocity. The film's title overtly capitalizes on the inextricability of the human dimension from the wolfish one. Literally translated, "*Jin-Roh*" indeed means "man-wolf," which should by no means be confused with "werewolf," the Japanese term for which is *okami-otoko*. Hence, the emphasis falls on the *natural* urge to prey upon other creatures, including members of their own species, that courses inexorably through the human race rather than on *supernatural* phenomena which, albeit harrowing, could be easily relegated to the province of harmless fantasy. It is in order to convey the grim image of a universe wherein no-one is unequivocally untainted, and in which destructiveness is the ineluctable consequence of even the most benevolent act, that Oshii chose to adopt the German version of the traditional fairytale, where the little girl herself consumes her mother's flesh. In a society that consists entirely of raptors and preys, the two roles are easily mixed up and, in the last analysis, just as easily inverted.

The film's cardinal virtue, in articulating these undeniably unsavory themes, resides with its clear-eyed avoidance of facile moralistic glosses. At

Jin-Roh: The Wolf Brigade (1998). Fuse and Kei tentatively tread the first steps of a doomed romance through a semifictional Tokyo in the process of constant demolition and reconstruction. A dreary compound of old backwaters on which time scarcely appears to have had any effect, ever-changing skylines and derelict limbos, the film's urban setting symbolically replicates the pervasive feelings of displacement and anomie under which its protagonists painfully labor. ©1999 Mamoru Oshii/BANDAI VISUAL • Production I.G.

the same time, *Jin-Roh* no less adamantly eschews any concessions to sentimentalism: it is noteworthy, in this respect, that the only kiss which the main characters allow themselves to savor belongs more in the sphere of comfort than in that of romance. Given its deliberately restrained tone, the movie may at first disaffect the viewer, and it is for this very reason that it benefits from repeat viewings (in much the same way as Oshii's live-action Kerberos features do). Moreover, *Jin-Roh* gains considerably from gradual assimilation due to an extraordinarily sophisticated technical execution that kept Production I.G busy for well over three years. Character designer Nishio Tetsuya's drawings (based on Okiura's own sketches) deliver one of the most accurate and solid renditions of human physiognomy to be found in the entire history of animation.

As George Wu has noted, *Jin-Roh*'s animational realism appears to be "influenced by Isao Takahata ... specifically Takahata's *Grave of the Fireflies* and *Only Yesterday*," and this is vividly borne out by the presentation of apparently insubstantial gestures that actually contribute volumes to the overall characterization. Wu cites as a paradigmatic instance the scene in which "Kei is walking" and "the hair above her ear falls down past her chin almost as if the animators themselves did not notice, but then a few beats later, her hand pushes her hair back in place." It is the artful casualness of the act that makes it memorable despite its utterly peripheral status at the level of the action.

It should also be noted, however, that even as it aimed for heightened photorealism, the animation team simultaneously sought to capture the affective essence of time-honored modalities of performance. The characters' expressiveness, in particular, is overtly consonant with the tradition of Noh theatre, where body language and objects are invested with central communicational powers over and above words. It is noteworthy, in this perspective, that Fuse and Kei are the characters endowed with the fewest lines of dialogue in the whole film.

In an interview for Production I.G with Tetsuya, conducted by Kenji Kamiyama (animation director) and also involving the participation of Kenji Horikawa (production manager) and Masanori Yoshihara (animator), Tetsuya has commented exhaustively on his involvement in Okiura's unprecedentedly daunting project, stressing that he "had never done a long feature in full vista," encompassing "over 10 thousand cels." Importantly, *Jin-Roh* is one of the very few films produced in recent years to have been animated almost entirely by recourse to hand-drawn cels. Tetsuya was to some extent sustained by an existing attraction to the ideological issues articulated in the film: "I had also been interested in the '70s student activists and security threat like the theme Oshii-san uses in his piece.... I'd actually done a storyboard on the topic of the student activists in the '70s for my graduation project.... A love story among the student activists." This topos, as noted earlier, has clearly been pursued by Oshii himself in the drafting of the script for *Jin-Roh* to maximum effect. However, Tetsuya could not merely translate his juvenile efforts into an apposite set of designs for *Jin-Roh* due to fundamental differences in his and the director's perceptions of the narrative: "Okiura-san's ideas are very different from those of mine so I can't include any of my ideas into the work I'm currently doing.... Only the details of their looks, things they carry, etc. were something that I had in my 'drawer' so I was able to utilize them, but the characters themselves were something that Okiura-san had to show me.... It was like a big culture shock for me ... everything seemed new to me. Every day was full of surprises."

Two major elements must be here taken into consideration, both of which are inextricably connected with Tetsuya's involvement in the execution of *Jin-Roh* as his first feature-length production. One of them, referred to above, is the sheer number of drawings required—a tantalizing task in and for itself but all the more so, in this specific context, as a result of Okiura's commitment to realism and to a decidedly non-digital approach to animation.[4] The other is the fact that Tetsuya, coming from a fundamentally TV series–centered professional background, had to learn a radically new working style that would enable him to cope with the relatively unsystematic and unpredictable character of cinematic animation. In the execution of a TV series, the character designer has stated, "[t]here is no time to think, debate or worry.... Everyone has their own task and knows exactly what to do. There is already a solid track and one needs only to follow the track" (Tetsuya). This was patently not the case with Okiura's feature, where the incremental testing, validation and indeed discarding of ever variable hypotheses consistently took precedence over any strict blueprints.

Jin-Roh has been hailed by numerous critics and commentators as one of the most uncompromising, thought-provoking and dexterously crafted animations ever made. Its richness, it could be surmised, owes much to the flawless synthesis of a realistically rendered mood of unrelieved moral darkness and a graphic sumptuousness that causes the gloom — paradoxical as this may sound — to become eerily resplendent. In accordance with Oshii's own aesthetics, therefore, it is from its stunningly detailed, melancholy beauty that the film's intrinsically ugly messages derive psychological and ideological potency.

Part Four
HUMANITY/VIRTUALITY:
OSHII'S POST-ROBOTIC VISION

Cyberspace. A consensual hallucination experienced daily by billions of legitimate operators, in every nation, by children being taught mathematical concepts ...

A graphic representation of data abstracted from the bank of every computer in the human system. Unthinkable complexity.

Lines of light ranged in the nonspace of the mind, clusters and constellations of data. Like city lights receding.
— *William Gibson 1995a, p. 67*

Cyberspace is created by transforming a data matrix into a landscape in which narratives can happen.
— *N.K. Hayles, p. 269*

23

Approaches to Cybersociety

Stylistically, the animated films discussed in this section are characterized by a thoughtful harmonization of traditional cel animation and state-of-the-art computer graphics that bears full witness to the Japanese animation industry's enduring commitment to the art of drawing even as it adventurously embraces innovative digital tools. *Avalon*, essentially a live-action feature, also offers a blend of tradition and experiment by integrating conventional footage with wholly computer-generated special effects and visual effects.

Furthermore, the films' daring amalgamation of the old and the new on the technical level is echoed by their treatment of narrative themes that consistently hark back to ancient lore and mythology, as well as traditional tales of both Eastern and Western derivation, while simultaneously embarking on futuristic speculations about mutating notions of identity and humanity in increasingly technocratic societies. *Blood: The Last Vampire* deploys a range of ground-breaking digital tools in arguably unprecedented ways and it is fundamentally for this reason that the film is deemed deserving of inclusion in this specific part of the book. *Avalon* and the *Ghost in the Shell* productions, for their part, marry the implementation of daring animational methodologies to a sustained and unsentimental philosophical assessment of the impact of technology on the body, on the mind and — hypothetically, at least — on the soul, too.

Avalon, on the one hand, engages with this elaborate topos with reference to the discourse of virtual reality — namely, a three-dimensional, highly photorealistic artificial environment simulated by means of computer hardware and software, which can be entered by recourse to special gear including gloves, earphones, goggles or full-body wiring. While feeding sensory input to the user, those devices concurrently measure the body's movements and display them onto a screen, hence meticulously monitoring the user's actions and reactions. The *Ghost in the Shell* films, on the other hand, articulate their preoccupations regarding the interpenetration of humanity and virtuality with reference to the figure of the *cyborg*, a portmanteau of *cybernetic organism*. This designates virtually anything that crosses the boundary between the organic and the mechanical. In recent and contemporary cinema and fiction, the term has tended to describe primarily a human being whose body has been taken over wholly or partially — and usually for the purpose of enhancing the organism's natural abilities — by electromechanical devices.[1]

Both *Avalon* and the *Ghost in the Shell* productions partake of many of the graphic, conceptual and broadly stylistic features that have come to be associated with the science fictional genre commonly dubbed "*cyberpunk*." As noted in the Introduction, the *cyber-* in cyberpunk refers to science and, in particular, to the revolutionary redefinition of the relationship between humans and machines brought about by the science of cybernetics.[2] Crucially, for the purposes of the present study, central to research in the field of cybernetics is the notion of the body as an electronic system: a communications network capable of absorbing information through the senses and of subsequently acting upon the information received. Concurrently, while the human body is conceived of as a machine, it is also considered viable to design machines which simulate the human organism. A machine so designed is precisely a cybernetic organism of the kind mentioned earlier — that is to say, a technological construct that replicates the human body on the basis of an understanding of the structural similarities between machines and living organisms. The virtual interchangeability of human bodies and machines is a recurring theme in cyberpunk and is specifically intrinsic to its representations of cyborgs.

If the *cyber-* component in the term cyberpunk alludes to the fact that the point of reference of this branch of science fiction is digital technology rather than intergalactic travel, the *-punk* element refers to a rebellious attitude rooted in urban subcultures. Cyberpunk's characters are people on the fringe of society: outsiders, misfits and psychopaths, struggling for survival on a garbage-strewn planet. William Gibson, the novelist generally regarded as cyberpunk's founding father, uses consistently the Japanese word *gomi*— "waste"— to designate the rubbish-infested environments inhabited by his varyingly dysfunctional characters.[3] What must be stressed is that the term *punk* is not employed literally by cyberpunk writers as a context-bound and context-specific subculture. Were this the case, cyberpunk would now be outdated. In fact, *punk* is used as a metaphor for rootlessness, alienation and cultural dislocation — experiences with which Oshii's Ash (*Avalon*), Kusanagi and Batou (*Ghost in the Shell* features) are only too intimately familiar. In Oshii's cyberpunk, no less than in Gibson's, the *punk* element could therefore be said to refer metonymically to virtually any form of subcultural disruption of the cultural fabric, played out among the debris of sprawling conglomerates.

The mediating factor between the potentially abstract configuration of life postulated by the digital framework (the *cyber-*) and the markedly physical outlook captured by postmodern subcultures (the *-punk*) resides in the field of biotechnology: the multifarious infiltration of the body by means of implanted circuitry, prostheses and genetic modification. Biotechnology — as dramatized by Oshii through the virtual-reality interface in *Avalon* and the genesis of cyborgs in the *Ghost in the Shell* features — partakes at once of the putatively disembodying computational dimension and of the intractably incarnated urban-posturban dimension. As the body is extensively invaded by technologies that seem to annihilate its materiality, the purging, honing and sculpting of the physiological apparatus concomitantly point to an ongoing fascination with the most indomitably material aspects of embodiment. In this respect, cyberpunk does not signal the demise of the body but rather stands out as an irreverent reinscription of the flesh at its most unnegotiably stubborn. In Oshii's cyberpunk cinema, as in Gibson's narratives, the body is undoubtedly altered by technology but never transcended. The material component, accordingly, goes on playing an axial role. As Bruce Sterling has observed, the corporeal traits of cyberculture are of vital importance to cyberpunk's representation of "the future from the belly up, as it is lived, not merely as dry speculation…. In Gibson's work we find ourselves in the streets and alleys, in a realm of sweaty, white-knuckled survival" (Sterling 1995, p. 11).

The cyberpunk motifs elaborated in *Avalon* and in the *Ghost in the Shell* films enable Oshii to maximize his inveterate proclivity to meditate upon the quintessentially unstable nature of human subjectivity, insofar as the elusive atmosphere of transience and unrelenting flux characteristic of that genre enables the director to create ideal backdrops for the depiction of his personae's inner struggles. At the same time, cyberpunk's persistent emphasis on the personal and collective destabilization of selfhood in the postmodern world affords scope for a systematic problematization of the relationship between the concept of identity and the art of animé itself. Indeed, the latter ultimately depends on sustained dislocations and transformations of the real that could be seen as analogous to those perpetrated by cyberpunk at its most effective. Susan Napier has evocatively captured this issue in the following statement: "[I]dentity in animé … cannot be taken for granted. The metamorphic process lying at the heart of the animated medium ensures that both characters and viewers can explore the rewarding, though sometimes oppressive, possibilities of creating and encapsulating worlds" (Napier, p. 116). The features examined in this part bravely endorse animé's commitment to the confrontation of such alternative dimensions, paradoxically portraying them as most graphically gorgeous precisely when they are also least amicable.

24

Blood: The Last Vampire

Winner of the Best Theatrical Feature Film Award at the World Animation Celebration held in 2001, *Blood: The Last Vampire* (dir. Hiroyuki Kitakubo) was the first theatrically released Japanese animation produced entirely by digital means. Oshii ideated the film's concept and original story and also took part in its making in the capacity of executive producer. The storyline itself is quite simple: a series of mysterious suicides are reported and a team of undercover agents is sent to investigate these suspicious events. Meanwhile, Saya — a nocturnally charismatic loner ostracized from both human and preternatural circles— is dispatched by a secret organization to vanquish the blood-sucking "chiropterans" (a race of hollow-boned shape-shifters) that have infiltrated human society and are actually responsible for the aforementioned deaths. Garbed in a typical Japanese school uniform quaintly incongruous with her fierce nature, and equipped with an ancient Samurai sword, Saya must penetrate the American school within the Yokota military compound, unearth the root of the scourge and quash it.

Saya is described as an "original," which — in the logic of the film — entails that the creatures she hunts and eliminates are actually her relatives (although *Blood: The Last Vampire* leaves the exact nature of the relationship tantalizingly unexplained). Throughout the bulk of the action, the heroine shows no compunction about destroying her kin. At the very end, however, Saya's decision to offer a few drops of her own blood to a chiropteran (which she has just slashed out of the sky with one single stroke of her formidable weapon) in order to alleviate its agony intimates some vestigial loyalty to the beleaguered species. This touch adds a realistic quality to a character that might otherwise have been perceived as a cardboard version of the "tough girl" stereotype. Saya's somewhat divided nature is corroborated by the vestimentary attributes alluded to earlier, the school uniform she dons for the main part of the film representing a concession to many fans' attraction to the fetish of ingenuous eroticism associated with schoolgirls in much anime, yet contrasting starkly with her portrayal as utterly emotionless, merciless and, quite frankly, inhuman.

Although *Blood: The Last Vampire* is not an overtly political movie, Oshii's ideological concerns can be detected, especially in the staging of the action against the backdrop of the Vietnam war and, implicitly, of issues surrounding the legality of Japan's indirect support of military operations. This aspect of the film is underscored, where setting is concerned, by the centrality of the Yokota Air Force Base whence the U.S. military machinery to be deployed in Vietnam is supplied. An intense mood of foreboding and violence dominates the compound as F4 combat planes take off in quick succession. The ending also carries a political message, as the character of the school nurse (who functions as an intradiegetic representative of the audience) draws an implicit comparison between the heroine's massacre of the monsters and human beings' ongoing slaughter of one another. Her reflections are made all the more ominous by the concomitant sight of a plane leaving the compound and by a radio report announcing revamped fighting in Vietnam. The closing credits unfold over digitally distorted live-action pictures drawn from news coverage of the conflict.

Being set in 1966, on the iconographic and representational planes *Blood: The Last Vampire* does not — and clearly *could not* without becoming utterly anachronistic — evince the degree of stunning refinement to be found in productions set in the more or less distant future. This, however, has not in any way prevented its makers from experimenting audaciously with the specifically technical element, in order to deliver a world picture that is indeed inspiringly visionary. There is even a sense in which the implicit contrast between the relative primitiveness of the technologies available to the film's characters in 1966 and the sophistication of those available to its makers in the twenty-first century serves to underscore the magnitude of Oshii's and his team's accomplishment.

Blood: The Last Vampire is characterized by extraordinary pictorial richness: an aspect of the production that is intriguingly counteracted by a no less remarkable narrative conciseness, as a corollary of which the audience is not supplied with protracted introductions to either the dramatis personae or their circumstances, and is invited instead to extrapolate the storyline from the action itself as this progresses. Abetted by effective character design, proficient voice acting and tension-building orchestral melodies that match ideally the action's mood, the film opts for an economically suggestive — rather than expository — approach that offers eloquent evidence for animation's ability to evoke memorable characters without recourse to narrative spoonfeeding. Furthermore, plenty of background information is disclosed by means of dialogue and flash shots, in a compelling alternation of rapidly paced and suspenseful sequences.

However, *Blood: The Last Vampire*'s ostensible reluctance to dwell on background information can be ascribed to pragmatically commercial no less than stylistic reasons. Indeed, the film constitutes just one portion of a multimedia project conceived by Production I.G that also comprises three novels (the first of which, *Night of the Beasts*, was penned by Oshii himself), a manga and a videogame for PlayStation 2. The endeavor to develop a narrative across a multimedia platform harks back to Oshii's—and the Headgear team's—creation of the extensive *Patlabor* saga. Spectators (primarily Western ones) who are not acquainted with the books and game related to *Blood: The Last Vampire* may experience a marginal sense of dissatisfaction in the face of the movie's narrative sparseness. This is a problem which the *Patlabor* franchise would not, by contrast, have posed due to the relatively free-standing character of each of its blocks. However, many audiences will have plausibly derived compensatory solace from *Blood: The Last Vampire*'s pioneering techniques and painterly opulence and, relatedly, from the realization that animé may have more to offer than a word-laden tale.

Furthermore, even though it is likely that some viewers would have wished to learn more about the protagonist of this macabre story, if not necessarily about the supporting personae, there is a surrealistically captivating aura surrounding Saya which could have easily been dissipated by a more exhaustive portrayal of her character, origins and destiny. As she races to hunt down the monsters before the school's Halloween party turns into a carnage far more horrific than even the most gore-relishing reveler would ever fancy, Saya remains cloaked in mystery. The sheer fact that she materializes out of an obscure and unmappable past and that, once her mission has been accomplished, vanishes again without trace and as expeditiously as she came contributes vitally to the sense of bewilderment which the animé seeks to evoke, and indeed maintain, to the end of the movie and beyond.

The sustained utilization of digital technology delivers highly detailed and smooth animation without, however, the viewer's awareness of CGI impairing the movie's overall realism. In fact, it is at times tempting to forget that what one is watching is an animated rather than a live-action film. This applies most typically to the action sequences involving transportation, where both warplanes and ground vehicles appear to have been shot in real life and in real time. Thus, *Blood: The Last Vampire* accomplishes a fluid synthesis of self-conscious artifice and mimetic credibility that captures the core aim of all animation — whether traditional or computer-assisted — as a wizardly evocation of convincing scenarios by the most patently manufactured means.

On the specifically technical plane, the movie derives its distinctive look from the melding of multiple tools, abetted by the persuasive deployment of different camera angles and by a solid direction unwilling to indulge in superfluous footage. Most importantly, it must be emphasized that all the character animation was initially hand-drawn and only subsequently scanned and manipulated by recourse to digital ink and paint, as well as the superimposition of lighting and textural effects. Japanese animation's steadfast commitment to traditional techniques as its foundations thus remains unscathed — indeed, even the textures used to render 3D CG objects were drawn in a conventional fashion prior to their incorporation into computers. The balance of manual and digital art is so immaculate that it is virtually impossible to differentiate between the graphic status of a computer-generated aeroplane, for instance, and that of the hand-drawn winged fiend on its trail: the traditional cel components, therefore, never stand out as lifeless cutouts in a digitally rendered 3D context, as is jarringly the case in other technologically eclectic productions of *Blood: The Last Vampire*'s own generation.

Also notable is the proclivity, revamped in the Oshii-directed feature *Ghost in the Shell 2: Innocence*, to draw the human figures with considerable graphic economy, which serves to make the lavishly detailed backgrounds and meticulously rendered props stand out as even more disquietingly and inspiringly poetic. As animation supervisor Kazuchika Kise has emphasized, a major difficulty in the handling of the specifically drawn element stemmed from the necessity of balancing each image's graphic intensity so that it would come across as satisfyingly slick and raw at once, and hence pithily convey the paradoxical synthesis of elegance and brutality on which Saya's own character is centered. "At first," Kise has noted, "the character came out too cartoon-like, no matter how hard we tried. So all the works inevitably became very clean and neat. Then I would say, 'No, it has to be more rough!' It was hard" (Kise). As in-between animation checker Chieko Ichimanda has explained, the problem was tackled by recourse to different "script sizes," which were introduced at the storyboard stage of the production process, each endowed with varying degrees of line-density and visual refinement. Thus, script A would feature "more detail and broader lines," script B would use "thinner" graphics but still contain "a moderate amount of detail," and script C would consist of perfectly "normal thin lines" of the kind one may expect to find in a basic sketch, which various animators could easily "trace." Subtle manipulations of even the simplest of lines, moreover, made it possible to evoke particular moods in an unobtrusively tasteful style. For example, a scene's entire atmosphere could be made "scarier" by simply adding a few lines on Saya's forehead to convey her ire, aggravation and estrangement: "something that most animators don't do to a *heroine!*" (Ichimanda).

Given its doubtlessly ground-breaking approach to the art of animation, *Blood: The Last Vampire* may well come to be regarded, as James

Cameron has contended, as "the standard of top quality in digital animation" (endorsement of *Blood: The Last Vampire* presented on the front cover of the Manga Entertainment DVD, Region 2, 2001). While the film clearly looks forward to the future of computer-generated imaging, however, it concurrently perpetuates a time-honored legacy steeped in Japan's artistic history and its inveterate commitment to visual stylization and graphic linearity. It would therefore be unjust to celebrate this accomplishment solely in terms of its innovativeness without acknowledging the glorious extent to which it has concomitantly enabled its creators to remain loyal to the art of drawing even as they endeavored to cultivate digital photorealism.

In the wake of *Blood: The Last Vampire*'s enthusiastic reception the world over, Production I.G decided to create a sequel of sorts that would develop Saya's story within a more decidedly modern setting, namely the TV series *Blood+* (directed by Junichi Fujisaku and aired in Japan from 8 October 2005). Oshii has contributed to the series in the capacity of co-planner, his involvement in the original production in an analogous role contributing substantially to the evocation of a cogent sense of thematic and narrative continuity across the two story arcs. What instantly strikes the viewer as a marked departure from the earlier film, conversely, is the overall approach to character design. The artist responsible for creating the original Saya and her hideous antagonist, Katsuya Terada, exhibited a distinctive preference for stern facial expressions and forceful body language, persistently imbued with an impalpable yet compelling sense of preternatural charisma. The character designer behind *Blood+*, Chizu Hashii, has endeavored instead to make Saya appear as normal as any attractive young woman situated in an animé context may be expected to be.

Beside reflecting a particular aesthetic predilection, the style favored by Hashii is quite in keeping with the new story's initially prosaic premises and atmosphere. Indeed, the TV series opens with a portrayal of Saya Otonashi as an ordinary teenager with a passion for athletics and a hearty appetite, who appears to lead a perfectly regular life with a loving family even though she suffers from a medical condition that requires her to undergo routine blood transfusions. The only somewhat unusual thing about her existence is her absolute inability to recollect anything she may have experienced prior to the past year, combined with inexplicable flashbacks of bloodshed and helicopters. After one of her periodic transfusions, Saya meets the handsome cellist Hagi, a highly proficient fighter with a mutated claw who, by merely kissing her in what could be read as a dark parody of the *Sleeping Beauty* topos, resuscitates the memory of her forgotten self: a warrior endowed with unearthly skills and a particular flair for exterminating vampiric shape-shifting monsters (once again designated as "chiropterans").

It gradually transpires that in the aftermath of the events depicted in *Blood: The Last Vampire*, Saya had ended up entombed in an Okinawa mausoleum belonging to the Miyagusuku family. The character of George (a supporting role in the feature film) had here worked as her keeper until the moment when she had eventually woken up, whereupon he had resolved to raise her as his own daughter. As Leslie Smith has pointed out, "Saya has no memories of her previous incarnation, and the first few episodes show her shock at trying to reconcile her teenaged self with the slayer that she once was, and the trained killer that she becomes at the taste of blood" (Smith). The heroine's discovery—and painful adjustment to—the unsavory truth regarding her origins and past actions indeed constitute the dramatic hubs from which the narrative proposed by the TV series derives both its momentum and its pathos.

25

Avalon

As argued in the next segment with reference to *Ghost in the Shell* and *Innocence*, Oshii is deeply concerned with the fate of humanity in the face of rampant invasions of the human body by technological extensions. *Avalon*, for its part, examines a different manifestation of technology's infiltration of the sensorium in the form of virtual reality. By dint of its status as a hybrid of live-action and animated CGI, moreover, the film draws attention to the technological significance of amalgamating disparate styles and media as a cinematographical correlative for the types of human-nonhuman fusions tackled by means of themes and imagery.

It can also be argued that *Avalon*'s composite nature as a seamless blend of conventional cinematography and CGI does not merely impact on its own distinctive look and feel but also on a broader understanding of the relationship between live-action cinema and animation, insofar as the CGI are no less animation, ultimately, than they are live-action. Hence, what the film contributes to hybridize, in the final analysis, is the very barrier between animated and non-animated spectacle. Comparable accomplishments can be found in the *Matrix* and *Lord of the Rings* trilogies, particularly in the use of the bullet-time technique (to be returned to later in this chapter), and in the generation of numerous synthespians (digital equivalents of actors) by recourse to motion capture and universal capture.[1]

While *The Matrix* is overtly indebted to *Ghost in the Shell*, *Avalon* is Oshii's way — among other things — of getting his own back, as it were, by fashioning an alternative version to the one proposed by the Wachowskis of the notion of a simulated universe. In Oshii's vision, the universe in question is an ultraviolent game structured around archetypal personas. As the film's prologue informs us, in the "near future" in which *Avalon* is set, "some young people deal with their disillusionment by seeking out illusions of their own — in an illegal virtual-reality war game. Its simulated thrills and deaths are compulsive and addictive.... The game is named after the legendary island where the souls of departed heroes come to rest — Avalon."

The island in question is told about in Arthurian legends and is said to be guarded by the Nine Sisters of Morgan Le Fay. Oshii's adoption of motifs drawn from classic Arthurian lore, and invigoration thereof through the infusion of vibrantly topical relevance into the old tales, are especially noteworthy. Also remarkable is the amalgamation of those mythological allusions with elements of his own personal philosophy, and ongoing preoccupation with the concepts of illusion, simulation, escapism, displacement and desire. Through an elegant reconceptualization of the ancestral themes of birth, death and rebirth, Oshii concurrently proposes a cutting critique of imperialism, militarism and oppressively ubiquitous surveillance strategies.

The game on which *Avalon* pivots is a compound of concepts drawn from not only the discourse of VR but also role playing games and videogames. As in most role playing packages, the film's players don headsets that serve to immerse their sensorium in the ludic realm and take part in the action as characters from certain ranks or classes (e.g., Warrior, Bishop, Thief), progressively augmenting their skills and accumulating experience points that enable them to progress upwards within the game's internal hierarchy. At the same time, Oshii's game abides by rules and principles familiar to players of videogames, especially the idea that in order to complete different levels, the participants have to defeat end-of-level leaders. *Avalon* reveals the influence of the role playing game *Dungeons and Dragons*, hugely popular in the 1980s, replicating the die used in that game through the prismatic shape seen on the protagonist's screensaver. The game *Wizardry* (designed in the 1980s by Robert Woodhead and Andy Greenberg) has also clearly inspired Oshii's narrative through its own handling of symbolic locations, level-based missions, and character categories and teams.

Although the game Avalon involves the lethal danger of its players becoming braindead while engaging with it, it also enables highly expert virtual warriors to make a profit out of the ludic venture. Among the most skilled subjects is Ash, a young woman who appears pathetically vulnerable in the context of the supposedly real world and its humdrum occupations but is capable of fighting with tremendous pluck within the simulation and of eking out a living by her efforts.

The dichotomy between Ash's experiences in the real world and her exploits in the virtual realm is reinforced by the film's emphasis on the timeless repetitiveness of her quotidian existence, in contrast with the adrenaline-charged action of the game-centered events. Nevertheless, while it is doubtlessly the case that in comparison with the bleak and rundown world putatively inhabited by Ash outside the game, the virtual world of Avalon is electrifying, the alternative existence it affords hardly seems more palatable. In essence, Avalon is indeed a colossal battlefield over which the spectral prospect of violent death hovers relentlessly, insinuating itself into the tiniest nooks and most secluded crevices of the hostile landscape.

Around Ash's own adventures revolve the destinies of other members of the now defunct team of Avalon players known as "the Wizard," namely Stunner, a player associated with the archetype of the Thief who finds it hard to perform single-handedly, and Murphy, a player rendered braindead by his quest for a secret level of the game dubbed "Special A," apparently only accessible with the aid of an elusive female known as "the Ghost."

Having pursued numerous leads in the hope of solving the mystery surrounding Special A and thus retrieving Murphy's absconded brain, and having encountered cryptic references to Arthurian legend in the course of her research, Ash discovers that her best chance of getting anywhere near the secret level is becoming a Bishop: that is, an exceptionally talented character type that can only be attained to by accumulating a vast amount of experience points. A meeting with an existing Bishop and the decision to form a new team with him lead to a tense action sequence from which Ash awakens to find that she has now entered "Class Real"—a highly advanced level of VR technology whose appearance contrasts starkly with the Avalon she is used to and recalls, in fact, a modern and lively European city.

Ash's task within Class Real is to destroy the "Unreturned" Murphy, which she does with aplomb only to discover, however, that her fulfillment of the assignment does not deliver her back to the real world after all: the customary "Mission Complete" signal is not, this time round, granted, and the message she receives instead is the befuddling caption "Welcome to Avalon." A deliberately open-ended finale, the message succinctly conveys the nebulousness of the boundary supposedly separating the virtual and the real, the evanescently dreamed and the empirically enacted. The film's ambiguous ending also implies the possibility of the entire action having taken place within a ludic domain — and of none of the levels visited by Ash, accordingly, being *real*— which potentially places the spectators themselves in the position of virtual players.

This theory would seem to be corroborated by the ostensibly deliberate omission of certain details: for example, the appearance of blank keyboards and of books filled entirely with empty pages could be justified by the fact that in a VR game, the actual existence of such minutiae does not matter — what matters is the players' ability and willingness to act as though the details were there. Further evidence for the comprehensively virtual character of the movie's reality is conceivably supplied by the sudden disappearance of Ash's dog. If *Avalon*'s world in its entirety consisted of a ludic space, this enigmatic occurrence could be explained on the basis that insofar as Ash is no longer in total control of her fate at this juncture in the narrative insofar as her actions are beings steered by the Bishop, the pet might have been removed by the more powerful player as a minor and hence dispensable adjunct to the game's world.

Avalon bears interesting affinities with David Cronenberg's *eXistenZ* (1999). This movie, so titled after the eponymous game on which the plot hinges, opens with the attempted assassination of game designer Allegra Geller by religious fanatics at a focus group. Allegra flees the blood-thirsty rage of the "Realists," who want "the demoness" destroyed for her unholy experiments in virtual reality, and soon comes to the conclusion that in order to ascertain whether or not the gaming equipment containing the original version of "eXistenZ" has been "infected" by the attempt on her life, she herself has to play the game. At this point, a series of unexpected ludic options is unleashed whereby it becomes increasingly difficult to tell who is who, and where "eXistenZ" begins or ends.

Paradoxically, although we might expect Allegra *not* to be surprised by elements of a game she herself has designed, she is by no means in control of the situation and of its random ramifications, and her adventures in the virtual space of "eXistenZ" suggest that even a program meticulously designed according to strict rules may run amok. At the same time, the movie intimates that simulations should not be dismissed as purely virtual toys devoid of material consequences through its emphasis on the entanglement of digital games with both lethal industrial rivalries and bigoted ideological agendas.

The complications inherent in this tangled situation fade into near insignificance, however, as the movie reaches its dénouement and we realize that each character is actually a participant in a game of "TransCendenZ"—the conception of the illustrious computer game designer Yevgeny Nourish—being played by another focus group that eventually culminates with the *real* Allegra Gellar and her partner professing to be "Realists" and assassinating the "demon Yevgeny Nourish." Cronenberg's obfuscation of the boundary between reality and virtuality, and his coupling of that topos with a daunting commentary on the lethal outcomes of blind fanaticism, are the traits that draw *Avalon* and *eXistenZ* most intimately together. Moreover, the two directors exhibit a shared proclivity for subtle and thought-provoking shifts of gears in the cinematographical orchestration of their thematic preoccupations.

Cinematographically, one of *Avalon*'s prime attractions lies with its employment of digital manipulation as a means of exploring Ash's various reality levels: the computer makes it possible for colors to be selectively stripped away from the image as the action shifts from one level to the next. The palettes used for the majority of the scenes set in the real world oscillate between stark monochrome and sepia, with more color filtering through to the image the further Ash moves from the frigidly inhuman technology of the game's spurious nirvana. Furthermore, in order to draw attention to the dissonance between the protagonist's putative reality and the virtual domain, the movie uses chromatic contrasts based on food imagery with remarkable graphic economy. For example, the colorless mush served in the Avalon canteen contrasts sharply with the luscious green and lurid red of the cabbage and meat prepared by Ash in her apartment, in order to provide her dog with an appropriately nutritious meal even though her own diet apparently consists exclusively of dry cereal, vodka and cigarettes.

The song used in the course of the film and in the conclusion reinforces this aesthetic of contrasts and indeed carries intensely ironical connotations, since its mention of the legendary Avalon's "apple groves," "heroes" and "faery" and its status as a "holy isle" is the very antithesis of Ash's world. The only link between the two dimensions, pathetically, is the ubiquity of "mist."

In assessing the specifically cinematographical dimension, it should also be noted, as Vince Leo has stressed, that "[f]or all of its high-concept theories about what is real and what is simulation, *Avalon* actually scores more points as a unique visual experience ... than as a richly detailed story," though it is also that in many commentators' eyes. "Oshii's brand of storytelling is inherently visual, utilizing symbols, icons and atmosphere to allow the viewer to piece together what's really going on" (Leo). Pursuing a cognate argument, Teri Tom maintains that *Avalon*

> is everything mainstream American cinema is not. Quiet. Deliberate. And disturbing. Not in an overtly violent or heavy-handed way — but one that is achingly truthful ... it has stunning imagery ... *Matrix*-like freeze-frame CGI ... even a little action in the game sequences. But unlike those sci-fi projects that give the genre a bad name, *Avalon* employs these devices in the service of asking the big questions. Loneliness. Isolation.... This is a *slow* film. And that is part of what makes it so compelling. We hear a lot these days about how we're constantly bombarded by stimuli. How we're unable to sit alone in silence because we might not like the company. Watching *Avalon* is a bit like that, as Oshii forces us to confront those issues that are usually buried under the superficial noise infecting most Hollywood films. *Avalon* is beautifully unsettling [Tom].

Oshii himself has confirmed the crucial importance of the themes of loneliness and isolation, and commented on their challenging technical repercussions for the representation of the affected characters at their least vivacious and dynamic:

> For the scenes in Ash's apartment.... I have sought to stress the suspension of time. My style draws inspiration from the European films I like best for their original way of "freezing" time, the sense of waiting. I like to dramatize time as lived by a person in a place where she finds herself alone. Gestures, attitudes, and facial expressions alter within that solitude. That's what concerns me. I take as much pleasure from shooting such scenes and expressions as I do from shooting the

characters in fight scenes. People are at their most sincere when they are on their own [Oshii 2002].

The opening sequence of *Avalon*'s highly sophisticated gameworld — with its rolling tanks, heavy-duty artillery fire, helicopter raids and amber-hued dilapidated edifices—is nothing short of awesome and fully encapsulates the film's cinematographical distinction. When bodies are hit, they flatten into 2D projections before disintegrating into myriad triangular fragments. Furthermore, Oshii felicitously deploys bullet-time technology in the explosions presented in this sequence. This technique relies on the use of slow motion to convey a comic-book quality to action scenes while, however, allowing the director to move the camera at regular speed. In practical terms, two motion cameras are placed at the beginning and at the end of the shot, and several still cameras are evenly spaced between them. Both motion picture cameras are rolled and each still camera is fired in rapid sequence, one after the other, to produce a series of images in which the point of view moves around the actors. The still pictures are then fed into the computer in order, and interpolation is implemented in order to create extra frames between the existing pictures and hence generate a smooth blend.

The use of Polish locations, filmed by indigenous cinematographer Grzegorz Kedzierski, contributes substantially to the evocation of an oppressively nightmarish atmosphere. The film, incidentally, was financed by Japanese investors but shot in Poland with an entirely Polish cast and crew, which makes it a distinctive hybrid on a further level beyond that of its technical execution. Furthermore, as Igor Sandman has emphasized, the "Eastern Europe acting style is so compatible with Mamoru Oshii's rhythms and atmospheres. The intensity of Ash's introspection is tangible thanks to Malgorzata Foremniak's attention to details. Bartek Swiderski gave so much personality to Stunner he is instantly considered as a friend while at the same time he inspires distrust in a pathetic way. The same goes for Dariusz Biskupski, from whom emanates such a wisdom" (Sandman). "Foremniak's terrifically understated performance," argues Tom, is the key factor that "holds Avalon together ... she conveys the sadness just beneath her detached exterior with a refreshing subtlety and ease" (Tom).

In evaluating the quality of the acting, human performers should not be the sole focus of interest, however. Critics have frequently commented on the cardinal role played by the figure of the basset hound in *Avalon* (and, in fact, throughout Oshii's output in its entirety). Where *Avalon* is specifically concerned, the centrality of the canine pet is touchingly underscored by the protagonist's habit of feeding him much better than she feeds herself, as borne out by the meticulously detailed and chromatically enticing sequences (alluded to earlier) in which she prepares his meals with exquisite tenderness and her body language invests the ingredients with sensuous palpability. However, what should be stressed more emphatically than has arguably been done thus far within the critical domain is Oshii's keen grasp of animal movement in this film, as indeed in animated productions wherein dogs also feature prominently.

The body language exhibited by Ash's dog is unquestionably one of the film's most memorable aspects, especially in the scene in which we first encounter the pet. As he hears Ash approaching the front door, his anticipation and excitement build up exponentially, crowned by an enthusiastic reception of the homecoming owner. As he proceeds to consume his dinner, the hound's floppy ears inexorably send bits of food flying out of the bowl and all over the floor. Later, the dog appears to be asleep as Ash sits at her computer, but subtle details in his posture indicate that he is actually awake and "keeping an eye" on the young woman, as it were. The dog's affectionate concern for his owner is even more vividly conveyed, in symbolic terms, in the later scene in which he appears uncharacteristically alarmed at the precise point at which Ash makes contact with the "Nine Sisters"— the promising but potentially hazardous link to the mysterious level of Avalon she seeks to penetrate.

A comparison between *Avalon*'s basset hound and his animated counterpart in *Ghost in the Shell 2: Innocence* will feasibly suggest that the cartoon creature's motion cumulatively displays greater fluidity and liveliness, which could be read as an indirect paean on Oshii's part to the unparalleled freedom of the animated medium. It should also be observed, however, that in directing the live-action and the drawn pets, Oshii has not merely explored the technical potentialities of two distinct art forms but has also endeavored to create two substantially different personalities. The heightened vivaciousness of Batou's pet in *Innocence* compared with the endearing ponderousness of Ash's dog corresponds to a generally more playful disposition. As a result, while in the later movie the figure of the basset hound serves largely to infuse an element of cheerfulness in an otherwise bleak reality, in *Avalon*, it metonymically encapsulates the entire film's unrelieved gloom.

Oshii's use of the image of the dog as a recursive trope also calls attention to the symbolic significance of this animal in Japanese culture. As J.C. Cooper notes, "Ainu[2] mythology has dogs stationed on the road to the otherworld at various points so that they can direct souls on their way and see that they go to the rightly deserved place. The dog is also considered psychic and can detect the presence of any ghost" (Cooper, p. 78). In *Avalon*, this symbolic function is elliptically underscored by the appearance of dogs watching Ash as she walks along the streets of both her own city and the metropolis in Class Real.[3]

The mood of ubiquitous perplexity instantly summoned up by *Avalon* right from its opening moments escalates precipitously in the sequence where we are gradually acquainted with one of the whole movie's most befuddling incidents: namely, the aforementioned vanishing of the protagonist's dog. As Ash approaches the front door of her humble abode, enters the space and goes about preparing a meal for the pet, we can hear him snuffling around. However, when she sets down the food bowl, he is nowhere in sight. Since he is hardly likely to have run away — let alone died of neglect — the most feasible explanation would seem to be that we are moving across diverse levels of virtual reality rather than dealing with clear-cut transitions between the inside and the outside of Avalon.

From this point onwards, the pace of Ash's quest accelerates. Having embarked upon thorough research into Arthurian lore in order to ascertain its relevance to the game from which she makes a meager living, she obtains additional, intriguing details from Stunner about the Special A dimension of Avalon (while the shifty Thief gorges himself on a luridly colored breakfast). It here transpires that a Bishop is present whenever the Ghost appears — not just any Bishop, to be precise, but one who is "Class-A Complete. An Archbishop, above Level 12." Stunner speculates that Ash might like to switch from Warrior to Bishop but needs double experience points to do so. Moreover, he argues, a player needs a party to back her or him up in order to succeed in such an expensive task. Finally, he taunts Ash by insinuating that she probably would not be able to pull it off anyway, though things might have been different if Murphy were still around. (This could be read as a hint at a past romantic liaison between the heroine and the braindead player.)

These allusions to Ash's future role in the VR game are dramatically developed in the ensuing segment of the film, as the character of the Bishop visits the heroine at her flat and she takes his intrusion fully on board by boldly declaring: "I want to form a party with you. The usual six members." The Bishop cryptically states that "[f]or the best players the game becomes its own reward," concomitantly making reference to the rumor according to which the Wizard team dispersed because "a certain Warrior ignored her orders and called 'reset.'" A flashback showing the Wizard's last mission appears to confirm the suspicion that it was indeed Ash's sudden panic that caused the assignment to fail. It is noteworthy, however, that Stunner will later assume responsibility for the party's dissolution ("It wasn't your fault that we got wiped out. The one who ran ... was me. I wanted to tell Murphy that."), and that Murphy himself will ultimately turn out to be true cause of the problem. Finally, the Bishop instructs Ash to meet him at "Flak Tower 22" at midnight the following day.

Ash's visit to the Avalon facilities, where she usually jacks into the game assisted by the Game Master, problematizes further the status of Special A as the Terminal Manager in charge at first denies that this level exists, and then qualifies her statement by saying that a level that you cannot reset from is no longer a game, implying that it does exist after all: "There's no such thing.... Not inside Avalon. No matter how real it seems, Avalon is just a game. But a programme you can't clear isn't a game anymore. That's why it's hidden away ... a forbidden field." Hence, it could be opined that Special A is not a game proper because it cannot be cleared by resetting — hence it cannot be considered, strictly speaking, to be a part of Avalon as such. These already thorny matters are by no means simplified by the disclosure that the Bishop has his own terminal and cannot, therefore, be tracked: he merely turns up in the game in his own terms as and when it suits his own schemes.

Once Ash has accessed virtual reality and located the Bishop, the enigmatic character explains that he works *for* the game, maintaining the balance of its disparate missions. The best game, he alleges, is "one you think you can clear but can't, one that looks impossible but isn't," and handling this state of affairs requires a knack of "finding out the subtle balance." Having completed an especially arduous mission involving the annihilation of a "Citadel"— a mighty battle tank — Ash discovers that she is still within the ludic realm without the option to "log off" as would customarily be the case. The Ghost next materializes by the wall that gives proper access to Special A: to enter that level, one must shoot the apparition just as she attempts to leave the wall. Ash manages to accomplish this feat and to pass through the gate, at which point the phantasmatic girl disassembles into a series of rectangular surfaces which then reel into a spiral of silvery blue light and eventually fade out altogether. Concomitantly, the VR surroundings fade to black and are replaced by swirling patterns of data. The protagonist's own body subsequently segments to be replaced by myriad orange digits, tangentially hinting at her utter assimilation to the intangible space of Avalon.

Ash is next seen in her own apartment — the dog's food bowl is there and so, rather mysteriously, is a virtual-reality chair. As the heroine removes her helmet, the computer monitor in the room displays the baffling message "Welcome to Class Real." The Bishop then materializes on the screen and announces that she has penetrated the wall guarded by the Ghost and entered Special A. This level of Avalon, according to the hooded player, is an extremely complex network of data and is almost flawless: to truly complete it, one last task must be undertaken and Ash is the appointed agent — namely, "finish off the Unreturned." The rules are relatively straightforward: Ash has "one pistol" and "one clip of ammunition" at her disposal; there are neutrals operating under free will who must not be harmed; there is no time limit. The only exit point for this mission is "completion" and no "reset," accordingly, is allowed. The Bishop finally states: "If you get back, you can be one of us," *us* referring to the creators of the alternative world encoded in the programme.

A tremendous amount of detail has undoubtedly been channeled into the construction of Special A. In approaching her mission, which will take her to the concert hall hosting the Filharmonia Narodowa's performance of a piece entitled *Avalon,* and publicized by means of a poster that exhibits a basset hound strongly reminiscent of her own former pet, Ash is even supplied with an apposite evening gown, high heels, a ring and earrings. The program creators' highly diligent take on the rendition of VR thus fittingly echoes Oshii's own meticulous approach to filmmaking, infusing the film with a riveting element of self-reflexivity.

In sharp contrast with Ash's putatively real city, the advert-packed metropolis into which the heroine emerges on her way to the ultimate assignment is unexpectedly smart, elegant, vibrant and—above all—colorful. Once Ash has reached her destination and met Murphy, the movie rapidly builds towards a climax that suitably encapsulates the concurrently perplexing and beguiling Chinese-box character of Avalon the game and *Avalon* the film in their entirety. Interestingly, from a cinematographical point of view, the melodic pace of the concert taking place in the background quickens at the same rate as the rhythm of the exchange between Ash and Murphy gains momentum. It is also worth noting, incidentally, that the exchange takes place in the concert hall garden, where the most conspicuous piece of ornamentation is a rather incongruously situated old cannon: this detail operates as an effectively concise reminder of the story's military dimension.

Ash asks Murphy if he came here just to be a vegetable in a hospital bed but Murphy advocates the genuine realness of Class Real, stating that he caused the Wizard party to disband because he wanted to "go all the way" in his own terms. He claims to have always believed that "[r]eality is nothing but an obsession that takes hold of us." "Why," he then adds, "shouldn't I make *this* my reality?" As they keep on arguing over the reality issue, Murphy maintains that when one of them shoots the other to death and the dead body does not disappear, the survivor will gain incontrovertible proof that the level they currently occupy authentically obtains. Nevertheless, Murphy's allegation is bluntly refuted by the fate met by his body once Ash has shot him. Seeing the character's supposedly corporeal substance dissolve in an explicitly computer-generated spiral effect, we cannot avoid questioning the veracity of his assertions. The scene that follows irrevocably confirms the empirically unverifiable nature of Class Real: while Ash approaches the concert hall, an enthusiastic round of applause is still audible in the background but upon entering the space she finds that it is almost entirely deserted — the sole exception being the now smiling Ghost standing on the stage. As alluded to earlier, the movie does not offer any conclusive resolution, the finale consisting, quite simply, of the starkly sibylline message "Welcome to Avalon."

26

Ghost in the Shell

Oshii's epoch-making cyberpunk feature *Ghost in the Shell* offers an inspired treatment of the arguably most elusive metaphysical, scientific and ideological question — namely, *what makes us human?* In both *Ghost in the Shell* and in its sequel *Ghost in the Shell 2: Innocence*, the director addresses this issue with reference to the incremental infiltration of both human organisms and mentalities by technological, artificial and synthetic components that cannot be unproblematically categorized as auxiliary prostheses but actually constitute integral parts of a person's being.

Ghost in the Shell is based on an immensely popular manga written and drawn by Masamune Shirow.[1] Several themes elaborated by Shirow's manga which Oshii's film problematizes deserve special notice in this context. Shirow's story arcs place considerable emphasis on the ever-growing sophistication of advanced cybertechnology, positing the figure of the "cyborg" as a "human whose body has been partially or almost completely altered by the use of substitute artificial organs and parts," endowed not merely with a "normal appearance" but also with lifelike physiological affects, including "oral sensation" (Shirow, p. 103 and "Author's Notes"). The manga also speculates that a synthetic sensorium is a handy tool in the peddling of "virtual-experience software" which "allows several members of the same sex to share in the enjoyment of a sexual experience, on several lines simultaneously." The more refined the "prosthetic body" in question, the more sensations are possible and the greater the entertainment provided accordingly is ("Author's Notes"). Shirow's emphasis on the pervasiveness of artificial bodies is jocularly reinforced, at one point, by the image of a waitress sporting a logo and a "Made in Japan" caption on her scantily clad backside (p. 123).

The film leaves out the cybersexual dimension altogether. Moreover, even though the protagonist herself, Major Motoko Kusanagi, is undoubtedly attractive, she is imparted a far less cute and substantially more somber mien by the film's character designer Hiroyuki Okiura than is ever the case in the parent text. Relatedly, where the manga humorously indulges in overt representations of nude female bodies that verge on soft porn and may even

185

Ghost in the Shell (1995). One of Oshii's most memorable pieces of visual poetry, Major Motoko Kusanagi's biotechnological "birth" vividly dramatizes the hybrid nature of the cybernetic organism as a seamless synthesis of machinery — epitomized by the cables jacked into the bioports that punctuate the character's body — and flesh — foregrounded by the palpable carnality of Motoko's feminine curves and by her fetuslike suspension in the digital equivalent of amniotic fluid. ©1995 Shirow Masamune/KODANSHA • BANDAI VISUAL • MANGA ENTERTAINMENT.

be interpreted as concessions to fetishistic scopophilia, in the film, nudity is employed as a means of succinctly conveying the main character's ultimate vulnerability as a concurrently physical and psychological dimension of her divided being, and hence an allusion to her inherent humanity.

No less central to Shirow's manga than the cyborg figure is the concept of "hacking"— namely, the technological operation that makes it possible to "brain-dive" into another person's sensorium and experience her or his situation as though one were actually inhabiting her or his body. A brain-diver can become an unlawful "ghost controller," penetrating other minds so as to brainwash them (pp. 17–20). A hacker, in Shirow's definition, is "a computer criminal who infiltrates other cyberbrains, steals information, manipulates data and programmes, plants viruses, and otherwise corrupts them" ("Author's Notes"). As shown later in this section, this notion plays a pivotal role in Oshii's plot.

Despite Oshii's deliberate engagement with the genius of the bizarre and the absurd in the elaboration of occasional aspects of *Ghost in the Shell*'s storyline and graphic register, the film's harrowingly topical cogency on the sociopolitical and economic planes can hardly be underestimated. Indeed, the movie constitutes primarily a trenchant critique of hierarchical and corporational mentalities, the abuse of authority and power, and humanity's haphazard romance with technology. Moreover, as Patrick Drazen has noted, even though *Ghost in the Shell* "will inevitably confuse first-time viewers, dealing as it does with the Byzantine round of backstabbings and powerplays that characterize Japanese politics in the future," the movie actually encapsulates harsh cultural realities:

> With the bursting of the economic bubble, Japanese politicians and the ruling Liberal Democratic Party had trouble finding anyone left to run the ship of state — especially after reports began surfacing of financial sweetheart deals between assorted politicians and business interests. Nobody seemed to be clean of the stain, and the tendency of those already in power to continue to rely on the old boy network to get things done only assured that nothing would get done. Skepticism turned to cynicism [Drazen, pp. 338–9].

The manga itself makes insistent reference to embezzlement, money-laundering, smuggling (of people no less than of goods), illegitimate transactions, the appropriation of public funds by unscrupulous individuals, diplomatic infractions, and the utterly unethical exploitation of spurious electoral manifestos.

Furthermore, Oshii's version of *Ghost in the Shell* complicates a number of ideological preoccupations adumbrated by the *Patlabor* features in that it comments dispassionately on the collusion of actual historical phenomena and technological advancement in a largely — though not undilutedly — dystopian vein. In this respect, the film could be said to substantiate Susan Pointon's arguments concerning Japan's attitude towards technology as a dubious gain rather than an unproblematic blessing: "It is obviously no accident," Pointon maintains, "that, in the years following the bombing of Hiroshima and Nagasaki and the subsequent evolution of the Japanese 'economic miracle,' Japanese cultural products ... have become progressively focused on narratives of technological oppression and premonitions of disaster" (Pointon).

The film foregrounds from the start the collusion of international politics and technological ventures in a scene dramatizing the covert meeting between a foreign dignitary and a computer programmer in which "Project 2501" is somewhat cryptically alluded to. Police forces make a theatrical entrance into the building and the dignitary instantly claims diplomatic immunity. Major Motoko Kusanagi presently descends from the top of the building to the level of the room where the fracas is occurring with the aid of a special cord, assassinates the foreign politician and escapes by donning "thermoptic camouflage" that enables her to merge with her surroundings. Kusanagi is a member of Section 9, a branch of the Ministry of Foreign

Affairs fighting technological terrorism and polarizing a wide range of political forces from various parts of the world, with their varyingly dubious economic and diplomatic priorities.

Like the Tokyo Metropolitan Police Special Vehicle Division 2 from the *Patlabor* productions and the Kerberos Panzer Cops from the Kerberos films, Section 9 is regarded ambivalently by both the government and the rest of the police hierarchy as a crucial component of the law-enforcing machine, on the one hand, and an embarrassingly uncompromising body of agents trained to kill without hesitation, on the other. Although no other organization or department would ever wish to get their own hands dirty through direct participation in the missions allocated to Section 9, Major Kusanagi's squad is more often grudgingly tolerated than positively recognized. As frequently, the scandalous information which its investigations repeatedly tend to disclose is conveniently pushed under the diplomatic carpet by the upper echelons of government and accordingly sanitized to suit the maintenance of existing alliances and interests.

The sequence just described is a paradigmatic example of Oshii's use of rapid-fire action sequences in the very opening of a film in order to set its tone and economically introduce themes destined to acquire cardinal importance at a later stage. A different take on technology is offered by the stunning montage presented under the opening credits in which Kusanagi's cybernetic birth is vividly depicted: the pace slows down dramatically, and roaring spectacle gives way to a daunting chapter of sheer visual poetry. An analogous sequence is proposed in the early segments of *Innocence* with comparable graphic and affective intensity.

A careful reconstruction of the story's somewhat baroque involutions and convolutions — which may necessitate repeat viewings — can help us situate the significance of the incident presented in the opening segment of the action within a broader context, and hence appreciate fully its ideological and philosophical implications. Such a reconstruction indicates that in the mid- to late 2020s, the Ministry of Foreign Affairs of the unnamed Asian country in which *Ghost in the Shell* is set decides to embark on a collaborative project with U.S. researchers in the field of artificial intelligence so as to develop a computer program capable of hacking into ordinary people, and hence controlling them to make them commit all manner of illegal deals on their behalf.

The program thus created, an unthinkably complex piece of software originally designated "Project 2501," becomes successfully operational and numerous crimes are perpetrated at its behest in various parts of the world. The most crucial tool used by the program to penetrate and manipulate other beings consists of prosthetic memories which the implanted subjects unquestioningly accept as genuine recollections. This theme echoes Ridley

Scott's *Blade Runner* (1982). Indeed, both Oshii's and Scott's films emphasize people's dependence on material vestiges of the past in the guise of photographs which, by supplying them with memories, are concurrently supposed to invest them with a sense of identity. Ironically, the photographic fragments of reality with which the felonious program provides its human marionettes are themselves a fabrication. In proposing that the human brain can be hacked into analogously to a computer, *Ghost in the Shell* is also redolent of Paul Verhoeven's *Total Recall* (1990) and Kathryn Bigelow's *Strange Days* (1996). It is precisely Project 2501's knack of governing its victims' minds and bodies that by and by gains it the nickname of "Puppet Master" or "Puppeteer" (*ningyouzukai*).

The program is deployed for the first time in the country of *Ghost in the Shell* in 2029, exactly at the time Oshii's story unfolds, as a means of resolving a thorny diplomatic conundrum. The Ministry of Foreign Affairs are eager to find a politically acceptable excuse to deport the former leader of an overthrown military dictatorship, Colonel Malez of the Republic of Gabel, who seeks asylum in their country. They therefore use the Puppet Master to hack into the brain of a petty criminal and implant a simulated identity therein, in order to induce him to believe he is a big-time violator of international law employed by the Embassy of Gabel to hack, in turn, into the brains of key diplomatic figures expected to participate in the negotiations, including the Prime Minister's personal interpreter. When the brain-hacked offender is arrested by Section 9 and it becomes clear that he has no connection whatsoever with his putative employers and is actually a mere pawn in the Puppet Master's massive operation, the situation takes an unpleasantly complicated turn.

It becomes increasingly evident that while the Puppet Master is presented as a dangerous criminal to be brought to justice, it is not actually the government's enemy but one of its most precious tools. Regrettably, just as the program promises to enable the Ministry of Foreign Affairs to smoothly solve a potentially embarrassing situation over the Malez issue, it unexpectedly manages to develop an independent identity and autonomous sentience, and break free. The reputation of the Ministry of Foreign Affairs is now sorely at risk and it is incumbent upon them to use any available weapon and measure to regain control over the rogue program. To achieve this aim, they lure the Puppet Master into a "designated body," that of a blonde female cyborg produced by the Megatech giants. However, the program and its host flee the factory, are run over by a truck and suspiciously turn up at the Section 9 headquarters. It is here that the Puppet Master makes itself sensationally heard by speaking through the cyborg torso rescued from the accident, and solemnly states: "I am not an AI.... I am a living, thinking entity that was created in the sea of information."

It now becomes clear that the transgressor, having attained consciousness, is aware of being a runaway from the government and hence seeks political asylum. Moreover, it transpires that the program is aiming to communicate specifically with Major Kusanagi. (The Puppet Master's desire to make contact with the heroine had emerged less conspicuously earlier on in the form of a spectral voice quoting from the Book of Corinthians 13, 11: "What we see now is only a dim image in a mirror. Then we shall see face to face.")

As the film races towards its elaborate climax, the cyborg torso is mysteriously abducted from Section 9, and the Major endeavors to retrieve it with the intention of "diving" into it so as to finally communicate with the Puppet Master and discover its true goal. The main motivation behind Kusanagi's actions, however, is her conviction that the entity is in a position to help her shed light on her own most intimate perplexities. Ripped apart by a multi-legged tank sent to stop her, the protagonist is saved by her loyal colleague Batou's antitank rifle and decides to interface directly with the Puppet Master by having her own remnants hooked up to the cyborg torso. The Puppet Master reveals that the reason it has persistently attempted to communicate with Kusanagi is that it aims to "merge" with her in order to gain the biological component it needs to ensure species survival. Through this unorthodox marriage, the Puppet Master avers, their "children" will be born into the "infinity of the Net." The entity is eventually destroyed but Batou manages to salvage Kusanagi's functioning remains and to rehouse her "ghost" in a new body—that of a schoolgirl, as it happens, due to the scarcity of viable "shells" on the black market.

Kusanagi's dive into the Puppet Master is both cinematically and diegetically crucial in establishing *Ghost in the Shell*'s iconic uniqueness. When the heroine enters the Puppet Master, the latter starts speaking through her mouth in a male voice. At the same time, the perspective shifts from Kusanagi's eyes to the Puppet Master's hosting body, so that we ourselves are encouraged to perceive the situation through the enigmatic entity rather than through the protagonist. The overall effect is a baffling sense of dislocation. From the viewpoint of Western liberal humanism, this strategy may be seen to allude to an irretrievably lamentable loss of selfhood and self-containedness, yet from an Eastern perspective, the dissolution of Kusanagi's identity and personal boundaries carries positive connotations. Indeed, it is consonant with the Japanese concept of *seishinshugi*: namely, spiritual catharsis and growth through suffering and self-deprivation. This idea is echoed by the Puppet Master's own words in the film's climactic sequence:

> Life perpetuates itself through diversity and this includes the ability to sacrifice itself when necessary. Cells repeat the process of degeneration and regeneration until one day they die, obliterating an entire set of memories and information,

only genes remain. Why continually repeat this cycle? Simply to survive by avoiding the weaknesses of an unchanging system.

Relatedly, it could be argued —following Susan Napier— that *Ghost in the Shell* "raises the possibility of technology's positive potential … in terms of the possibility of spiritual development." The problem, in this respect, is that this possibility is granted to a cyborg, not to a human, and indeed the film "does not offer … much hope for the organic human body, which is seen essentially as a puppet or a doll … to be manipulated or transformed by outside sources" (Napier, p. 105).

It is also noteworthy, however, that the central cyborg character is herself not presented as unambiguously strong but rather as "both powerful and vulnerable." This is borne out by the opening sequence, where the Major's dauntlessness is counterpointed by hints at her potential weakness:

> Because the viewer is at first not privy to the fact that this is a carefully arranged assassination, his or her first reaction to Kusanagi's fall is one of unease. She is … prey to the currents of the air … her body encapsulates both presence and absence, signified first by her disembodied voice outside the window, and then by the next scene in which … we see her become invisible … allowing the viewer to suddenly see, through the disappearing outlines of her body, the vast electronic high-tech city toward which she falls [p. 109].

Kusanagi's ambiguity is reinforced by the film's depiction of her physical appearance in terms of a fairly stereotypical notion of feminine sexiness replete with alluring curvaceousness, and its concurrent emphasis on the fact that even when she appears to be nude, she is actually donning technologically enhanced flesh-colored body suits intended to abet her performance — and thus again insinuating her latent vulnerability.

Endowed with a 95 percent artificial body throughout the bulk of the action, Kusanagi is understandably plagued by doubts concerning the actual extent of her humanity. As Jonathan Clements and Helen McCarthy aptly remark, this aspect of her personality makes the Major "an angst-ridden platoon leader … who can't leave the service because, like the original *Bionic Woman*, parts of her are government property" (Clements and McCarthy, p. 141). "Cyborgs like myself have a tendency to be paranoid about our origins," Kusanagi reflects at one point. "Maybe there wasn't a real me in the first place and I'm completely synthetic." Propelled by these torturing quandaries, she forces herself in defiance of both safety and logic to engage in scuba-diving expeditions, even though the weight of her cybernetic enhancements could easily drag her into the ocean's depths for good, in order to test her emotions and, specifically, her very ability to experience fear, elation or pleasure. In the climactic sequence wherein the Major witnesses the Puppet Master's transfiguration, her humanity is vividly demonstrated by the welling up of tears in her eyes. This scene corroborates the film's proposition, voiced through Batou, that "even a doll can seem to have a soul" — a topos destined to be invested with fresh resonance in *Innocence*.

Oshii's most insistently (and almost obsessionally) revisited theme throughout his corpus to date — namely, the interpenetration of reality and fantasy — strikes once more sonorous chords in *Ghost in the Shell*. In representing simulated-experience technologies, the movie radically challenges conventional humanist models of memory and hence unsettles related notions of reality. If an individual's brain is hacked into and she or he undergoes a simulated experience while in a conscious state, the experience could be said to partake in equal measures of fantasy and reality. On one level, the event is unreal insofar as it did not actually take place in the real world. Yet, on another level, it cannot be dismissed as a mere delusion on the person's part insofar as it emanated from a *real* program running inside his or her violated nervous system.

In assessing the aliveness of cyborgs in *Ghost in the Shell* — and indeed in its sequel — it is important to acknowledge the influence of Shinto upon Oshii's vision. According to the world view promulgated by Japan's official religion, all sorts of objects and substances (including rocks) host spiritual and dynamic energy. Relatedly, *manga-ka* Shirow has stated: "I think all things in Nature have 'ghosts.' This is a form of pantheism, and similar to ideas found in Shinto.... There are, after all, humans who act more like robots than robots" (Shirow, "Author's Notes"). As Drazen has noted, "Japan has ... spent centuries coming to terms with machines that seem human. *Karakuri ningyou* — clockwork wooden dolls that resembled people — were first built in the Tokugawa period [1603–1867]. Such dolls would 'bow' their heads while carrying cups of tea on a tray. Lifting a cup from the tray would stop the doll until the cup was replaced" (Drazen, p. 340). One such automaton features at a crucial point in *Innocence*.

It is also useful, in evaluating *Ghost in the Shell*'s dramatization of close encounters between humans and machines, to appreciate the frequently equivocal and sometimes overtly paradoxical nature of the association between technology and animation itself. As James Clarke argues, a

> product of the mechanized, modern age, animation often tells stories that play up the usually hapless relationship between humans and their inventions.... Somewhat ironically, it was by mocking and parodying the modern world of machines that animation really broke into mainstream culture, itself becoming a mass-produced form involving huge numbers of animators, painters, designers and technicians [Clarke, pp. 2–3].

Moreover, the "tradition of the animated film is also ... the starting point for people's appreciation, understanding and sheer enjoyment of the magic of what we now think of as special effects" (p. 2). Relatedly, "[t]oday's live-action films are becoming increasingly live-action-animation fusions, most notably *Star Wars: Episode I*, *The Matrix* and *The Lord of the Rings* trilogy" (p. 10). *Ghost in the Shell* fully confirms the central incidence of technology in the animated medium as a set of both themes and tools. At the same time, by rivaling live-action cinema at the level of image quality, the film invites us to reflect on the contemporary phenomenon highlighted by Clarke, whereby animation can no longer be regarded as a second-rate form seeking — and generally failing — to emulate its live-action counterpart but should actually be approached as something of a prerequisite for the cinematic process in its entirety.

A major corollary of digitization is that special effects, once relegated to cinema's margins, have become the staple of computer-assisted filmmaking, for the reason that they capitalize on the generation of images independently of external referents. However, animation has always done this — well before the advent of CGI — and it could therefore be argued that animation is the form that lies at the very foundations of contemporary cinematography.

In the domain of digital cinematography, animation does not merely pertain to techniques used to bring cartoon-like characters to life. In fact, it permeates the entire film-making apparatus, playing a crucial role in the rendition of both architectural and organic structures. The importance of animation in digital cinematography points to an intriguing shift in the history of film, which Lev Manovich has described as a partial return to the medium's infancy. Manovich maintains that the early techniques from which cinema evolved "all relied on hand-painted or hand-drawn images" and that "[i]t was not until the last decade of the nineteenth century that the automatic generation of images and their automatic projection were finally combined." It was at this point that the art of animation came to be banished to the very periphery of the history of moving images: "[o]nce the cinema was stabilized as a technology, it cut all references to its origins in artifice" and animation became a "bastard relative." What live-action cinema seemed to disapprove of most sanguinely was animation's most distinctive feature: namely, the fact that it "foregrounds its artificial character, openly admitting that its images are mere representations," where live-action cinema, by contrast, "works hard to erase any traces of its own production process.... It denies that the reality it shows often does not exist outside of the film image."

Over the past two decades, however, the rapid expansion of digital tools and their increasing deployment by the film industry have meant that the techniques marginalized by cinema in order to efface its artificiality (e.g., front and rear projection, matte paintings, green-screen and blue-screen photography) have been regaining pivotal status: the "[m]anual construction and animation of images gave birth to cinema and slipped into the margins ... only to reappear as the foundation of digital cinema. The history of the moving image thus makes a full circle. Born from animation, cinema pushed animation to its boundary, only to become one particular case of animation in the end" (Manovich).

Ghost in the Shell innovatively partakes of recent developments in the field of computer graphics, and has played an important historical role in rescuing animation from its Cinderella-like position by implicitly drawing attention, thanks to the stunning photorealism of many of its scenes, to live-action cinema's own dependence on animational strategies. To this extent, it eloquently confirms Manovich's argument. In the production of the film, Oshii's team resorted consistently to Digitally Generated Animation (DGA), the ensemble of processes through which hand-drawn cels, CGI, live-action footage and audio are amalgamated and translated into digital data that can be further manipulated in the computer. Computer-generated graphics encompass three interrelated category: digital cel work; visual displays; and images as they are perceived by the cybernetically enhanced brains of the key characters.

Digital cel work refers both to the use of computers for compositing purposes and to computer-assisted camera work. One of the most distinctive aspects of the latter in *Ghost in the Shell* is the use of distortion to convey particular moods and emotions: a classic case is supplied by the shot of Kusanagi's face in the foreground during the key sequence in which she rides a boat down a Newport canal with Batou, reflecting on the meaning of humanity. Here the protagonist's features and proportions are subtly distorted in order to evoke her gnawing doubts on the subject and her mounting apprehension as she catches a glimpse of what looks just like her double. (This sequence will be returned to later in this chapter.) Also notable is the employment of filters intended to create perspectival effects: for instance, the scene where the major is shown facing the viewer with the towering Newport edifices behind her, seeming to get gradually smaller and to disappear into the background as the background, in turn, appears to advance towards the foreground and engulf her, deploys those tools to evoke an overwhelming sense of claustrophobia.

Digital cel work also includes the adoption of ground-breaking TIMA software, specifically in the sequences where thermoptic camouflage is donned. This enables the CGI team to isolate individual frames of a background and to manipulate or deform them independently so that the initial background remains undisturbed. The warped frames are then superimposed on the original scenario to convey the impression of the cloaked character's motion against it without affecting its actual images and textures.

Visual displays are grids whose purpose is to offer graphic visualiza-

Ghost in the Shell (1995). From the vertiginous heights of futuristic Newport City, Major Motoko Kusanagi prepares to descend upon her unsuspecting victim in the opening sequence of Oshii's epoch-making cyberpunk thriller. The exaggerated perspective, extremely low camera angle, somber atmosphere, and play with vertical and diagonal lines to suggest dynamism even in static frames are among the director's best-known trademarks. ©1995 Shirow Masamune/KODANSHA • BANDAI VISUAL • MANGA ENTERTAINMENT.

tions of various aspects of future technology, such as maps of wired brains and analogously advanced cybernetic and biotechnological apparatuses, as well as electronic maps that are accessed by the characters in the course of their missions by recourse to interfaces plugged directly into their sensorium. Images as perceived by the brain, for their part, reveal how the filmic characters themselves perceive their surroundings when they are hooked up to vast data networks by means of cables. Both the visual displays and the images perceived by the brain are rendered in the typical green hue that has been conventionally associated with filmic representations of digital technology since Ridley Scott's *Alien* (1977) and has more recently been immortalized by the *Matrix* trilogy and its non-cinematic tie-ins and spin-offs.

    Ghost in the Shell's cityscapes, so rich in detail and chromatic nuances as to frequently appear to have been filmed from life, were executed with the assistance of the Rotoscope. This device, patented by Max Fleischer in 1917, projects live-action footage frame by frame onto a small screen, upon which drawing paper is placed. Animators can trace the live-action figures in each frame, thus achieving stunningly realistic results. (A formidable instance of the implementation of this technique can be seen in the representation and animation of the Fairy Godmother in Disney's *Cinderella* [1950].)[2]

Although the movie's inspiring adoption of state-of-the-art technology deserves careful consideration, its simultaneous devotion to traditional animation should not be underestimated. This is borne out by the collaborative efforts of various members of Oshii's team. Art director Hiromasa Ogura was responsible for ideating animation backgrounds based on a highly and refreshingly unconventional use of the relationship between light and shadow, whereby in scenes with stark contrasts between lit and dark portions (of which there are several), the dark ones were made incrementally darker until none of their details could be identified, and illuminated ones remained bright throughout and filled with intensely visible details. The animation director Toshihiko Nishikubu was especially concerned with accomplishing realistic visual and special effects in the rendition of the action pieces, and worked especially hard on the sequence depicting Kusanagi's confrontation with the tank with the objective of communicating convincingly the impression of bullets hitting different surfaces— adding sparks in the case of metal but not in that of stone — to transcend the animational stereotype whereby sparks are unthinkingly thrown in whenever a bullet makes impact with any material whatever.

Ghost in the Shell exerted a vital influence at both the thematic and the visual levels on the Wachowski brothers' seminal film *The Matrix* (and its sequels), as well as on the series of animated shorts collected under the title of *The Animatrix* (dirs. Andy and Larry Wachowski, *et al.*). Salient similarities between Oshii's production and the Wachowskis' work are also thrown into relief by *The Art of the Matrix*, a documentary volume that explicitly substantiates the allegiance to Japanese cinema of those recent instances of Western cinema by clearly demonstrating that the storyboards underlying the *Matrix* films and animations are akin not just to comic books in general (as storyboards often are) but specifically to manga, due to their incorporation of that medium's distinctive use of formal features redolent of camera actions.

As far as Oshii's cinematographical approach is concerned, *Ghost in the Shell* is made especially memorable by the dynamic capture of light as a means of enhancing a setting's credibility (e.g., in the rendition of vehicles and adverts) or, alternatively, of suspending realism so as to conjure up a feeling of prismatic magic (e.g., in the scenes where a rainfall refracts the light in quasi-kaleidoscopic chromatism). The reflections and refractions of light in and through water —from vast expanses to single droplets— are also imaginatively handled. At the same time, in order to mirror visually the ethically shadowy character of the world he portrays, Oshii resorts to a studious use of chiaroscuro effects— most notably, in the shots where shadows inundate people's faces and sink them into unfathomable darkness. A significant proportion of the setting's forbidding feel emanates from Oshii's handling of the disorientingly shifting perspectives of skyscrapers in relation to the vehicles driving past them.

Cinematographically, one of the most unforgettable sequences offered by *Ghost in the Shell* is indubitably the aforementioned depiction of Kusanagi's cybernetic genesis. This dramatizes the cyborg's concurrently organic and technological assemblage, seamlessly harmonizing the two dimensions in order to evoke their inextricable interconnection. The major is first portrayed as an abstract set of digital data. She next takes the shape of a minimalistic anatomical frame, as various implants are inserted into the skull area so as to programme the cyborg's functions. The character then proceeds to assume incrementally more realistic — and hence more overtly human — physiological attributes: her flesh-encased body floats in a fetal position within a vat filled with a substance reminiscent of amniotic fluid and is eventually ejected into the world as a full-fledged adult.

No less memorable is the pillow sequence located midway through the movie, lasting two minutes and thirty-four shots and paradigmatically typifying the director's approach to montage. This is the sequence, referred to earlier, in which the major and Batou are seen riding a boat down a Newport City canal. The audience is invited to look through the protagonist's eyes at a motley gallery of lonely and somber individuals uncaringly licked by urban neon as they plod along the rain-filled streets. Backed up by an appropriately haunting musical score, the sequence communicates a potent sense of the human condition at large as a situation of atomized disconnection, and thereby prompts us to reflect upon Kusanagi's personal dilemma regarding the extent of her own humanity as a corollary not so much of her cyborg status as of her existing at all. It is precisely the tormenting intimation of loneliness that ultimately makes the major human, and accordingly enables her to hear whispers in her "ghost," over and above any physiological markers. This is therefore the sequence in which one can sense most palpably the heroine's vulnerable humanity. It is at this juncture, as Drazen observes, that one fully appreciates that "[s]he is, in spite of heightened strength and abilities, an ordinary mortal, asking the same old questions mortals have asked since the dawn of time: Who am I? Is there a reason why I'm here? What happens after I die?" (Drazen, p. 340). At one point, as the boat gently drifts past a glass-fronted café, Kusanagi suddenly sees a woman equipped with precisely the same model of cybernetic body as her own on the other side. A further Kusanagi lookalike features later in the sequence in the guise of a mannequin in a departmental store display.[3]

Although reflections play a prominent role in virtually all of Oshii's productions, their use in this film is especially pervasive and significant insofar as they serve as cinematic parallels for the story's thematic focus on the tropes of identity and selfhood, and for its preoccupation with the precariousness of an individual's boundaries. A moving commentary on the issues of humanity and identity that concisely summarizes the entire movie, the canal sequence fully testifies to Oshii's penchant for ideating scenes and sequences imbued with wordless pathos. On the specifically cinematographical plane, Oshii establishes a tantalizing tension at the beginning of the sequence between the shots that are perceived from the protagonist's point of view and the supposedly more objective shots of streets and edifices taken from high angles. Within the montage, Oshii deftly accommodates all the most distinctive traits of his characteristic signature: water, reflective surfaces, narrow passages, metropolitan crowds, artificial beings and, of course, a waggy-tailed basset hound.

The orchestration of sound effects contributes vitally to the overall atmosphere, conveying a realistic sense of motion as sounds become louder or softer in accordance with the characters' movements towards or away from the action's focal point. As a result, the spectators are immersed in the spectacle by virtue of not only what they see but also what they experience acoustically. Silence itself, at acutely suspenseful points in the filmic narrative, can be affectingly heard.

Cumulatively, on the cinematographical plane, *Ghost in the Shell* comes across as a film of contrasts. It undeniably offers the violent gun-fights, high-speed chases and voluptuous feminine curves that many manga fans customarily cherish. Yet, most viewers will ultimately remember it as a pensive contemplation of fundamentally existential issues. These, as indicated, are articulated principally with reference to Kusanagi's perception of her hazy subjectivity, and to germane reflections on the nature of her origins and destiny. The wistful tone that these troubling speculations evoke finds a perfect iconic correlative in Oshii's depiction of rain-drenched cityscapes wherein visions of architectural decay, semiotic overload (*infomania*) and overall sense of alienation symbolically fuel the central character's personal apprehension of unrelieved solitude.

Ghost in the Shell is therefore simultaneously melancholy and cerebral, lyrical and savage, concisely terse and fluidly meandering, just as its protagonist is at once a ruthless titanium-reinforced *shell* and a lonely, emotionally fragile *ghost*. *Innocence* will elaborate these visual and thematic elements to engender a multi-faceted universe, endowed with a mesmerizingly dreamlike, yet piercingly provocative, aura.

27

Ghost in the Shell 2: Innocence

Oshii's keen ability to pose questions about science fiction's essential cornerstones and to lay bare multiple connections between that genre and our quotidian lives, all the time cultivating an approach to visuals that pushes the boundaries of the animation format, has reached something of an apotheosis with *Ghost in the Shell 2: Innocence*. All of the axial preoccupations evinced by Oshii's cinema since the mid-1980s have made a spectacular return in *Innocence*. At the same time, this film is his first production to concentrate explicitly on Japan since *Patlabor 2*. More than in any of Oshii's earlier movies, in *Innocence* the science fictional substratum is indeed firmly anchored in indigenous tradition, and particularly in the beliefs and rituals associated with the *ningyou* (doll) figure. Though eager to chart the mutating significance of the organism in contemporary and approaching technoscapes, *Innocence* is ultimately more concerned with the human elements that manage to subsist in the face of invasive technologies than in how such technologies alter humanity.

If *Ghost in the Shell*'s intelligent meditation on the human soul was deservedly hailed as a ground-breaking achievement in 1995, when the Japanese animation industry was still busy establishing its trademark by means of huge-eyed magical schoolgirls and giant robots, *Innocence* has transcended even more radically the genre ghetto by launching its predecessor's existential preoccupations into the stratosphere, and ushering us further into the future of cybertechnology than any filmmaker has ever done before.

The film is set in 2032, three years from where *Ghost in the Shell* left off, and revolves around the Special Anti-Terrorist Agent Batou (a supporting character in *Ghost in the Shell*), employed by Public Safety Division Section 9. The prequel's heroine, Major Kusanagi, has putatively dissolved into the ether merely leaving behind a disembodied, spectral voice which Batou loves unconditionally and indeed describes as his "guardian angel." Kusanagi is listed as "missing" while government agents are still looking for her in the knowledge that she is likely to possess top-secret information regarding the notorious "Project 2501."

The plot's convolutions are predicated upon the premise that by 2032, the dividing line between humans and technological apparatuses will have faded virtually beyond recognition. This theme is introduced right from the start in a mesmerizingly beautiful sequence that dramatizes in a stylized fashion the genesis of cybernetic organisms. While redolent of the sequence unfolding under the opening credits of *Ghost in the Shell* in which Major Kusanagi's "birth" is articulated, the sequence offered by *Innocence* is technically more sophisticated, thus attesting to the exponential refinement of computer-assisted animation since 1995. However, the two sequences somewhat complement each other insofar as they could be regarded as companion pieces within the broad context of Oshii's self-reflexive employment of digital technology as a means not merely of flaunting his team's technical flair but also—and more importantly—of commenting on the generation of technohuman syntheses at the thematic and diegetic levels of filmmaking.

A solitary, expressionless and hulking cyborg, Batou nonetheless preserves his humanity in his unfaltering pursuit of justice and in his deeply loyal attachment to his pet basset hound, an unbiased witness to human folly in both its crassest and its most pathetic manifestations.[1] The unobtrusively realistic shots in which Batou affectionately tugs the dog's soft ears out of his feeding dish, having prepared the microwavable dinners that constitute the only luxury in his modest dwelling, are among the most heartbreakingly memorable in the entire movie. Beside the hound, other unforgettable images proposed by *Innocence* are likewise associated with organic life, including a fish in its bowl and the meticulously detailed plumage of a seagull.

A paradigmatic instance of Oshii's central preoccupation with the vicissitudes of the human element as it struggles to endure in the face of increasingly intrusive technologies is supplied by the scene in which the main character, whose wounded biotechnological arm has been replaced with a limb cloned from his own DNA on the basis that this procedure is more time- and cost-effective than healing the original, wonders: "where's my real arm?" As he flexes his new—utterly synthetic and yet utterly realistic—fingers, the doctor replies phlegmatically, "We threw it out," evincing no sign of acknowledgement of, let alone sympathy towards, the existential dilemma coursing through the tortured protagonist's cyberbrain. Throughout the film, the character is portrayed as a calculatingly clever mental gymnast, as well as a physically imposing killing machine. However, as Julian Boyance has aptly remarked, he is also "startlingly conflicted for a cyborg.... Going to such outlandish lengths as to have an expensive 'real' dog, a tense moment of danger is created when [he] goes to buy liquid rather than dry dog food. Unknowingly hacked into, Batou goes on a berserk shooting spree in a crowded grocery store.... Our hero's conflicted nature gives [him] an appealing sardonic edge that belies a soft interior" (Boyance).

Batou and his mostly human partner Togusa (whose humanity is underscored by a tormenting fear of deserting his family) are responsible for investigating a case involving a malfunctioning gynoid — namely, a lifelike female doll with eerily supple limbs designed for sexual entertainment — that went berserk and murdered her owner. In the wake of the murder, numerous other dolls go awry, dismally tearing their humanoid skin apart as their eyes and internal gears pop out of their comely faces in a veritable glut of technological grotesquerie.

As Batou and Togusa endeavor to delve into the seemingly inscrutable manufacturing defect across the city's retrofuturistic underbelly, having to fight off thugs, suffer brain hacks and negotiate with corrupt corporate executives and devious bureaucrats, they inspect a CSI lab, a *yakuza* haunt and a cyborg factory, on the trail of an elusive software programmer called Kim who may be responsible for the crime and its gorily bizarre aftermath. Indeed, all the malfunctioning gynoids turn out to come from the same place, the corporation Locus Solus, an industrial giant revolving around Kim that vaunts an eccentric crew of highly skilled techno-artisans residing in a disused battleship off the coast of China. The sequences set in the villain's palatial residence, replete with some of the most hypnotizingly beautiful architectural and ornamental details ever seen in the animated medium to date, holographic simulations of humans, birds, plants and roaring flames, and a colossal music box splendidly rendered down to its minutest cog and wheel, evince total dedication to the punctilious representation of all sorts of materials and textures, lighting effects and chromatic pyrotechnics.

Diegetically, the sequences constitute alternate facets of the massive cybermaze created by Kim to avert Batou and Togusa from the case. Batou manages to break free, to release Togusa and to capture the criminal, and proceeds to search for further incriminating evidence intended to ascertain incontrovertibly Kim's part in the murders by infiltrating the villain's doll factory. Although the criminal's brain-hacking stranglehold has been neutralized, there has also been sufficient disruption in the system to awaken the dolls hosted within the factory. The frantic gynoids mercilessly attack the protagonist, who is rescued just in the nick of time by a reincarnation of Major Kusanagi's ghost in a doll's body. It transpires that Kim's company had kidnapped children and used a ghost-dubber to create degraded replicas of their souls for implantation into the dolls, and thus endow the artifacts with a higher degree of humanity that one would expect to encounter in the domain of artificial intelligence. A programmer had then tried to help the children by weakening some of the constraints placed on the copied ghosts, which had enabled the children themselves to induce the dolls to cause problems that would attract the attention of the relevant authorities and eventually lead to their rescue. Batou's "guardian angel" shuts down the system, thereby losing an arm in a scene vividly reminiscent of the sequence in which she dives into the Puppet Master in the first *Ghost in the Shell* film. She then promises Batou that she will always be on his side within the vast digital matrix before disappearing once more and leaving merely the doll's empty "shell" behind.

The case at the heart of *Innocence* is not merely a matter of law and order, however. In fact, while presiding over a criminal investigation, Batou concurrently ponders intractable existential questions concerning the essence of humanity and humans' inveterate tendency to immortalize their image in synthetic counterparts, alluded to by recourse to tangential quotations and aphorisms drawn from Confucius, René Descartes, John Milton, Jakob Grimm, Isaac Asimov, Jean-Luc Godard, Ludwig Wittgenstein and the Bible. Intertextuality is undoubtedly one of *Innocence*'s defining cachets. Oshii took great care in selecting relevant quotations and interleaving them seamlessly with the dialogue, and has acknowledged Godard as the pivotal influence behind his adoption of this particular approach. *Innocence*, incidentally, echoes Godard's *Alphaville* in both its cumulative visual rhythm and, more specifically, in the representation of Locus Solus. The integration of textual elements from other authors and stories is a means, according to Oshii, of foregrounding cinema's flair for ongoing self-renewal insofar as the insertion of a preexisting piece of language into a novel production does not only enrich the latter but also revitalizes the former's emotional and intellectual import.

Innocence thus both develops and problematizes *Ghost in the Shell*'s thematic concerns, while concurrently taking full advantage of the tremendous advancement of digital technology since the creation of the earlier movie, to deliver some of the most stunning visuals ever yielded by an animé production. Nevertheless, the manually drawn component retains cardinal importance in Oshii's aesthetic vision. The result is a blend of polished and elegantly edited traditional 2D animation (used mainly in the drawing of the characters) and eye-meltingly gorgeous 3D CGI (employed for the machinery and the backgrounds). The film was four years in the making and the festival segment alone took up over a year, ultimately providing a "perfect match of sound and image ... something Hitchcock and Bresson spent their lives searching for ... 'pure cinema,' something that is unable to be reproduced in comic books, TV shows, or novels" ("*Destroy All Monsters* Review of *Innocence*").

The chromatic palettes are subtly orchestrated, ranging from golden, washed-out sepia and amber hues (in contrast with its predecessor's preference for cool green and blue tones) to darkly sumptuous nuances for the more explicitly futuristic nocturnal scenes. At the same time, the animation's overall style faithfully reflects Oshii's customary devotion to the rendition of the minutest facets of his imaginary universes:

> I enjoy making the world [of the film] as detailed as possible. I get absorbed in the finer points—like what the back of a bottle label looks like when you see it through the glass. That's very Japanese, I suppose. I want people to go back to the film again and again to pick up things they missed the first time [Oshii 2004a].

Above all, as stated in a press release coinciding with the screening of *Innocence* at Cannes, Oshii adamantly believes that the "strength of Japanese animation is based in the designer's pencil. Even if it mixes 2D, 3D and computer graphics, the foundation is still 2D. Just doing 3D does not interest me" (Oshii 2004b).

As in much animé, so in Oshii's films generally and in the *Ghost in the Shell* productions specifically, eyes play a crucial role as telling indicators of a character's personality, disposition and intent. At times, the action depends almost exclusively on the nuances of ocular motion, as Oshii is frequently more inclined to communicate the pathos of a specific shot or scene by capitalizing on the merest glance than by animating the entire body. Paradoxically, the display of a character's response to a situation by recourse to such expressive minutiae often succeeds in evoking the shot or scene's dramatic intensity more eloquently and more enticingly than the overtly sensational adoption of full-bodied action. Moreover, the characters' eyes rarely appear to be still insofar as the vagaries of light and shadow upon their receptively moist surfaces continually endows them with chromatically dynamic radiance. This technique plays a pivotal role in the infusion of vitality into even the most ostensibly stereotypical or cardboard persona (e.g., the gangsters confronted by Batou and Togusa in their investigation).

The pupil holds pride of place in eye animation within the domain of animé generally (and Oshii's works are no exception), feelings being often conveyed precisely by the play of light on the pupil, rendered in the guise of white circles of varying diameters, and through its total dilation at times of heightened emotion. An illustrative example of situations in which eyes are accorded an especially prominent role, drawn from the first *Ghost in the Shell* feature, is the scene showing Kusanagi's reactions to the sight of her surroundings upon emerging from her cybernetic birth: her expression comes across as simultaneously apprehensive and inquisitive and gains pathos from the unspoken suggestion that at this stage in the narrative, the character combines the innocence of the newborn and the experience of an adult. Most intriguing, where the handling of ocular animation in both of the *Ghost in the Shell* films is the concerned, is Oshii's ability to invest Batou's countenance with a tremendous variety of feelings—ranging from outrage to affection, from anger to dejection—through the skilful representation, paradoxical as this may sound, of the flickers of light flashing across the cyborg's utterly blank, expressionless eyes. Given the centrality of the character of Batou in the second *Ghost in the Shell* feature, it could be argued that Oshii's handling of this particular animational strategy constitutes one of the film's cinematographically most memorable traits.

Where cinematography is concerned, no less striking is Oshii's deployment of the camera as a means of orchestrating poetically refined visual tableaux, penetrating all possible angles and offering alternative perspectives on a given scene. A perfect example is supplied by the sequences in which Batou and Togusa confront the villain Kim in his mansion. The three concatenated sequences tease the audience's memory with nightmarishly Proustian gusto by reiterating the same nexus of events with subtle shifts of pace and pattern, as well as variations in emphasis and rhythm. This play with our mnemonic faculties parallels the film's ubiquitous preoccupation with the role played by recollections in defining the essence of humanity.

All three sections of the movie open in the same quintessentially surreal location: a carpeted octagonal deck bearing an enormous sculpture with a no less titanic foot as its pedestal and leading to Kim's mansion by means of an equally carpeted and seemingly endless footbridge stretching across a vapory abyss. Varyingly subtle variations on this opening set enable Oshii to characteristically suspend the boundary between reality and illusion, prompting the audience to wonder to what extent the images on offer reflect Batou's and Togusa's actual perceptions of tangible entities, and to what they visualize the impalpable figments concocted by Kim to sustain his exquisitely diabolical domain. In all three variations on the same basic sequence, Batou and Togusa traverse the improbable bridge and enter a magnificent hall wherein a huge music box of kaleidoscopic complexity and a magnificent staircase tower above a gleaming floor.

The first version of the sequence introduces us to artificial renditions of Major Kusanagi as seen at the end of the first *Ghost in the Shell* feature, absorbed in the act of touching the polished floor as though it were a digital interface in order to summon up cryptic codes, and of Gabriel the basset hound. The synthetic character of these two entities is confirmed by the fact that when Batou's cybernetic brain scans their bodies, the message he receives unequivocally states: "Biological Reaction Negative." The protagonist is next seen hurrying along corridors into which multi-colored light filters through majestically executed stained-glass windows. The mansion's intricate architecture and decor are minutely depicted, offering a mesmerizing plethora of chromatic palettes, decorative patterns and stylistic motifs, as well as illusory chambers filled with eerily photorealistic holograms. Its multifarious materials and textures, moreover, appear throughout their inebriating profusion to have been patinated with the translucent pages of a dark yet alluring history of secrecy and subterfuge.

Prompted by Togusa, Batou then enters Kim's luxurious study, where the cybercriminal finally makes an appearance in the shape of a mechanical corpse attached to cables that intriguingly recall a puppeteer's strings. The sequence reaches its climax as Togusa, having accepted a cup of tea from a *ningyou* waitress in Kim's service, opens a hidden closet wherein an extremely complex architectural model is stored, and is seemingly sucked into a kind of black hole. At this point, we are led back to the octagonal platform.

In this sequence, the character of Kim comments on the relationship between humans and dolls in ways which shed light on the movie's whole philosophy: "The human," he maintains, "is no match for a doll, in its form, its elegance in motion, its very being. The inadequacies of human awareness become the inadequacies of life's reality. Perfection is possible only for those without consciousness, or perhaps endowed with infinite consciousness. In other words, for dolls and for gods." He then adds "animals" to the list, stating, as conclusive evidence for his hypothesis, that "Shelley's skylarks are suffused with a profound, instinctive joy. Joy we humans, driven by self-consciousness, can never know."

The second variation — in which Kim features again as an automaton but is also endowed with Togusa's somatic attributes—culminates with Batou's face bursting and revealing a disturbing mechanical constitution beneath the illusion of flesh. In this sequence, Kim's speculations tackle another pivotal theme that resonates not only throughout *Innocence* but also Oshii's overall cinematic exploration of the relationship between the natural and the synthetic, the animate and the inanimate: "The doubt is whether a creature that certainly appears to be alive, really is. Alternatively, the doubt that a lifeless object might actually be alive. That's why dolls haunt us. They are modeled on humans. They are, in fact, nothing but human. They make us face the terror of being reduced to simple mechanisms and matter ... science, seeking to unlock the secret of life, brought about this terror. The notion that nature is calculable inevitably leads to the conclusion that humans too, are reducible to basic, mechanical parts."

The third variation, where Kim assumes Batou's mien, offers a more markedly spectacular climax than the previous ones, as massive explosions devastate the futuristic city, Togusa is ostensibly shot in the chest, and his torso splits asunder to reveal in turn an artificial skeleton. The metamorphoses undergone by Togusa in this scene and by Batou in the climactic shot of the preceding variation graphically encapsulate the "terror" ensuing from the realization that the human organism may amount to a mere machine expounded upon by Kim earlier in the film. The action then shifts to a close-up of Togusa — very much alive but evidently troubled — holding the same cup he had earlier obtained from the *ningyou* as Batou, having realized that his partner's "e-brain" has been fed "a tangle of virtual experience," intervenes and puts an end to the cybernightmare.

On all three occasions, the Kusanagi replica's manipulation of invisible codes, apparently embedded in the phantasmagoric floor of the mansion's hall, conjures up words that eventually turn out to be secret messages specifically addressed to Batou. In the first version of the sequence, the word in question is *aemaeth*, which means "truth" in Hebrew (alternative spelling: *emeth*). This refers to the *Sigillum Dei Aemaeth* or Seal of God's Truth — namely, "a pictorial seal given to Dee and Kelley by the Angel Michael in an early seance held on the 14th of March 1582.... This seal was then to be used in all seances in the form of wax replicas placed under each of the legs of the table" ("*Sigillum Dei Aemaeth [Emeth]*"). The link between "*aemaeth*" and the esoteric tradition of divination is discreetly perpetuated by Oshii's film in the deployment of the character of the synthetic Kusanagi as a sort of medium providing Batou with a symbolic connection to another world — not the world of the departed, in this case, but the no less perplexing universe of mystery and intrigue underpinning Kim's nefarious operation. The latter could indeed be regarded as a technological adaptation of the mythological Hades at its least agreeable. Moreover, the angelic legacy associated with the *Sigillum* is echoed by Batou's aforementioned reference to the major as his "guardian angel."

An equally interesting symbolic use of the term *aemaeth* — arguably even more directly relevant to the world portrayed in *Innocence* — consists of its traditional employment as a means of instilling life into artificial beings that could be regarded as legendary forerunners of Oshii's own dolls, mannequins and cybernetic organisms: that is to say, the *golems*. These are clay statues modeled according to the reflection of a face in a mirror, into which animating energy is infused by registering on their face that very word. Should the *golem* become harmful by acquiring excessive independence, it would be possible to neutralize it by erasing the syllable "*ae-*" and leaving only "*maeth*," which means "death." This is indeed the term evoked by the artificial Kusanagi in the second variation — plausibly to allude to the rapidly intensifying threats to which Batou and his partner are exposed as a corollary of Kim's brain-hacking ploys.

The metamorphosis of "*aemaeth*" into "*maeth*" is instrumental to Batou's realization that Kim's palace is a lethal trap, since it is by recalling the version of the *golem* legend as recounted by Jacob Grimm that he arrives at the conclusion that "no truth would be found within these walls." The sinister implications associated with *"maeth"* are dissipated by the eventual appearance, on the hall's floor, of the digits "2501"— the Puppet Master's official designation in *Ghost in the Shell* which Batou and Kusanagi agree, at the end of that film, to adopt as a private password should they ever meet again. Symbolic of the Major's undying loyalty to her cyborg partner and hence of positive energy, "2501" also becomes, by extension, a reassuring signifier of life in contrast with the grisly perversity of Kim's world. Moreover, as hinted at earlier, it turns out that Kusanagi's "ghost" is the very agent responsible for breaking through the firewalls which enable Kim to further his brain-hacking plan and that, having penetrated the simulation, she has employed the coded variables *"aemaeth," "maeth"* and "2501" precisely to alert Batou to the villain's deceptive schemes.

The movie's visual multidimensionality is matched by the prismatic quality of its soundtrack, which ranges from the choral melodies and traditional drum music already used in *Ghost in the Shell*, through the epic cadences used for the most overtly spectacular sequences, to the mellowness of the closing tune "Follow Me," executed by the jazz singer Kimiko Itoh and set to the second movement of Joaquin Rodrigo's *Concierto de Aranjuez*— arguably the most soothingly melancholy animé theme song ever conceived. Moreover, the collusion of lights, colors and aural effects in the film's most overtly surreal portions comes across as disturbingly fitting — uncannily hyperperfect, as it were. These moments are made all the more impressive by the studious juxtaposition of incurably squalid, damp and shadowy underworld scenes, on the one hand, and the awe-inspiring yet demented opulence of the explicitly retrofuturistic urban-scapes, on the other.

A number of different doll types are encountered along the way, including a damaged and mute android, a female automaton virtually indistinguishable from a human, a bunch of robots burned in effigy by a revenge-thirsty human crowd, and a man who has adopted the semblance of a corpse in the conviction that this will enable him to transcend human frailty. Batou himself becomes more and more akin to an artificial doll as the film progresses, his initial cyberorganic makeup requiring additional mechanization as a result of a near-fatal wound. Through the eyes of these various non-human — or only barely human —characters, Oshii delivers a variety of alternative perceptions of the human species, recursively emphasizing the insolence and dishonesty that the dolls inevitably detect in their organic counterparts. What the doll-based sequences dramatize most potently is the corruption of innocence.

The problem with the anthropomorphic constructs ideated by humans to perpetuate to infinity their self-image and hence keep temporarily at the bay their awareness of ineluctable finitude and puniness in the face of the crushing vastness of the cosmos at large is that they are designed to be *perfect*. To this extent, they are bound to disappoint, in their presumed role as satisfying copies of living people, simply insofar as they fail to capture the ultimately most distinctive attribute of not only humanity but also aliveness in general. The review of *Innocence* published in *Ain't It Cool News* eloquently validates this point as follows:

> We can try all we want to create a reasonable facsimile of life, but we'll never succeed, because the best we can do is perfection. One character quips that perfection is for "dolls and deities," for those either devoid of consciousness or hyperconscious. We can create a perfect doll, but we can never reproduce life because life is all about imperfection. This movie is about our glorious failures, and it is those failures that ultimately give us our innocence [*"Ain't It Cool News Review of Innocence"*].

In line with this argument, it could be maintained that the trait that renders the character of the basset hound Gabriel so genuinely and vibrantly alive is the very fact that he is *not* perfect — the emphasis elliptically placed on his naughty behavior in his owner's absence in the first scene devoted to Batou's return home effectively underscores this notion. Togusa, too, is rendered authentic by his imperfection — specifically, his haunting sense of vulnerability. As for Batou, his imperfection is touchingly conveyed by the doubts he begins to harbor concerning the status of his own "ghost" once it has transpired that the gynoids, too, host souls of sorts: to what extent does a cyborg ultimately differ from a doll? Aramaki, the Section 9 chief, intimates that humanity and imperfection are inextricably intertwined by positing the human condition as one of perpetual erring, the term simultaneously alluding to the state of wandering and to that of committing more or less irreparable mistakes.

In the aforementioned press release published at the time of *Innocence*'s screening at Cannes, Oshii commented as follows on his use of non-human and semi-human personas:

> [e]conomic recession ... corporate downsizing ... violent crime ... it is this culture of fear and anxiety[2] that I want to depict cinematically ... For some reason, people have always created robots in their own image. I wonder why? I don't suppose that the human figure is the most practical shape for industrial robots. What is it about people that makes them do such illogical things? I thought that exploring this question from the doll's point of view would help me better understand human nature.... The movie does not hold the view that the world revolves around the human race. Instead, it concludes that all forms of life — humans, animals, and robots — are equal. In this day and age when everything is uncertain, we should all think about what to value in life and how to coexist with others ... what we need today is not some kind of anthropocentric humanism. Humanity has reached its limits [Oshii 2004b].

This message is corroborated by Oshii's observations in the course of an interview for *Midnight Eye* conducted by Nicholas Rucka later that year (23 September 2004), where he comments on the gradual erosion of corporeal integrity in contemporary societies, while also frankly admitting to *Innocence*'s autobiographical dimension:

> Since people are all starting to lose part of or all of their "bodies," they need to associate themselves with something else to identify themselves. It could be dogs like myself, or it could be cats or other animals. It does not need to be living things. It could be machines, cars, computers, cities, just about anything but yourself. That's how you find your lost "bodies" ... people are definitely losing their human forms. Animals have always stayed the same, and continue to do so in the years to come, but humans are always changing, and they need to change, with the development of technology. However, they should not fear the change or evolution, but rather accept it and learn to live with it.... This movie is about me and my dog [Oshii 2004c].

Asked by Mark Schilling (on behalf of *The Japan Times*) to comment on the proposition that "[d]olls are an important motif in *Innocence*, but the attitude toward them is quite different from that of a film like *Toy Story*," Oshii riposted:

> In *Toy Story* the dolls are just objects that humans bring to life, for their own amusement. The Japanese have a different view: they think that dolls have a spirit. That's why when they no longer have any use for a doll they just don't throw it away in the trash. They would be afraid to do that; the doll might put a curse on them. So they take the doll to a priest, who performs a ceremony [*kuyo*] to appease its spirit. I believe that myself, that dolls have a spirit. They're not just objects to have fun with ... but that has nothing to do with a specific religion. Children have similar feelings about dolls—if they love a doll enough, they feel that it's alive. That feeling is universal. It's not something they're taught—they just feel it somehow [Oshii 2004a].

Furthermore, Oshii has stressed his intention to steer clear of anthropocentrism and hence to invest his artificial creatures with distinctively non-human attributes—even though his dolls are deliberately executed with anthropomorphic precision in order to convey with unnerving impartiality the idea that humans are "obsessed with recreating themselves" (as stated in the film itself). Indeed, in the *Japan Times* interview quoted above, the director has also remarked: "In *Toy Story*, the dolls move and talk like human beings. It's hard to tell them from the human characters. But when you animate dolls that way, you lose what makes them special, their individual spirit. It's a lot harder to animate dolls so they still look doll-like. That was the toughest part of the film for me." So as to emphasize the extent to which other—human or robotic—characters also participate in the mood of rampant artificiality that defines *Innocence* from beginning to end, Oshii has made their own "movements

... somewhat doll-like. Even their expressions are more doll-like than human."

All the dolls are lovingly represented, and their rendition is indeed grounded in punctilious background research on the director's part involving visits to several doll museums throughout both Japan and the West. A life-size, ball-jointed doll executed by the Japanese sculptor Simon Yotsuya, displayed in a Sapporo museum, provided inspiration for the design of the villain Kim, while the latter's mansion was based on a doll's house and giant music box seen in the spa town of Atami. Especially influential was the work of the Surrealist artist Hans Bellmer (1902–1975), whose dolls Oshii first saw as a student — and, on his own admission, fell in love with, intrigued by the way each body part was so beautifully crafted that one never tired of looking at it. Oshii inspected Bellmer's dolls again at the International Center of Photography in New York in the course of fieldwork specifically associated with *Innocence*. In visiting New York to be reunited with Bellmer's work after a thirty-year gap, Oshii also found the city's architecture enormously inspiring by virtue of its ingrained possession of an atmosphere of Gothic ominousness and of vertiginous perspectives akin to those he had been aiming to convey in *Innocence*.

In Berlin, Oshii had opportunity to study the dolls rumored to have shaped Bellmer's own imagination and at La Specola museum in Florence,[3] he saw wax anatomical models molded (creepily but very appositely in the logic of *Innocence*) from actual corpses. La Specola indeed constitutes a veritable cornucopia of simultaneously chilling and enrapturing bodies, rendered all the more uncanny by their value as scientific documents even as they appear more at home in the most consummately macabre cabinet of curiosities than in a natural history collection. A specific texture known as *bisque* was deliberately adopted in the rendition of the film's dolls, its porcelain smoothness but relatively warm feel—compared with glass— matching Oshii's intention to portray those characters as overtly artificial, yet elliptically sentient, vulnerable and, above all, innocent.

In iconographic and broadly cultural terms, the dolls depicted in *Innocence* could be regarded as latter-day equivalents of the courtesans of old. The figure of the courtesan is firmly embedded in Japan's visual tradition, having for long constituted a favorite subject among *ukiyo-e* artists. This is eloquently attested to by the woodblock prints of the eighteenth and nineteenth centuries executed by renowned masters such as Kikumaro (active in the 1800s), Harunobu (c. 1725–1770), Utamaro (1753–1806), Koryusai (active between around 1765 and 1784) and Anchi (active around 1700–1720). As "pictures of the transient show," a possible translation for the term "*ukiyio-e*," those works sought to capture the mocking ephemerality of pleasure and beauty. It is hardly surprising, therefore, that they should often have elected the image of the courtesan — with its well-established connotations — as a fittingly recurrent emblem.

Oshii's representation of the gynoids also harks back, albeit elliptically, to the *ukiyo-e* tradition insofar as in both cases, the pleasure-providing object is situated in an economically specific context. *Innocence*'s dolls are manufactured so as to satisfy the carnal desires of wealthy industrialists and entrepreneurs, gangsters and politicians belonging to particular strata of society within the film's hypothetical time-scale. In the case of the *ukiyo-e*, "the transient show" which courtesans were intended to epitomize referred specifically to the ever-shifting world of urban delights and fashions of the Edo period, and particularly to the red-light district of Yoshiwara towards which the increasingly affluent middle classes tended to gravitate.

Alongside dolls, the other innocent categories of being presented in the film are children and dogs: specifically, children such as Togusa's daughter and dogs such as Batou's basset hound, namely, the cyborg's only surviving link to his own ancestral innocence and indeed the principal evidence for the enduring merit of the concepts of joy and happiness in the entire movie. The twin victimization of dolls and children is brought home precisely by the fact that copies of children's ghosts are made to be implanted into the artificial beings as a means of investing them with a modicum of humanity. As the children are thus violated (in a fashion redolent of Philip Pullman's *Northern Lights*), the dolls are concurrently turned into virtual thieves branded by an indelible stain of culpability — and thus robbed of their original innocence — even though they are not truly accountable for any obvious trespass or infamy. It is barely surprising that they should strive to regain that state through self-destruction.

The antithetical modality, where ethics are concerned, finds its starkest incarnation in the character of Kim, who seems to live exclusively for himself and his own unremitting betterment. The villain's disconnection and unwillingness to interact with any other form of life is encapsulated by the very name of his company, "Locus Solus" indeed consisting of a literal translation into Latin of the phrase "isolated place." Moreover, Oshii has posited the image of the mirror as a symbol of self-absorption and, by extension, egoism and accordingly furnished Kim's mansion with a plethora of reflective surfaces, including opulent marble and polished gold. The forbidding atmosphere of glacial and rigid selfishness surrounding Kim's existence — which those substances succinctly capture — also extends to the vestimentary preferences exhibited by his city's inhabitants: an unmasked monk is at one point visible in the crowd witnessing the splendid festival parade but by and large all the locals, including children, hide behind masks in order to conceal their actual — and almost certainly corrupt — selves from the inquisitive looks of others. One even gets the impression, at times, that so shallow and uncaring these people have become that what they are really hiding, ultimately, is not their true individualities but the fact that they no longer possess any such thing as a personal identity. Intriguingly, when the gynoids commit suicide, their faces literally blow up like crumbling masks — an image which could be read as their agonizing recuperation of an atavistic state of innocence.

Innocence contains an explicitly somber dimension, paradigmatically captured in the lines, delivered by the protagonist, "life and death come and go like marionettes dancing on a table; once their strings are cut, they easily crumble." Yet, the film is also, in its own peculiar (and very possibly idiosyncratic) vein, a hymn to life in its fostering of an ethos of symphonically coordinated harmony for disparate species of both organic and synthetic creatures. Thus, although *Innocence* is dark, sad, languidly introspective and even downright painful at times, it nonetheless strikes positive notes. It does so, primarily, in its exploration of the various tactics — often vapidly inane yet arresting in their tenacity — deployed by humans in their quest for happiness, offering hints and hypotheses but no patronizing conclusions. The words voiced by the supporting character of Aramaki may well turn out to be the best piece of advice for one to follow: "walk alone, with few wishes, committing no sin, like an elephant in the forest."

In keeping with Oshii's reluctance to dish out definitive resolutions for either his characters or his viewers, *Innocence* ends on a note of destabilizing ambiguity, tentatively poised between incredulity and acquiescence. Indisposed to either sanitize or sentimentalize the import of the film's philosophical dimension, Oshii deliberately celebrates ambiguity and irony over dogmatism, and diversity over uniformity, in the recognition that human virtues and flaws are always inextricably intertwined.

The subtext consistently coursing through both of the *Ghost in the Shell* features ultimately amounts to a sustained contemplation of the status of contemporary and futuristic technologies as novel versions of myth and magic. Technological advancement, it is suggested, does not represent a clear-cut departure from the proverbially irrational rhythms of animistic spiritualism in the direction of rationalist certainties. In fact, the new "machines" portrayed by Oshii's cinema draw life and vibrancy from their imbrication with traditions that blatantly predate not only cybernetics but industrial technology, as well. The religious and mythological allusions mentioned in the evaluations of the *Ghost in the Shell* movies offered in the preceding pages persuasively testify to this hypothesis.

Accordingly, Oshii's cyberpunk modality marks the shadowy territory where the *golem* and the cyborg, esoteric systems and state-of-the-art digital technology, alchemy and bionics meet and merge in mutual suffusion, and where such encounters, in turn, usher in a cinematic universe of unquestionably unique resonance. In David Chute's evocative words (used to describe the first film but arguably also applicable to the sequel), the *Ghost in the Shell* universe constitutes "an artfully fabricated mechanism with discernible life-signs, a factory product with a human soul. Its traditional cel-animation techniques are augmented with swatches of glittery computer graphics, but what matters most is that its complicated story and sophisticated themes are consistently interesting ... it's an entertainment machine with functioning grey matter" (Chute).

28

Ghost in the Shell: Stand Alone Complex

Ghost in the Shell: Stand Alone Complex, produced by Production I.G, headed by director Kenji Kamiyama and originally sketched by Masamune Shirow, comprises two television series, broadcast in 2003 and 2004. These were inspired by the world portrayed in Oshii's *Ghost in the Shell* features, yet develop independent story arcs. Thus, although it may tempting to conceive of *Stand Alone Complex* as something of a prequel to the *Ghost in the Shell* movies, it would be fairer to its creators to approach it as an alternate version of the *Ghost in the Shell* universe than as its ancillary appendage. It should also be noted that it is much closer to the manga series at the level of character design than either of the features is, and is principally concerned with complex character interactions.

In an interview conducted by the animé expert Fred Patten, Oshii has commented on *Stand Alone Complex* and on the degree of his involvement in its execution as follows: "[*Innocence* and *Stand Alone Complex*] were both planned at the same time. I was not involved with the TV creation at all, although in the second season of *Stand Alone Complex*, the *2nd Gig*, I was involved in writing some plots." In response to Patten's question regarding the cerebral density of both the second *Ghost in the Shell* feature and the television episodes, Oshii stated: "I think that *Stand Alone Complex* … did not really have a philosophical plot. It has more of a realistic plot. All of the problems that the modern world is having or is facing right now are being explained or talked about … these kinds of stories can be more easily accepted by the TV audience than a complete fantasy or science-fictional story, which has no association to the real world" (Patten 2004).

The episodes are divided into two categories: complex episodes and stand-alone episodes. The complex episodes are those that deal explicitly with the show's principal story arc — namely, the "Laughing Man Incident" — whereas the stand-alone episodes consist of isolated occurrences independent of the central plotline. However, several of the stand-alone episodes are thematically — if not overtly — connected with the Laughing

Man topos. The Laughing Man is a top-class hacker, able to infiltrate at will not merely computers but human minds as well. His trademark logo, his skills, and his agenda have made him a legend, but the questions of how much is myth and how much is fact quickly become the object of heated debate as new cases revolving around this enigmatic figure start proliferating.

The phrase "Stand Alone Complex" refers to the phenomenon whereby independent entities are ostensibly capable of engaging in coordinated action due to the rapid and nearly perfect flow of information in the series' cybernetic universe. "Tachikomas," artificially intelligent minitanks, are skillfully deployed as a counterpoint to this phenomenon. They synchronize perfectly with each other, sharing their experiences to such an extent that they cannot even tell which unit actually underwent the experience in question. Yet, they are ostensibly able to develop a sense of individuality even though this was not initially a component of their programming. By adopting the broader tapestry of a multi-episodic structure, the series is more about Section 9 in its entirety than Major Kusanagi as an individual agent. However, Kusanagi is still very much at the forefront in most of the episodes and we are even allowed to capture some vague allusions to her otherwise unfathomable background — most notably in Episode 8 of the first series, "Missing Hearts." In its engagement with a broader debate regarding the ethics of organ replacement, organ harvesting, life extension and cybernetics as a whole, the episode elliptically offers a rare look into Kusanagi's past that hints at the possibility of her rebirth as a cybernetic organism not having been entirely a matter of free will or choice on her part. At the same time, other characters deemed relatively marginal to the gist of Oshii's own plots are also given opportunity to develop throughout the run.

As in Oshii's features, however, what ultimately drives *Stand Alone Complex* is neither an individual character nor sets of personae as such but rather the exploration of the increasingly hazy boundaries separating humanity and machines as the two become almost inextricably intertwined. Each episode offers a twisting and relatively self-contained story, while concurrently relating in various ways to the complete arc, enabling the overall series to deliver a military-political technodrama with a dark, cyberpunk-oriented metaphysical twist. Among the series' most profound preoccupations are the issue of both personal and collective responsibility in a thoroughly networked world, and cognate concerns emanating from the tension between nationalism and globalization.

Stand Alone Complex dramatizes the familiar cyberpunk themes of corporate manipulation and larceny, brain-hacking, organ theft and cloning (among several other related issues), occasionally supplying gruesome depictions of the body's intractable materiality and graphic reminders of its vulnerability regardless of cybernetic enhancement. Echoing Oshii's films, the television episodes make frequent references to intricate philosophical conundrums. An intriguing instance is offered by "Meme" (Episode 6, first series), the narrative underpinning of which is the concept, promulgated by Richard Dawkins in *The Selfish Gene* (1976), that an analogy obtains between the way in which genes propagate themselves across the gene pool and the way in which units of cultural information (ideas, values, patterns of behavior) are transferred from one individual to another by non-genetic means and principally by imitation.

A rather disturbing motif — also pivotal, as we have seen, to *Ghost in the Shell 2: Innocence* — is articulated by Episode 7 in the first run, "Idolater," where we are faced with the idea that synthetic replicas of the human body may be realistically animated through the installation therein of soul-like effigies. Indeed, as Kusanagi investigates the case revolving around the seemingly immortal and ubiquitous revolutionary leader Marcelo Jarti, the major discovers that there are multiple Jartis. It eventually transpires that these entities have been created with the assistance of a "ghost-dubbing" machine — redolent of the apparatus deployed in *Innocence* — capable of copying a person's "ghost" at will, and by implanting numerous copies thus obtained into a veritable swarm of cloned bodies.

Like Oshii's *Ghost in the Shell* movies, *Stand Alone Complex* portrays several futuristic technologies. Among these, an axial role is played by the cyberbrain, a product of revolutionary advancement in the field of neural augmentation technology. The cyberbrain results from the implantation of exceptionally sophisticated electronic mechanisms directly into a person's cerebrum, as a result of which information-processing and mnemonic capacities are exponentially enhanced. The implanted subject, moreover, becomes capable of ubiquitous access to digital networks, of wireless communication — which can simply be *thought* into existence — and of a formidable knack of retrieving, digitizing and encrypting the most disparate data and sources. *Stand Alone Complex* also depicts both exhaustively and convincingly possible user interfaces for this technology. Concurrently, the potential disadvantages of neural augmentation are addressed with reference to a fictional disease, indigenous to the universe of the series, known as "Cyberbrain Closed Shell Syndrome." The phrase designates a type of autism occasioned by cyberbrain implants.

Nanoscience and nanotechnology — branches of science and engineering dedicated to the design and production of electronic devices and circuits on the ultra-small scale of individual atoms — also feature prominently in the show's futurescape though they are not deemed to have developed, by the year 2030, much beyond the experimental stage. As in Oshii's features, a key technology represented in the series is thermoptic camouflage. This enables both human members of Section 9 and their Tachikoma tanks to activate a stealth system whereby they can blend in almost seamlessly with their surroundings. However, though virtually invisible to the naked eye and undetectable by radars and infrared sensors, the system is yet to be perfected for it cannot compensate for abrupt changes in lighting and atmospheric conditions and for especially calamitous impacts.[1]

Notions of identity, individuality and interaction are central to the series, and are typically articulated with consistent reference to the role played by memory in the genesis and shaping of subjectivity. Frequent allusions are made to the possibility of a person's—or machine's—mnemonic faculties being either erased or transferred from one entity to another, and to the feasible effects of such practices on the definition of selfhood and personality. For example, in Episode 18 of the first series, "Lost Heritage," a boy is implanted with the memories of his father. The implant radically alters his mental functions, leading him to attempt to assassinate a foreign dignitary: an act that neither the father nor the son in themselves would have ever contemplated. The series repeatedly intimates that identity is inseparable from the omnipresent flow of information in the digital age—and, by implication, from the media and apparatuses through which this flow is generated, divulged and (often nefariously) edited.

The animation is crisp and polished: the backgrounds are meticulously executed, and the character designs effective—although the panty-clad major may come across as rather too gratuitous a concession to a potential spectatorship of horny teenagers. Yoko Kanno's soundtrack complements ideally the series' overall tenor, and the opening theme "Inner Universe," in particular, constitutes a felicitous match for the trippy mood of the entirely computer-generated visual prelude that introduces each episode. The background music is where Kanno's soundtrack shines forth in its full colors, contributing a sense of pathos and even gravitas to the action without ever degenerating into noisy pretentiousness.

Stand Alone Complex bears eloquent witness to the accumulated skills and proficiency of the Production I.G team, incorporating all the lessons learnt in the execution of the *Ghost in the Shell* features, as well as other films produced in the years separating the two. The television episodes are arguably less moody than Oshii's films where the animation style is concerned, presumably in keeping with the requirements of the medium through which they have been disseminated and especially with a TV audience's general preference for action-oriented shows over sustained verbal cogitation. However, the attention to detail is rarely short of spectacular in the rendition of the tiniest architectural, ornamental and vestimentary elements. Furthermore, the consistent employment of depth-of-field shots, of digitally generated chromatic grading and environmental effects, and of cel-shaded computer models contributes vitally to the visual impact of the entire televisual package. As Rob Lineberger has pointed out, "[i]f the devil is in the details, consider *Stand Alone Complex* angelic. The blacks are deep and the colours are rich, but the series maintains a realistic palette. The animation is glossy, smooth, and bright. If you took *Blood: The Last Vampire*'s lush visuals and wrapped them around four solid stories, you'd get *Stand Alone Complex.*... When *Stand Alone Complex* is quiet, you pick up on many subtle details that sell the environment. When it is loud, you're rocked out of your seat" (Lineberger). Ultimately, the series' cumulatively elegant rhythms result precisely from the dexterously balanced alternation of those two contrastive modalities.

The ruminations that generously garnish Oshii's cinematic fare tend to be replaced, in the show, by sequences that encapsulate Shirow's vision in dynamic action rather than dialogue. Oshii's predilection for stationary moments of reflection can nonetheless be detected in Episode 9 of the first series, "Chat Chat Chat," which revolves around a group of characters sitting in a virtual room conversing with one other, and hence consists entirely of rapid-fire dialogue. Moreover, the existential concerns articulated in the *Ghost in the Shell* features remain poignantly pervasive throughout *Stand Alone Complex*: the shift is in emphasis, not substance. To this extent, the series does full justice to Oshii's legacy on the conceptual plane even where it stylistically departs from his distinctive tone.

29

Post-Innocence
Developments

Oshii's most recent projects have enlisted all the various facets of his multifarious expertise, involving him in script writing, direction and multimedia design. In the first capacity, he has been engaged in penning the screenplay for Kenta Fukusaku's *Eru no Ran* (Production I.G), a film based on the 1990 riots that took place in the Kamagasaki district of Osaka, involving brutal confrontations between workers and the police.[1] In the second, Oshii has returned once more to the directorial chair to execute the live-action feature *Tachigui — The Amazing Lives of the Fast Food Grifters* (*Tachiguishi Retsuden*). Executed by Production I.G and due for release in Japan in spring 2006, the film is based on the original novel written by Oshii himself and published in serial format between 2000 and 2003. The president of Studio Ghibli Toshio Suzuki, once before employed in a live-action Oshii production — namely *Killers: .50 Woman* — also appears in this film.[2] It was at one stage rumored, incidentally, that Oshii would be animating *Tachiguishi Retsuden* by recourse to stick-and-paper puppets, the technique deployed in the production of *Minipato* towards which Oshii professedly harbors a marked attraction.[3]

As noted in the overview of the film offered by the official Production I.G Web site, "This project attracted numerous prominent figures from different genres, visual, SF, animation, who have all come together to share a vision and take part in the film, including Japan's top producer, Toshio Suzuki of Studio Ghibli" ("*Tachigui*: Overview"). *Tachigui*, a term that literally designates the concept of "standing and eating" and may be roughly translated into English as "fast food," has been a long-standing source of fascination for Oshii. In the live-action film *The Red Spectacles*, for example, he deployed this theme to unique dramatic effect by turning it into a political metaphor, and by specifically associating the country's enslavement to an increasingly totalitarian regime with the promulgation of laws intended to stifle conviviality — and hence the danger of seditiousness — by prohibiting the consumption of meals by seated groups of people in public, and by strictly limiting the range of popular fast-food dishes available, with crucial repercussions for a burgeoning fast-food black market. The same theme also plays a prominent part in the short live-action film *Killers: .50 Woman*, where a seemingly endless provision of snacks of pluri-culinary provenance constitutes the most assiduous and compelling screen presence throughout.

Oshii believes that *tachigui* in Japan is not only a ubiquitous commodity, encompassing both Western imports and indigenous products, but also— more importantly — a cultural marker whose evolution over time throws light on the country's socioeconomic history. By focusing on the *Tachiguishi*, or Fast Food Grifters, the heroes of an as yet uncharted history of Japan stretching from the immediate aftermath of the Second World War through the protest movement of the 1960s to the eve of the Bubble economy, Oshii's film offers a novel take on the discipline of historiography.

The characters include the legendary Fast Food Grifter Tsukimi Ginji (who also features in *The Red Spectacles* as a character with highly dubious ethical credentials); the beautiful Fast Food Grifter lady Kitsune Croquette O-Gin; Cold Tanuki Masa, whose notorious end draws the public's attention to the existence of Fast Food Grifters in Japanese society; and Hamburger Tetsu, responsible for rocking the whole American fast food industry.[4] As the aforementioned Production I.G site states, the "Fast Food Grifters are the phantoms that rise and fall with the shifting diet-styles. They are the dissenting heroes that left their names on the dark side of dietary culture with their glare. Now their legend revives, strong as ever."

In the third capacity mentioned above, Oshii has contributed to the Japan Expo 2005 held in the Aichii Prefecture and devoted to "Nature's Wisdom." Oshii's installation deserves notice, in this particular context, both as an artwork in its own right and as testimony to Oshii's ecopolitics. Indeed, the Expo constitutes the first post-Kyoto initiative to have mobilized disparate industrial sectors on an international scale in the promulgation of a positively green agenda, engaging with the repercussions of globalization and of the evolution of information and communication networks upon the natural environment, and documenting the pursuit of a sustainable and choral coexistence of all natural forms.[5]

Considering that Oshii's focus has gradually progressed from political issues regarding militarism, technological misappropriation and economic iniquity towards an unsentimental study of the meaning and boundaries of humanity itself, his recent concentration on the viability of the concept of environmental balance seems a perfectly logical development within the socioethical trajectory of his oeuvre. In the handling of this project, no less than in the direction of both animated and live-action films, Oshii evinces once again a penchant for disarmingly lucid presentation and impeccable design. In view of its felicitous combination of thematic, stylistic and technical traits that could be deemed pivotal to Oshii's output in its entirety, a brief evaluation of this particular project therefore seems an apposite exit point for this study.

Oshii's task consisted of creating the concepts and supervising all the designs for one of the zones of the pavilion named "Mountain of Dreams," wherein several companies sought to deploy their innovative, cutting-edge tools and methodologies to celebrate the interactions of Nature, science, craftsmanship and technology. The pavilion's overall mission was phrased as follows by its organizers and sponsors:

> The 20th century mainly progressed as a human-centered quest for ever-greater efficiency of living. As a result, the Earth's natural environment has been severely damaged. The most important mission for humanity in the 21st century is to solve this problem and restore the Earth to its splendour. This issue must be addressed on a global scale.[6]

Oshii's particular zone, "Open Your Mind," featured the first Experiential Video Space to be displayed at an international exhibition. It used one of the world's largest floor video screens (comprising ninety-six 50-inch monitors and measuring approximately 600 m^2), enabling visitors to walk through an experiential space and to modify at will their visual perspective. The video images themselves integrated computer graphics and live-action footage of the natural world, and were projected simultaneously not only on the gigantic floor screen but also on huge monitors placed both on the walls and overhead. As in Oshii's most famous cinematic productions, so in "Open Your Mind," the overall atmosphere owed much of its uniqueness to Kenji Kawai's inspired audio accompaniment.

As argued in the course of this book, Oshii's animé productions consistently hark back to traditional motifs embedded in Japanese history and lore. Likewise, the design used in the context of the Expo sought to capture the flavor of a time-honored legacy by evoking the image of Mt. Fuji as a symbol of Japan and, specifically, by echoing its representation in the woodblock print "Red Fuji," executed by Katsushika Hokusai in the Edo period. This same historical era, moreover, is laden with symbolic connotations of direct relevance to the spirit of the Expo in virtue of its commitment to the harmonious coexistence of human beings and all other forms of life.

Oshii's animé— alongside live-action productions explicitly inspired by animé's visual rhetoric — serve to remind us as powerfully as that art form has hitherto been capable of doing that animation is not only a means of bringing a fantasy world into existence but also a means of compelling us to look at our own world differently. Indeed, its goal is arguably not to *recreate reality* but rather to *communicate a view of reality*. The perspectives conveyed by the films here examined encompass diverse reality levels that invite comparably manifold audience responses. The intrinsic multi-accentuality of Oshii's cinema is largely a corollary of his most distinctive characters' psychological and emotional complexity. Indeed, Oshii's works deliver a varied gallery of artificial replications of humanity that ultimately serves as a speculative, even visionary, commentary on the nature of technology's potential destinations and of the paths which human beings may tread in their pursuit.

However, the director's reflections on synthetic humanity do not merely constitute futuristic hypotheses of the kind one habitually encounters in science fiction film and fiction. In fact, they also— and more intriguingly — point to ontological and epistemological concerns of an eminently existentialist character, inviting us to ponder what imaginary depictions of artificial humanity may tell us about actual human beings— about what we are, and how we might come to know what we are. Above all, Oshii persistently draws attention to the anthropocentric thrust inherent in the urge obdurately evinced by human beings to replicate themselves, intimating that the desire to fill the world with humanoid entities— and indeed to invest non-human animals with anthropomorphic connotations — does not stem from some god-given strength but from a fatal weakness and the concomitant need to compensate for such a failing.

By disseminating effigies of humanity across the globe (and, ideally, the cosmos' countless galaxies), humans desperately endeavor to plug the gaps which they themselves, in their natural forms, are quite at a loss to tackle. Those gaps consist of lacunae in our grasp of humanity's place in a by and large unchartable universe. What renders them especially menacing is the ever lingering fear that if it is the case — as various developments in modern science have sought to demonstrate — that the natural world is an ensemble of interacting and interreacting elements comparable to the cogs and wheels of a machine, there is no incontrovertibly reliable way of proving that human beings are not mechanical, too. As we incessantly populate the planet with replicas of humanity, we thus endeavor to keep at bay the twin specters of what we do not know and what we do not want to know.

Where Hollywood cartoons tend to foster the doctrine of anthropocentrism by insistently capitalizing on the charm of creatures such as cute talking animals, living toys and dancing tableware (to mention but a handful of examples), Oshii's movies take their audiences into alternative realities that are patently dominated by neither humans nor humanism. At times, Oshii seemingly invests non-human figures with quasi-human faculties and proclivities. Thus, we encounter otherworldly demons (*Urusei Yatsura*), hyperskilled cyberdogs (*Dallos*), *mecha*-based automata (*Patlabor*), dolls (*Ghost in the Shell* and its sequel), and deeply sensitive basset hounds (*Avalon* and *Ghost in the Shell 2: Innocence*). However, what directs the narrative is not a yearning to tame the natural world by translating it into an array of approximations to humanity. In fact, what Oshii's films consistently communicate is a profound and not seldom pained sense of empathy with Nature's countless manifestations and with their own distinctive forms of consciousness and aliveness.

In resorting to the medium and language of animation, which constitutionally depends for its very existence on the construction of artificial creatures, and further emphasizing the trope of synthetic humanity by recourse to robots, cybernetic organisms, *mecha* suits, hybrids and aliens, Oshii's cinema encourages us to observe these figures' constructedness and to reflect on how they have been brought into being by animators and technicians. In so doing, it implicitly reminds us that we, too, are in some way constructed — by the culture we inhabit, by the language we speak and are spoken by, and indeed by the codes and conventions of the entertainment industry itself, animé included.

It is, arguably, in accordance with a subconscious apprehension of this essential kinship that audiences are able to identify with the artificial beings portrayed by Oshii in varying degrees, and to empathize with their ideals, misgivings and fears. Regardless of whether one initially approaches cyborgs such as Major Kusanagi or Batou, or human-machine composites such as the Kerberos agents of the Patlabor corps as heroic models or shrinks from them as eerie monsters, the identification process is likely to occur, albeit subliminally. This is largely attributable to the fact that even at their most self-possessed and ostensibly impregnable, those characters are invariably tormented by doubts and anxieties concerning their identities and their duties, and thus echo, allegorically, the quintessentially human afflictions discussed earlier.

Oshii's assiduous revisiting of this nexus of ideas, alongside cognate concerns of a political and philosophical nature, eloquently attests to the director's determined refutation of the stereotypical notion that animated films are kids' stuff. In addition, the conceptual range of Oshii's productions is complicated by their tenacious defiance of inflexible binary oppositions at the level of characterization, as a result of which the protagonists and their foes are never primly categorized with reference to doxastic definitions of good and evil but are actually imbued with credible doses of each. For Oshii, strict classifications are incongruously preemptive in a pervasively networked universe which, as the character of Major Kusanagi states in the closing frames of *Ghost in the Shell* is, quite uncompromisingly, "vast and infinite."

Filmography

Please note the following designations of Oshii's contribution (in diverse capacities) to each film:

D   Director
w   Writer
p   Producer
c   Concept Designer or Plot-Sketching Advisor

^{D,W} ***Angel's Egg*** (1985). Original Title: *Tenshi no Tamago*. Status: Original Video Animation. Director: Mamoru Oshii. Original Story: Oshii, Yoshitaka Amano. Screenplay: Oshii. Producers: Hiroshi Hasegawa, Masao Kobayashi, Mitsunori Miura, Yutaka Wada. Executive Producer: Yasuyoshi Tokuma. Production Companies: Tokuma Shoten, Studio DEEN. Music: Yoshihiro Kanno. Length: 71 minutes. Animation Director: Yasuhiro Nakura. Art Directors: Lee Hyun Se, Shichiro Kobayashi, Yoshitaka Amano. Character Designer: Yoshitaka Amano. Sound Director: Shigeharu Shiba.

^D ***Avalon*** (2001). Original Title: *Abaron*. Status: Live-Action Feature Film. Director: Mamoru Oshii. Screenplay: Kazunori Itoh. Producer: Atsushi Kubo. Co-Producer: Shin Unozawa. Executive Producers: Naoyuki Sakagami, Toru Shiobara, Shigeru Watanabe. Production Companies: Bandai Media, Dentsu, Nippon Herald Films, Inc. Music: Kenji Kawai. Length: 106 minutes. Art Designer: Tanake Watabe. Digital Art Director: Hiroyuki Hayashi. Production Designer: Barbara Nowak. Cinematography: Grzegorz Kedzierski. Visual Effects Supervisor: Nobuaki Koga. Mechanical Designer: Atsushi Takeuchi. Sound Director: Kazuhiro Wakabayashi. Cast: Malgorzata Foremniak (Ash), Wladyslaw Kowalski (Game Master), Jerzy Gudejko (Murphy), Dariusz Biskupski (Bishop), Bartek Swiderski (Stunner), Katarzyna Bargielowska (Receptionist).

^C ***Blood+*** (2005). Original Title: *Blood+*. Status: Animated TV Series. Director: Junichi Fujisaku. Original Story: Production I.G/Aniplex. Co-Planner: Oshii. Production Companies: Production I.G/MBS/Aniplex. Music: Mark Mancina. Animation Director: Akiharu Ishii. Art Director: Junichi Higashi.

Character Designer: Chizu Hashii. CGI Director: Makoto Endo. Mechanical Design: Kenji Teraoka. Director of Photography: Koji Tanaka. Colour Designer: Yumiko Katayama.

^{B,C} **Blood: The Last Vampire** (2000). Original Title: *Blood: The Last Vampire*. Status: Animated Feature Film. Director: Hiroyuki Kitakubo. Original Story: Production I.G, Team Oshii (Visual Concept). Screenplay: Kenji Kamiyama. Producers: Ryuji Mitsumoto, Yukio Nagasaki. Executive Producer: Mamoru Oshii. Production Companies: SPE Visual Works, Sony Computer Entertainment, Production I.G, IPA. Music: Yoshihiro Ike. Length: 48 minutes. Animation Director: Shinji Takagi. Art Director: Yusuke Takeda. Character Designer: Katsuya Terada. CGI Director: Tokumitsu Kifune. Sound Director: Keiichi Momose. Colour Designer: Katsue Inoue.

^D **Dallos** (1983–84). Original Title: *Darossu*. Status: Original Video Animation. Director: Mamoru Oshii. Screenplay: Hisayuki Toriumi. Production Companies: Pierrot Project Co., Ltd., Bandai, Yomiuri. Music: Hiroyuki Nanba, Ichiro Nitta. Length: 30 minutes x 4 episodes. Animation Director: Toshiyasu Okada. Art Director: Mitsuyoshi Nakamura. Character Designer: Toshiyasu Okada. Mechanical design: Masaharu Satou. Sound director: Shigeharu Shiba.

^D **Ghost in the Shell** (1995). Original Title: *Koukaku Kidoutai*. Status: Animated Feature Film. Director: Mamoru Oshii. Original Story: Masamune Shirow. Screenplay: Kazunori Ito. Producers: Yoshimasa Mizuo, Ken Matsumoto, Ken Iyadomi, Mitsuhisa Ishikawa. Executive Producers: Teruo Miyahara, Shigeru Watanabe, Andy Frain. Production Company: Production I.G. Music: Kenji Kawai. Length: 80 minutes. Animation Director: Toshihiko Nishikubo. Art Director: Hiromasa Ogura. Character Designer: Hiroyuki Okiura. Mechanical Designers: Shoji Kawamori, Atsushi Takeuchi. Weaponry Designer: Mitsuo Iso. Sound Director: Kazuhiro Wakabayashi. Colour Designer: Kumiko Yusa.

^{D,W} **Ghost in the Shell 2: Innocence** (2003). Original Title: *Koukaku Kidoutai 2: Inosensu*. Status: Animated Feature Film. Director: Mamoru Oshii. Original Story: Masamune Shirow. Screenplay: Oshii. Producer: Mitsuhisa Ishikawa. Executive Producer: Toshio Suzuki. Production Company: Production I.G. Co-Production Company: Studio Ghibli. Music: Kenji Kawai. Length: 99 minutes. Animation Directors: Toshihiko Nishikubo, Naoko Kusumi. Art Director: Shuichi Hirata. Character Designer: Hiroyuki Okiura. CGI Director: Hiroyuki Hayashi. Machine and Vehicle Designer: Atsushi Takeuchi. Sound Director: Randy Thom. Colour Designer: Kumiko Yusa.

P,C *Ghost in the Shell: Stand Alone Complex* (2002–2004). Original Title: *Koukaku Kidoutai: Stand Alone Complex.* Status: Animated TV Series. Director: Kenji Kamiyama. Original Story: Shirow Masamune. Screenplays: Kenji Kamiyama, Shotaro Suga, Yoshiki Sakurai, Dai Sato, Junichi Fujisaku, Nobuhisa Terada. Visual Concept: Mamoru Oshii (2nd "gig"). Plot-Sketching Advisor: Oshii (2nd "gig"). Executive Producers: Mitsuhisa Ishikawa, Shigeru Watanabe. Production Company: Production I.G. Music: Yoko Kanno. Length: 30 minutes x 26 episodes. Animation Directors: Takayuki Goto, Masahiro Sato, Kyoji Asano, Akihisa Maeda, Ken'ichi Yamaguchi, Jyun Uemura. Art Director: Yusuke Takeda. Chief Character Designer: Makoto Shimomura. Mechanical Designers: Kenji Teraoka, Shinobu Tsuneki. CGI Director: Makoto Endo. Sound Effects: Daisuke Jinbo. Colour Designer: Yumiko Katayama.

W *Jin-Roh: The Wolf Brigade* (1998). Original Title: *Jin-Roh.* Status: Animated Feature Film. Director: Hiroyuki Okiura. Original Story: Mamoru Oshii. Screenplay: Oshii. Producers: Minoru Takanashi, Hidekazu Terakawa. Executive Producers: Mitsuhisa Ishikawa, Shigeru Watanabe. Production Company: Production I.G. Music: Hajime Mizoguchi. Length: 98 minutes. Animation Director: Kenji Kamiyama. Art Director: Hiromasa Ogura. Character Designer: Nishio Tetsuya. Weaponry Designer: Kazuchika Kise. Vehicle Designer: Sadafumi Hiramatsu. Sound Director: Kazuhiro Wakabayashi. Colour Designer: Yumiko Katayama.

D *Killers: .50 Woman* (2002). Original Title: *Killers: .50 Woman.* Status: Live-Action Short Film (in a 5-episode anthology). Director: Mamoru Oshii. Anthology Co-Directors: Kazuhiro Kiuchi, Shundo Ohkawa, Takanori Tsujimoto, Shuji Kawata. Length: 115 minutes (overall).

W *Minipato* (2001). Original Title: *Minipato.* Status: Animated Shorts (3 episodes). Director: Kenji Kamiyama. Original Story: Mamoru Oshii. Screenplay: Oshii. Producers: Atsushi Sugita, Masahiro Fukushima, Ryuji Mimoto. Production Companies: Bandai Visual, Production I.G. Music: Kenji Kawai. Length: 12 minutes. Animation Director: Nishio Tetsuya. Art Director: Hirosama Ogura. Character Designer: Nishio Tetsuya. Sound director: Kazuhiro Wakabayashi. Colour Designer: Nagisa Yasube.

D *Mobile Police Patlabor*, OVA 1 (25 April 1988–25 June 1989). Original Title: *Kidou Keisatsu Patoreibaa.* Status: Original Video Animation. Director: Mamoru Oshii. Original Story: Masami Yuuki. Screenplay: Kazunori Itoh. Production Company: Sunrise. Music: Kenji Kawai. Character Designer: Akemi Takada. Mechanical Designer: Yutaka Izubuchi.

W *Mobile Police Patlabor*, OVA 2 (22 November 1990–23 April 1992). Original Title: *Kidou Keisatsu Patoreibaa.* Status: Original Video Animation.

Director: Various. Original Story: Masami Yuuki. Screenplay: Various; Mamoru Oshii: Episodes 7, 8, 10, 13. Production Company: Sunrise. Music: Kenji Kawai. Character Designer: Akemi Takada. Mechanical Designers: Yutaka Izubuchi, Yoshinori Sayama.

^W *Mobile Police Patlabor* TV Series (11 October 1989–26 September 1990). Original Title: *Kidou Keisatsu Patoreibaa*. Status: Animated TV Series. Director: Naoyuki Yoshinori. Original Story: Headgear. Screenplay: Various; Mamoru Oshii: Episodes 3, 9, 14, 29, 38. Production Company: Sunrise. Music: Kenji Kawai. Character Designer: Akemi Takada. Mechanical Designers: Yutaka Izubuchi, Yoshinori Sayama.

^D *Patlabor 1: The Mobile Police* (1989). Original Title: *Kidou Keisatsu Patoreibaa*. Status: Animated Feature Film. Director: Mamoru Oshii. Original Story: Masami Yuuki. Screenplay: Kazunori Itoh. Producers: Shin Unozawa, Taro Maki, Makoto Kubo. Production Company: Production I.G Tatsunoko. Music: Kenji Kawai. Length: 98 minutes. Animation Directors: Koji Sawai, Kakuchika Kise. Art Directors: Hiromasa Ogura, Hiroaki Sato, Hiroyuki Mitsumoto. Character Designer: Akemi Takada. Mechanical Designers: Yutaka Izubuchi. Sound Director: Shigeharu Zanza. Colour Designers: Sayuri Ike, Masatsugu Arakawa.

^{D,W} *Patlabor 2: The Movie* (1993). Original Title: *Kidou Keisatsu Patoreibaa: The Movie 2*. Status: Animated Feature Film. Director: Mamoru Oshii. Original Story: Masami Yuuki. Screenplay: Kazunori Itoh, Oshii. Producers: Shin Unozawa, Tsuyoshi Hamawatari, Mitsuhisa Ishikawa. Executive Producers: Tetsu Uemura, Makoto Yamashina. Production Company: Production I.G Tatsunoko. Music: Kenji Kawai. Length: 113 minutes. Animation Directors: Toshihiko Nishikubo, Kakuchika Kise. Art Director: Hiromasa Ogura. Character Designers: Akemi Takada, Masami Yuuki. Mechanical Designer: Shouji Kawamori, Yutaka Izubuchi, Hajime Katoki. Sound Director: Naoko Asari. Colour Designer: Kumiko Yusa.

Patlabor WXIII: Movie 3 (2002). Original Title: *WX3: Kidou Keisatsu Patoreibaa*. Status: Animated Feature Film. Director: Fumihiko Takayama. Original Story: Masami Yuuki. Screenplay: Miki Tori. Producers: Atsushi Sugita, Masahiro Fukushima. Executive Producers: Kazumi Kawashiro, Keiichi Kosaka, Shigeru Watanabe. Production Companies: Bandai Visual, HEADGEAR, Madhouse Studios, Production I.G. Music: Kenji Kawai. Length: 107 minutes. Animation Director: Takuji Endo. Art Director: Takashi Watabe. Character Designer: Hiroki Takagi. Mechanical Designers: Shouji Kawamori, Yutaka Izubuchi, Hajime Katoki. Sound Director: Toshiki Kameyama.

^{D,W} *The Red Spectacles* (1987). Original Title: *Akai Megane*. Status: Live-Action Feature Film. Director: Mamoru Oshii. Original Story: Oshii. Screenplay: Kazunori Itoh, Mamoru Oshii. Producers: Daisuke Hayashi, Shigeharu Shiba. Production Company: Bandai Visual. Music: Kenji Kawai. Length: 116 minutes. Cinematography: Yousuke Mamiya. Sound Effects: Yasufumi Yoda. Cast: Shigeru Chiba (Koichi Todome), Machiko Washio (Midori Washio), Hideyuki Tanaka (Soichiro Toribe).

^{D,W} *Stray Dog: Kerberos Panzer Cops* (1991). Original Title: *Stray Dog Keruberosu Jigoku no Banken*. Status: Live-Action Feature Film. Director: Mamoru Oshii. Original Story: Oshii. Screenplay: Oshii. Producers: Sumiaki Ueno, Daisuke Hayashi. Executive Producers: Shigeru Watanabe, Noboru Yamada. Production Company: Bandai Visual. Music: Kenji Kawai. Length: 95 minutes. Cinematography: Yousuke Mamiya. Model Production Art Director: Hisashi Yasui. Weapon Effects: Kikuo Notomi. "Protect-Gear" Designer: Yutaka Izubuchi. Sound Director: Naoko Asari. Cast: Shigeru Chiba (Koichi Todome), Yoshikazu Fujiki (Inui), Takashi Matsuyama (Man in White), Eaching Sue (Tang Mie).

^{D,W} *Tachigui—The Amazing Lives of the Fast Food Grifters* (2006). Original Title: *Tachiguishi retsuden*. Status: Live-Action Feature Film. Director: Mamoru Oshii. Original Story: Oshii. Screenplay: Oshii. Executive Producer: Mitsuhisa Ishikawa. Production Company: Production I.G. Music: Kenji Kawai. Length: 100 minutes. Cast: Mako Hyoudou (Kitsunecroquette no Ogin), Mitsuhisa Ishikawa (Nageki no Inumaru), Kenji Kawai (Hamburger no Tetsu), Katsuya Terada (Frankfurt no Tatsu).

^{D,W} *Talking Head* (1992). Original Title: *Talking Head*. Status: Live-Action Feature Film. Director: Mamoru Oshii. Original Story: Oshii. Screenplay: Oshii. Producers: Hiroki Miyagawa, Shin Unozawa. Executive Producers: Katsuji Murakami, Kyoichi Mori. Production Company: Bandai Visual. Music: Kenji Kawai. Length: 105 minutes. Cinematography: Yosuke Mamiya. Animation Director: Yoshinori Kanada. Art Director: Hidefumi Hanaya. Sound Director: Masashi Iwahashi. Cast: Shigeru Chiba (I), Tomoko Ishimura (Tamiko), Fumihiko Tachiki (Handawara).

^{D,W} *Twilight Q2: Labyrinth Objects File 538* (1987). Original Title: *Towairato Q2: Meikyuu Bukken File 538*. Status: Original Video Animation (1 episode). Director: Mamoru Oshii. Original Story: Oshii. Scenario: Kazunori Ito. Production Company: Studio DEEN. Length: 25 minutes. Animation Director: Shinji Otsuka. Character Design: Akemi Takada.

^{D,W} *Urusei Yatsura Movie 2: Beautiful Dreamer* (1984). Original Title: *Urusei Yatsura: Byuutifuru Dorimaa*. Status: Animated Feature Film. Director: Mamoru Oshii. Original Story: Rumiko Takahashi. Screenplay: Mamoru

Oshii. Producer: Hiroshi Hasegawa. Executive Producer: Hidenori Taga. Production Companies: Kitty Films, TOHO. Music: Katsu Hoshi. Length: 90 minutes. Animation Directors: Yuuji Moriyama, Kazuo Yamazaki. Art Director: Shichiro Kobayashi. Character Designer: Kazuo Yamazaki. Sound Director: Shigeharu Shiba.

Urusei Yatsura Movie 4: Lum the Forever (1986). Original Title: *Urusei Yatsura: Ramu za fouebaa*. Status: Animated Feature Film. Director: Kazuo Yamazaki. Original Story: Rumiko Takahashi. Screenplay: Toshiki Inoue, Kazuo Yamazaki. Producers: Hiroshi Hasegawa, Yoko Matsushita. Executive Producer: Hidenori Taga. Production Company: Kitty Films. Music: Fumi Itakura. Length: 93 minutes. Animation Director: Tsukasa Dokite. Art Director: Torao Arai. Character Designer: Akemi Takada. Sound Director: Shigeharu Shiba. Colour Designers: Sadako Yonemura, Yuko Nishikawa.

[D] ***Urusei Yatsura Movie 1: Only You*** (1983). Original Title: *Urusei Yatsura: Onri Yuu*. Status: Animated Feature Film. Director: Mamoru Oshii. Original Story: Rumiko Takahashi. Screenplay: Tomoko Komparu. Producer: Yuuji Nunokawa. Executive Producer: Hidenori Taga. Production Companies: Fuji Film, Kitty Films. Music: Izumi Kobayashi, Fumitaka Anzai, Kohji Nishimura, Masamichi Amano. Length: 101 minutes. Animation Directors: Katsumi Aoshima, Endo Yuichi, Magoichi Takazawa. Art Directors: Arai Torao, Shichiro Kobayashi. Character Designers: Akemi Takada, Magoichi Takazawa. Mechanical Designer: Masahito Yamashita. Sound Director: Shigeharu Shiba. Colour Designer: Chieko Ishiguro.

[D,W] ***Urusei Yatsura TV Series*** (14 October 1981–19 March 1986). Original Title: *Urusei Yatsura* ("Those Obnoxious Aliens"). Status: Animated TV Series. Directors: Mamoru Oshii, Kazuo Yamazaki; Oshii: Season 2, Episodes 22–43 (1982), Season 3, Episodes 44–54 (1982), Season 4, Episodes 55–77 (1983), Season 5, Episodes 78–106 (1983). Original Story: Rumiko Takahashi. Screenplays: Tadashi Fukui, Keiji Hayakawa, Hiroyuki Hoshiyama, Kazunori Itoh, Hiro Iwasaki, Ichiroh Izumi, Shusuke Kaneko, Hiroshi Konishikawa, Tomoko Konparu, Akira Nakahara, Yukiyoshi Ohashi, Oshii, Rumiko Takahashi, Masaki Tsuji, Yu Yamamoto. Production Companies: Fuji Television Network Inc., Kitty Films, Studio Gallop, Studio Pierrot Co., Ltd. Music: Various. Character Designers: Various.

Chapter Notes

Preface

1. Cavallaro, Dani. *Cyberpunk and Cyberculture: Science Fiction and the Work of William Gibson* (London: Athlone, 2000).

2. Cavallaro, Dani. *The Animé Art of Hayao Miyazaki* (Jefferson, N.C.: McFarland, 2006).

Chapter 1

1. In examining the transnational exchange between Japan and the West undertaken through the language of animation, it is also worth noting that the first animé export to the West was Seitaro Kitayama's *Momotaro* (1917), a film shipped to France even before enjoying its domestic release. (The character of Momotaro was revamped in the 1940s at the government's behest and transformed into a national hero for war propaganda purposes.) In the course of the Occupation, Japan was exposed to Disney and began to develop a particular approach to the art of cel animation that indubitably constitutes contemporary animé's prototype. In 1958, the president of Toei Douga sent Sanae Yamamoto's *Hakujaden* (*The Legend of the White Serpent*, released in the US in 1961 as *The Panda and the White Serpent*) to the Venice Children's Film Festival where it was awarded the Grand Prix. *Shounen Sarutobi Sasuke* (1959, released in the US in 1961 as *Magic Boy*) was also the recipient of this prestigious award and accordingly recruited by MGM. Toei Douga's reputation grew rapidly in the West and its features sold impressively across the global market.

Chapter 2

1. The other animations screened at Cannes prior to *Innocence* were:

- *Dumbo*, dir. Ben Sharpsteen, 1941
- *Peter Pan*, dirs. Clyde Geronimi, Wilfred Jackson and Hamilton Luske, 1953
- *Fantastic Planet*, dir. René Laloux, 1973
- *Shrek*, dirs. Andrew Adamson and Vicky Jenson, 2001

Beside *Innocence*, the other animated feature exhibited at the Festival in 2004 was *Shrek 2* (dirs. Andrew Adamson, Kelly Asbury and Conrad Vernon, 2004).

Chapter 5

1. Intriguingly, few imaginable lifestyles could be more at odds with the entire experiential or adventure imperative than Oshii's own. For instance, in a press release coinciding with the screening of *Innocence* at Cannes, Oshii has stated: "[e]conomic recession ... corporate downsizing ... violent crime. We live in a cruel and frightening world. For some time now, I've been working in the animation industry — a sinful world unto itself — and frankly, I have gotten tired of dealing with people in general. Sometimes, I imagine eliminating all human interaction and spending the rest of my life at home in Atami, relaxing and soaking in a hot spring. I feel old — everyday, I have to force myself to go to work" (Oshii 2004b). In an interview conducted by Peter Oberth, he has likewise answered the question "What are your future plans [after *Innocence*]?" with the words: "To spend some valuable time back home with my dogs, cat and wife" (Oberth). In spite of these deep reservations concerning the value of social relations, the director's ethical tenets and creative drive prompt him to remain involved in cinematic production.

Chapter 6

1. A paradigmatic instance of multi-layered Japanese wordplay, the title *Urusei Yatsura* has no direct English equivalent. The first word, *urusei*, is a deliberately idiolectic mispronunciation of the Japanese word *urusai* ("obnoxious," "aggravating," "noisy"). The second word, *yatsura*, is the plural form of *yatsu* ("person"). Hence, the title could be translated as "obnoxious people." However, it should concurrently be taken into consideration that *Uru* is also the name of the fictional planet whence the Oni (a pivotal set of dramatis personae in the series) originate. Moreover, the *kanji* (Chinese character) used to write *sei* means "star" (pronounced *hoshi* when it occurs as a free-standing word rather than as part of a compound), which entails that *Urusei Yatsura* could plausibly mean "noisy-star people" or perhaps "aggravating people from planet Uru." The standard pronunciation is *oo-roo-say yat-soo-rah*.

2. According to the most comprehensive fan Web site dedicated to the universe of *Urusei Yatsura*, Tomobiki, Takahashi is

> without a doubt, the most commercially successful female comic book creator in the world, having sold well over 100 million copies of her works in Japan alone. This landmark doesn't even include international sales, which are considerable. She remains one of the first female *manga-ka* to write comics aimed at young males. However, her comics continue to be universally popular with both boys and girls. Both adult and child. With the combination of her highly in-demand comics, the influential animated series that spawned from her works and the endless merchandising, it isn't hard to see how she's become the richest woman in Japan (Tomobiki on Rumiko Takahashi).

Takahashi's subsequent hits include the inspiring manga behind the hugely popular TV series *Maison Ikkoku* (1986), *Ranma 1/2* (1989) and *Inuyasha* (2000). The artist's knack of investing even the most improbable situations with a warm sense of psychological realism, fully demonstrated by *Urusei Yatsura* in spite of its salad-day positioning in Takahashi's career, is unflinchingly confirmed by those later works.

3. Ataru's bad luck is putatively ascribable to his birth on a day that was at once Friday the 13th, the date of a catastrophic earthquake, and *Busumetsu*, "the day the Buddha died" in the traditional lunar calendar. His very name signifies cosmic ill fortune, *Ataru* literally meaning "to get hit" and *Moroboshi*, "falling star."

4. On *Setsubun* — the day in the old calendar supposed to mark the end of winter and coinciding with the 3rd or 4th of February in our calendar — people still practice the custom of scattering soy beans outside the house (a symbolic way of averting the evil eye) whilst chanting *Oni wa soto, fuku wa uchi* ("Oni out, good luck in").

Chapter 8

1. "The name 'Mujaki' is a multilayered pun. Literally translated, it means 'guileless' or 'innocent.' However, when written with the proper *kanji*, it takes on an entirely different meaning: 'The Demon That Interferes with Dreams.' It is the second meaning that Sakura is referring to when she says 'as the name says, you are an evil demon who delights in manipulating dreams, and planting the seeds of evil in people'" (*Beautiful Dreamer*: Unofficial Liner Notes).

Chapter 9

1. The process of remediation is certainly not a stranger in the context of the Western film industry as a whole, particularly where Hollywood is concerned. Indeed, it would be arduous to refute, in evaluating that particular universe, Robert Shaye's proposition that "[e]ntertainment is one of the purest marketplaces in the world" (Shaye, p. 75). The industry's imbrication with the logic of product placement and the concomitant production of myriad ancillary goods that frequently turn out to be even more lucrative than the cinematic productions with which they are associated is confirmed by the evolution of marketing and investment policies over the past couple of decades. Richard Maltby has comprehensively documented this phenomenon:

> In the early 1980s, world-wide sales of *Star Wars* goods were estimated to be worth $1.5 billion a year, while *Batman* (1989) made $1 billion from merchandizing, four times its box-office earnings. *Jurassic Park* (1993) went so far as to advertise its own merchandizing within the movie: at one point, the camera tracks past the Jurassic Park gift shop, showing a line of T-shirts, lunch boxes, and other souvenirs identical to the

ones available for purchase in the lobby of the theatre…. In 1999, the total retail value of the licensed product market was estimated to be more than $70 billion a year, and the most successful movie series existed most prominently as brands or franchises [Maltby, pp. 190–1].

Chapter 10

1. The Greek word for "fish," *ichthus*, was used by the early Christian worshippers susceptible to imperial persecution as a coded term for the name of Jesus, consisting of an acronym for the phrase *Iesus Christos Theou Uios Soter*: "Jesus Christ God's True Son."

Chapter 11

1. "One of television's most rightly revered series, *The Twilight Zone* (CBS, 1959–64) stands as the role model for TV anthologies. Its trenchant sci-fi/fantasy parables explore humanity's hopes, despairs, prides and prejudices in metaphoric ways…. Creator Rod Serling wrote the majority of the scripts, and produced those of such now-legendary writers as Richard Matheson and Charles Beaumont. The series featured such soon-to-be-famous actors as Robert Redford, William Shatner, Burt Reynolds, Robert Duvall, Dennis Hopper, Carol Burnett, James Coburn, Charles Bronson, Lee Marvin, Peter Falk and Bill Mumy, as well as such established stars as silent-film giant Buster Keaton, Art Carney, Mickey Rooney, Ida Lupino and John Carradine. An often worthy revival series ran on CBS from 1985 [to] 1987" (*Twilight Zone*: "*SciFi.com* Review").

2. "The mother of all Japanese monster TV series. Master effects guru Eiji Tsuburaya launched his own production company in the mid-1960s and created this 28-episode series that was a cross between *The Twilight Zone* and *The Outer Limits*. Highly respected as one of the most well produced series, Tsuburaya reportedly stopped after 28 episodes only because his crew was fatigued by all the effort they had put into each show" (*Ultra Q*: "Review, *Godzilla and Other Monster Music*").

3. Memorable graphic associations of marine creatures and aeroplanes have more recently been proposed by *Patlabor WXIII: Movie 3* (dir. Fumihiko Takayama, 2002) and "After the Rainy Day" (dir. Shui-Cheng Tsai, 2005). The opening sequence presented in the former features the image of a malfunctioning plane shedding a veritable deluge of large fish and other sea species. The latter, an animated short in which a small boy's reveries as he plays with his rocking-horse in the course of a tediously wet day gradually give way to a full-fledged vision, culminates precisely with the protagonist's toy plane's metamorphosis into an actual plane, which the boy gleefully flies amidst a lyrical swirl of tropical fish.

Chapter 14

1. The reader may benefit from the following panoramic visualization of the evolution of the *Patlabor* universe from its embryonic conception by the *manga-ka* Masami Yuuki and by future members of the "Headgear" team to its coming to fruition as a multimedia franchise of arguably unprecedented scope:

> *Jailazard* (Preliminary Concept, c. 1981); *Lightning Garrakres* (Preliminary Concept, c. 1982); *Vidor* (Preliminary Concept, 1982–83); *Mobile Police Patlabor OVA 1* (OVA Series 1 [7 episodes], 1988–89); *Patlabor 1: The Mobile Police* (Feature Film, 1989); *Mobile Police Patlabor TV Series* (TV Series [47 episodes], 1989–90); *Mobile Police Patlabor OVA 2* (OVA Series 2 [16 episodes], 1990–92); *Patlabor 2: The Movie* (Feature Film, 1993); *Minipato* (Animated Shorts [3 episodes], 2001); *Patlabor WXIII: Movie 3* (Feature Film, 2002)

2. "The Bubble economy was the period (running roughly from the mid-'70s to 1990) when the relative value of the Japanese yen increased at an overwhelming rate, especially following the Plaza Accord in 1985. Since the growth was predicated on stock investment rather than an actual increase in capital or productivity, inflation caused the 'Bubble' economy to burst in the early '90s. This, in turn, precipitated the East Asian stock market collapse of the mid-'90s" (Suchenski).

Chapter 15

1. Notably, the villain's family name — Inubashiri — contains the root word "*inu*" (literally meaning "dog") which also composes the bulk of the name of the Kerberos agent placed by Oshii in a lead role in the live-action film *Stray Dog: Kerberos Panzer Cops*, Inui. Though arguably quite peripheral, this

lexical detail is nonetheless worthy of observation as a concisely telling clue to Oshii's distinctive approach. More specifically, it could be argued that Oshii's cinema derives much of its unique flavour from the director's punctilious attention to the minutest details and, relatedly, to their recursive utilization across diverse media and genres as a way of weaving an internally coherent intertextual tapestry out of seemingly discrete and unrelated cinematographical enterprises.

The recurrence of the *"inu"* root, in this respect, may be considered meaningful on two counts. At one level, it underscores the director's almost obsessive tendency to import into his productions the talismanic significance which he appears to attribute to the canine presence by whatever means may seem plausible in any one given context. At another level, the particular association of *"inu"* with rogue cops, terrorists and fugitives from the law points to Oshii's symbolic coupling of these dubious personas not just with the image of the dog in general but specifically with that of the stray dog — the outsider, the outcast, the pariah. This ploy enables him to communicate a liminal feeling of sympathy with the wrongdoer as a figure that cannot be unproblematically damned for failing society insofar as he, too, has in turn been failed by his fellow humans.

Chapter 16

1. This bird is invested with multifarious symbolic connotations by different facets of Japanese mythology and lore. Though often regarded as an evil omen and bearer of bad fortune (especially when heard croaking in the evening, as opposed to the early morning or noon), the crow (*karasu*) is also thought to be a messenger of some deities and spirits (*kami*). In numerous tales, the crow is employed as a symbol of filial piety on the basis of the bird's presumed proclivity to care for its grizzled parents.

Chapter 17

1. Although Japan has not been allowed to play a military part outside its borders in the aftermath of the Second World War, in 1992 the national Diet (the government's legislative branch) passed a UN Peacekeeping Cooperation Law that would permit the JSDF to participate in UN-coordinated operations under certain conditions. In the same year, the JSDF took part in UN missions in Mozambique and Cambodia. This development constituted an alarming scenario for Oshii since, as pointed out by the character of Arakawa, the basic fact that it was precisely an aggressive military disposition that led Japan on the brink of disaster in the first place cannot and should not be ignored.

Chapter 18

1. "Godzilla (*Gojira*) is a giant, amphibious, dinosaur-like fictional creature first seen in the Japanese-produced 1954 *kaijuu* ... film *Gojira* produced by Toho Film Company Ltd.... Godzilla has three primary abilities: regeneration, amphibious mobility, and an atomic fire beam. Godzilla is also extremely durable and can resist almost all physical assaults. The atomic fire beam is Godzilla's trademark skill. Although much of Godzilla's significance as an anti-war symbol has been lost in the transition to pop culture, the nuclear breath remains as a visual vestige of the creature's early Cold War politics.... *Gojira* was first released in the United States in 1955 in Japanese-American communities only. In 1956, it was adapted by an American company into *Godzilla, King of the Monsters*, edited and with added, principal scenes featuring Raymond Burr, and this version became an international success. As a result, the monster came to be known as 'Godzilla' also in Japan.... Godzilla was originally an allegory for the effects of the hydrogen bomb, and the unintended consequences that such weapons might have on Earth.... Much of Godzilla's popularity in the United States can be credited with TV broadcasts of the Toho Studios monster movies during the 1960s and 1970s" (Wikipedia.org, s.v. "Godzilla").

2. Given *Patlabor 3*'s generic affiliation to the *daikaijuu* tradition, it is worth noting that the film *Godzilla Versus Biollante* (1989) analogously features a scientist who creates a top-notch monster by crossing cells obtained from the body of his dead daughter with a rose.

3. a. "The 1995 Great Hanshin Earthquake (M=6.9), commonly referred to as the Kobe earthquake, was one of the most devastating earthquakes ever to hit Japan; more than 5,500 were killed and over 26,000 injured. The economic loss has been estimated at about $US 200 billion. The proximity of the

epicentre, and the propagation of rupture directly beneath the highly populated region, help explain the great loss of life and the high level of destruction" ("Kobe Earthquake [1995], Japan").

b. "Aum Shinrikyo is a Japanese religious cult obsessed with the apocalypse. The previously obscure group became infamous in 1995 when some of its members released deadly sarin nerve gas into the Tokyo subway system, killing 12 people and sending more than 5,000 others to hospitals.... It was the most serious terrorist attack in Japan's modern history, causing massive disruption and widespread fear in a society that is virtually free of crime.... Aum Shinrikyo is a doomsday cult whose teachings are based on tenets borrowed from Hinduism and Buddhism ... at the centre of the group's belief is reverence for Shoko Asahara, Aum's founder, who teaches that the end of the world is near. The police have portrayed the nerve gas attack as the cult's way of hastening the apocalypse" (*Terrorism: Questions and Answers*).

4. Although *Patlabor 3* was released after *Avalon*, its soundtrack was composed earlier.

Chapter 19

1. Interestingly, the artists and animators involved in the production of *Minipato* took it upon themselves to supply viable voices for their puppets, thus temporarily assuming the role of actors. This decision lends full credence to Ed Hooks's contention that "a good animator must go through the ... process of motivating his characters on a moment-to-moment basis" (Hooks, p. 5). Furthermore, it could be argued that animators are always marginally akin to actors insofar as in manipulating their characters in terms of both physical actions and emotional reactions, they have to develop and sustain particular performing styles.

2. <http://www.oshiimamoru.com/>

Chapter 20

1. According to Foucault, a "discourse could be described as a set of recurring statements that define a particular cultural object (e.g., madness, criminality, sexuality) and provide the concepts and terms through which such an object can be studied and discussed. Discourses produce distinctions between what can and what cannot be said

about an object and establish who has the right to say whatever can be said. The fact that statements occur with regularity in a culture does not mean that they constitute a logical or coherent system. Indeed, Foucault rejects conventional notions of history as a linear chronology of facts and emphasizes instead its incongruities and ruptures. Discourses, accordingly, are characterized by discontinuity and do not evolve according to a predictable temporal trajectory. This is borne out by the Latin etymology of the term discourse: *dis* = 'in different directions' + *currere* = 'to run.' Each era produces different discourses through which the subject may be objectified according to the ruling values, beliefs and interests of its society. Whatever we may call the truth is always embodied in historically contingent discourses. Indeed, Foucault denies the existence of any reality outside or beyond discourse" (Cavallaro).

2. Oshii will again draw allegorical connections between laws intended to regulate the public consumption of food and the broader priorities of specific political regimes in *Tachigui — The Amazing Lives of the Fast Food Grifters (Tachiguishi Retsuden)*, a live-action film based on his own novel (here addressed in the Epilogue).

3. Damian Cannon has commented thus on the stylistic uniqueness of Chris Marker's 1962 film: "*La Jetée* is almost totally composed of individual frozen pictures, since it is a photo-montage with sparse narration ... the essential story is projected in surprising detail for such a short piece. In part this effect is achieved through the choice of superlative black-and-white photographs; these are grainy enough and shot in such a way that the immediate impression is of wartime photojournalism whilst the events captured suggest far more than they illustrate. By altering the time for which each shot is held (at times a quick succession of similar images approximates to film) a tight grasp of pace and a certain level of suspense is achieved. Interestingly, perhaps the most significant result of *La Jetée* is that the basic structures utilised in cinema are stripped bare and revealed unadorned" (Cannon). These remarks apply no less fittingly to Oshii's distinctive utilization of frozen frames, montages and a carefully varied shooting pace. Cannon's words also constitute an apposite assessment of Oshii's own tendency to capitalize on the atmospheric effects of stark chromatic contrasts, his concentration on the apparently least conse-

quential details of a scene, and his determination to foreground the cinematographical artifice without kowtowing to the aesthetic and ideological requirements of mimetic realism.

Chapter 21

1. In this regard, the hit woman's character is vividly redolent of the figure of the librarian presented in Haruki Murakami's *Hard-Boiled Wonderland and the End of the World* (originally published in 1985). (Murakami, incidentally, shares with Oshii a keen taste for the interpenetration of the factual and the oneiric, lucidity and preposterousness.) Murakami's librarian has a tendency to devour an extravagant amount of dishes of the most diverse culinary orientation without her shape or weight being in the least affected, which she attributes to "gastric dilation," and understandably describes as "frightening.... Most of my salary disappears into my stomach" (Murakami, p. 91).

Chapter 22

1. Okiura had already worked on Katsuhiro Otomo's *Akira* (1988) and on Oshii's *Ghost in the Shell* (1995), and his development had been deeply influenced, in the process, by Otomo's work in his capacities as a manga artist and writer and specifically by his preference for a realistic approach to graphics and the overall sense of design.

2. *Jin-Roh* was released in France earlier than on home turf, presumably to gauge the nature of its reception abroad before testing domestic audiences. The film's early release in France regrettably precluded its nomination for the first ever Academy Award for Best Animated Feature introduced in 2002. Its reception at numerous international film festivals, including those hosted in Brussels, Annecy, Berlin, Porto and Singapore, was undilutedly enthusiastic.

3. It is worthy of consideration, in this respect, that the tale of *Little Red Riding Hood* has spawned legion variations on the core narrative with which most Western readers will be familiar. The version of the tale chosen by Oshii as the metaphorical skeleton for *Jin-Roh* is by no means the only available permutation of the story deemed to allude to weighty adult concerns. Indeed, as Jack Zipes has persuasively argued in *The Trials and*

Tribulations of Little Red Riding Hood, the majority of those related texts carry political, psychological and ethical connotations of significant gravity. In tracing the development of *Little Red Riding Hood* over the centuries and subjecting to close analysis thirty-five of the most influential versions of the story—from its inception as a folktale to its adaptation by the Brothers Grimm, Walter De La Mare, James Thurber, Alphonse Daudet, Anne Sexton, Olga Broumas and others—Zipes demonstrates that the tale has plenty to say about issues of violation, manipulation and abuse. This critical volume thus supplies an intriguing correlative for Oshii's own filmic narrative.

4. Oshii has stated that he would have utilized computers more extensively than Okiura has done, especially for camera work and water-related effects. Yet, Oshii has also emphasized that computers should not be regarded purely as transmutational tools in the manipulation of frames. In fact, he believes that they can be used most imaginatively when their mechanisms are allowed to work in tandem with more traditional instruments and methodologies: "I've learned quite a bit while working on *Ghost*. A computer can do more than just a simple digital processing. You can use it for the analog world as well, especially for the vertical movements of the camera and lens effects" (Oshii 1997).

Chapter 23

1. According to Antonia Levi, animé's first cyborg was the eponymous hero of Osamu Tezuka's *Tetsuwan Atomu* (*Astro Boy*):

> Although designed as a children's show, *Tetsuwan Atomu* already showed some of the moral questioning and general sense of unease that characterize animé's attitude towards cyborgs. *Tetsuwan Atomu* was essentially a tragic character. He was created by a scientist to replace a dead child. When his failure to grow revealed his essentially artificial nature, he was rejected by his "father" and left to create his own place in an uncaring world. He succeeds and *Tetsuwan Atomu* does not focus heavily on the tragic ramifications of his predicament, but it remains there [Levi, p. 44]

The pitiful element inherent in the figure of the cyborg, potently communicated by both of the *Ghost in the Shell* movies, resides with their mounting awareness that the enhancement of natural abilities goes ineluctably hand in hand with an attenuation of their humanness.

2. The word "cybernetics" was introduced in 1948 by the mathematician Norbert Wiener (1894–1964) in a book titled *Cybernetics, or Control and Communication in the Animal and the Machine*. Cybernetics derives from the Greek word "*kibernetes*," which means "steersman," to imply that control should be a form of steersmanship, not of dictatorship. Wiener believed that biological bodies and mechanical bodies are self-regulating systems connected by the basic fact that both work in terms of control and communication. Moreover, Wiener divided the history of machines into four stages: the Golemic age (a pre-technological world), the age of clocks (seventeenth and eighteenth centuries), the age of steam (late eighteenth and nineteenth centuries) and the age of communication and control (the era of cybernetics). To each of these stages corresponds a different model of the physical organism: the body as a magical clay shape, as a clockwork mechanism, as a heat engine and, finally, as an electronic system. *Ghost in the Shell 2: Innocence* could be said to constitute, amongst other things, a capsulated history of the evolutionary pattern theorized by Wiener insofar as it spins subtle threads of connection between the pre-industrial figure of the *golem* and the post-industrial figure of the cyborg by means of visual and rhetorical allusions to diverse mechanical and industrial apparatuses.

3. It should also be noted, in this regard, that cyberpunk and Japan are linked on various levels, as numerous Western writers in this genre have adopted Japanese words and locations, whilst Japan itself was quick to embrace cyberpunk and, relatedly, to use its ingredients in the construction of somber sci-fi plots with a markedly international dimension, which could eloquently comment on the country's experience of globalization.

Chapter 25

1. The phrase "motion capture" refers to the process whereby external devices can be used to capture movement data from various live sources and then transmit it to the computer, where the data are applied to a virtual actor. The real performers on the motion-capture stage wear black bodysuits equipped with retroreflective markers, or sensors. Optical cameras positioned on tripods with red lights at their bases are blind to the performers and only record the movements of the reflections of their own red lights onto the markers.

Reputedly ideated in the execution of the *Matrix* sequels, universal capture is a form of motion capture designed to focus on facial performance: five high-definition cameras are arranged in a semi-circle around the actor and photograph him or her from every possible angle, recording skin texture, pores, follicles and expression lines down to the minutest detail. These can then be stored in image libraries and applied to the faces of CG characters as appropriate.

2. The Ainu were the original inhabitants of Japan, based in the Northern regions and especially Hokkaido, and were renowned for their highly imaginative animistic beliefs.

3. Given Oshii's consistent allusions to Arthurian lore, it seems worth mentioning that a very interesting canine figure whose name briefly appears in the course of Ash's quest for the Nine Sisters, also features in that tradition in the guise of the Crop-Eared Dog: a "creature," in Ronan Coghlan's words, "who despite his dogginess, was fully able to converse in human speech" (Coghlan, p. 82). Likewise notable Arthurian beings with canine connotations are the "Dogheads," fierce (albeit not always monstrous) opponents of the legendary king who were putatively related to ancient populations of both Irish and Iberian descent, namely the Conchind and the Cunesioi respectively.

Chapter 26

1. Masamune Shirow, the *manga ka* ("comic book writer") behind the hypnotic universe of *Ghost in the Shell*, self-published the first volume of his manga series *Black Magic* in 1983 as a student at the Osaka University of Art, where he had initially sought to study oil painting. *Black Magic* caught the eye of the publishing company Seishinsha, who asked Shirow to become a professional in the field of comic-book production. The first work he published in that capacity was *Appleseed*, a story staged in a dystopian, post-apocalyptic society and centred on two cops' battle against the terrorists who plague the city of Olympus. Although the story's general mood anticipates *Ghost in the Shell*, a

crucial aspect of the later work — namely, bioengineering — is only peripherally alluded to. *Appleseed* was animated as an OVA in 1988 (dir. Kazuyoshi Katayama) and as a feature-length movie in 2004 (dir. Shinji Aramaki).

2. The rotoscope could be regarded as a forerunner of digital motion capture (mocap), the extrapolation of motion data from live performers by electronic means and application thereof to computer-generated characters. The *Matrix* sequels (notably in the depiction of the ubiquitous Agent Smith) and the *Lord of the Rings* films (particularly in the rendition of the persona of Gollum) make prominent use of these "synthespians."

3. This does not actually imply that the Kusanagi lookalikes are of the same biotechnological quality as the major. Shirow's comments on Kusanagi's appearance are here worthy of consideration: "Major Kusanagi is deliberately designed to look like a mass-production model so she won't be too conspicuous. In reality, her electrical and mechanical system is made of ultra-sophisticated materials unobtainable on the civilian market. If she appeared too expensive, she might be suddenly waylaid on a dark street some night, hacked up, and hauled off to be sold" (Shirow, "Author's Notes"). Nevertheless, such a technical consideration does not in any way diminish the pathos of the character's intense feeling of personal dislocation in the face of the anonymous replicas.

Chapter 27

1. The basset hound had previously featured in the first *Ghost in the Shell* production in three forms: adverts for the brand of dog food reintroduced in *Innocence*; the photograph of the brain-hacked offender's pet; and the dog on the bridge in the famous canal sequence. A special item which few Oshii fans would want to miss, distributed around the time of *Innocence*'s theatrical release, consists precisely of a *Basset Box* replicating in the minutest detail the boxes of *Bashido* dog food purchased by Batou in the course of the film, containing a T-shirt displaying the adorable hound, a selection of "Gabriel" pins, and a sticker advert for the "Stray Dog" brand of beer consumed by the cyborg — an explicit reference to Oshii's live-action film of the same name.

2. Intriguingly, this is also how Michael Moore, the eventual winner of the Palme

D'Or in the year of *Innocence*'s shortlisting for the Cannes award, described the world depicted in his documentary *Farenheit 9/11*.

3. A further Italian influence can be observed in the aerial sequence marking Batou's and Togusa's descent towards Kim's eerie city, its cathedral a clear echo of the Duomo in Milan.

Chapter 28

1. Research into the scientific and technological viability of thermoptic camouflage is currently being undertaken by Tachi Lab, a specialist laboratory in the fields of virtual reality and telexistence based in the Graduate School of Information Science and Technology at the University of Tokyo. Tachi Lab's assessment of their progress to date can be inspected at the following address: <http://projects.star.t.u-tokyo.ac.jp/projects/MEDIA/xv/oc.html>.

Chapter 29

1. a. Source: <http://club.nokia.co.jp/tokyoq/weekly_updates/anime/anime-0508.html>.

   b. "Kamagasaki, one of Japan's most infamous slums, was the site of nine days of violence when angry day labourers protested after a police chief was arrested for taking bribes, and 2000 riot police were called in. The protesters, mostly men in their 50s and 60s, fought with the riot police using fists and rocks against shields and nightsticks. The violence continued for nine days with hundreds of injuries.... Today, in an effort to spruce up its image, Kamagasaki has been renamed Airin, but it still has a bad reputation because there are more than 30,000 day labourers and as many as 90 yakuza offices there" (*The Kamagasaki Riots*, <http://www3.tky.3web.ne.jp/~edjacob/danger%20japanics.htm>).

2. Source: <http://www.nausicaa.net/miyazaki/newspro/latest_news.shtml>.

3. Source: <http://club.nokia.co.jp/tokyoq/weekly_updates/anime/anime-0504.html>.

4. Notably, the fox (*kitsune*) and the raccoon (*tanuki*) are mythical animals, endowed with magical and metamorphic powers, deeply embedded in Japan's most ancient lore.

5. Oshii's pavilion was not the sole contribution to the event made by a practitioner

from the animé industry, since the section devoted to architectural harmony between humans and the natural environment also contained a faithful replica of the traditional Japanese countryhouse central to Hayao Miyazaki's *My Neighbour Totoro*.

6. Source: <1.exp02005.0r.jp/en/venue/pavilion_private_h.html>.\

Bibliography

It cannot be guaranteed that all of the Web site addresses provided in this bibliography are currently available and accessible due to the intrinsically volatile nature of the World Wide Web. However, all the sites here cited were active at the time of their consultation in the preparation of this book (June 2005–March 2006).

"*Ain't It Cool News* Review of *Innocence.*" 2004. <http://www.aintitcool.com/display.cgi?id=17814>.

Angel's Egg Script. <http://www.cultivatetwiddle.com/angelsegg/angelscript.txt>.

Arnold, M. 2004. "Japanese Animation and the Animated Cartoon." *Midnight Eye.* <http://www.midnighteye.com/features/animated_cartoon.shtml>.

Arsenau, A. 2003. "*DVD Verdict* Review of Mamoru Oshii's *Talking Head.*" <http://www.dvdverdict.com/reviews/talking-head.php>.

Bakhtin, M. 1984. *Rabelais and His World.* Trans. H. Iswolsky. Bloomington: Indiana University Press.

Bakhtin, M. 1993. *Problems of Dostoevsky's Poetics.* Trans. C. Emerson. Minneapolis: University of Minnesota Press.

Beautiful Dreamer: Unofficial Liner Notes. <http://home.swipnet.se/~w-66939/uy/uymovie2.html#5>.

Beveridge, C. 2003. "*Animé on DVD* Review of *Mobile Police Patlabor* Original Video Animation 1." <http://www.animeondvd.com/reviews2/disc_reviews/2317.php>.

Big Apple Anime Fest— Mecha in Animé— 2003. <http://www.fansview.com/2003/baaf/083003a.htm>.

Bolter, J.D. and R. Grusin. 2000. *Remediation: Understanding New Media.* Cambridge, Mass.: MIT Press.

Bordwell, D. 2005. *Figures Traced in Light: On Cinematic Staging.* Berkeley, Los Angeles and London: University of California Press.

Boyance, J. 2004. "*Movie Vault* Review of *Ghost in the Shell 2: Innocence.*" <http://www.movie-vault.com/archive/>.

Bryson, N. 1983. *Vision and Painting: The Logic of the Gaze.* London: Macmillan.

Cannon, D. 1997. "*Movie Reviews UK*: Review of *La Jetée.*" <http://www.film.u-net.com/Movies/Reviews/Jetee.html>.

Cavallaro, D. 2001. *Critical and Cultural Theory: Thematic Variations.* London: Continuum.

Chute, D. 1996. "The Soul of the New Machine." Review of *Ghost in the Shell* originally published in *Film Comment* magazine, September. <www.geocities.com/Tokyo/Island/3102/ghost.htm>.

Clarke, J. 2004. *Animated Films.* London: Virgin Books.

Clements, J. and H. McCarthy. 2001. *The Animé Encyclopaedia.* Berkeley, Cal.: Stone Bridge Press.

Coghlan, R. 1993. *The Illustrated Encyclopaedia of Arturian Legends.* Shaftesbury, Dorset; Rockport, Mass.; Brisbane, Queensland: Element Books.

Cooper, J.C. 1992. *Symbolic and Mythological Animals*. London: Aquarian Press.

Crandol, M. 2002. "Review of *Patlabor: The Mobile Police* (TV Series: DVD Vol. 1)." *Animé News Network.* <http://www.animenewsnetwork.com/reviews/display.php?id=279>.

Crandol, M. 2003. "Review of *Patlabor: The Mobile Police* (TV Series: DVD Vol. 4)." *Animé News Network.* <http://www.animenewsnetwork.com/reviews/display.php?id=432>.

Dahmen-Ingenhoven, R. 2004. *Animation: Form Follows Fun*. Basel: Birkhauser.

Dawkins, R. 1976. *The Selfish Gene*. Oxford: Oxford University Press.

"*Destroy All Monsters* Review of *Innocence*." 2004. <http://destroy-all-monsters.com/gitsinnocence.html>.

Drazen, P. 2003. *Animé Explosion: The What? Why? & Wow! of Japanese Animation*. Berkeley, Cal.: Stone Bridge Press.

Ebert, R. 2004. Interview in *Grave of the Fireflies* Double Disc Special Edition. Disc two. Optimum Releasing. DVD.

Elder, R.K. 2003. "*Chicago Tribune* Review of *Patlabor WXIII: Movie 3*." <http://www.rottentomatoes.com/m/xviii_wasted_13_patlabor_the_movie_3/>.

Erick. 2004. "*Beyond Hollywood.com* Review of *Patlabor: The Movie 3*." <http://www.beyondhollywood.com/reviews/patlaborthemovie3.htm>.

Foucault, M. 1973. *Madness and Civilization*. Trans. R. Howard. New York: Vintage.

Foucault, M. 1979. *Discipline and Punish: The Birth of the Prison*. Trans. A. Sheridan. New York: Vintage.

Fredericks, C. 1982. *The Future of Eternity*. Bloomington: Indiana University Press.

Garcia, R. 2001. "Alive and Kicking: The Kung Fu Film Is a Legend." *Bright Lights Film Journal*, issue 31. <http://www.brightlightsfilm.com/31/hk_alive.html>.

Gibson, W. 1995a. *Neuromancer*. London: HarperCollins.

Gibson, W. 1995b. Quoted in M. Harrison, *Visions of Heaven and Hell*. London: Channel 4 Publications.

Godzilla on Wikipedia.org. <en.wikipedia.org>, s.v. "Godzilla."

Havis, R.J. 2003. "*Hollywood Reporter* Review of *WXIII*." <http://www.hollywoodreporter.com/thr/article_display.jsp?vnu_content_id=1791902>.

Hayles, N.K. 1996. "Virtual Bodies and Flickering Signifiers." In *Electronic Culture*, edited by T. Druckrey. New York: Aperture.

"Hong Kong Martial Arts Cinema." *Zhang Ziyi CSC*. <http://csc.ziyi.org/filmography/cthd/wuxiafiction/hkcinema.html>.

Hooks, E. 2000. *Acting for Animators*. Portsmouth, N.H.: Heinemann.

Ichimanda, C. 2001. Interview in "The Making of *Blood: The Last Vampire*." Manga Entertainment. DVD.

Imamura, T. 1953. "Japanese Art and the Animated Cartoon." *The Quarterly of Film, Radio and Television,* spring.

Izubuchi, Y. 2003. "Production Notes," booklet accompanying the *WWIII: Patlabor* Ultimate Edition DVD (Pioneer Entertainment, 2003).

Johnson, S. 1999. User's Guide to *Delirious Film*. <http://www.deliriousfilm.com/guidepg.html>.

Jones, J. 2001. "Things Fall Apart." *The Guardian*, 11 October.

Kawai, H. 1995. *The Japanese Psyche: Major Motifs in Fairytales of Japan*. J.G. Donat, ed. Einsiedeln, Switzerland: Daimon.

Kawai, K. 2003. "Production Notes," booklet accompanying the *WWIII: Patlabor* Ultimate Edition DVD (Pioneer Entertainment, 2003).

Kise, K. 2001. Interview in "The Making of *Blood: The Last Vampire*." Manga Entertainment. DVD.

"Kobe Earthquake (1995), Japan." 2000. University of Washington, Soil Liquefaction. <http://www.ce.washington.edu/~liquefaction/html/quakes/kobe/kobe.html>.

Kristeva, J. 1989. *Black Sun: Depression and Melancholia*. Trans. L. Roudiez. New York: Columbia University Press.

Lent, J.A. 2001. Introduction to *Animation in Asia and the Pacific,* edited by J.A. Lent. Bloomington and Indianapolis: Indiana University Press.

Leo, V. 2003. "*Qwipster.net* Review of

Avalon." <http://www.qwipster.net/avalon.htm>.

Levi, A. 2001. "Myths for the Millennium: Japanese Animation." In *Animation in Asia and the Pacific,* edited by J.A. Lent. Bloomington and Indianapolis: Indiana University Press.

Lineberger, R. 2004. "Review of *Ghost in the Shell Stand Alone Complex — DVD, Volume 2.*" <http://www.dvdverdict.com/reviews/gitsv012.php>.

Makosuke. 2004. "*AAW* Review of *Urusei Yatsura.*" <http://animeworld.com/reviews/uruseiyatsuratv.html>.

Maltby, R. 2003. *Hollywood Cinema.* Second edition. Oxford: Blackwell Publishing.

Manovich, L. 2001. "Digital Cinema and the History of a Moving Image." In *The Language of New Media.* Boston: MIT Press. Extracts at <http://www2.unibo.it/parol/articles/manovich.htm>.

Murakami, H. 2003. *Hard-Boiled Wonderland and the End of the World.* London: Vintage.

Murayama, M. 1963. *Thought and Behaviour in Modern Japanese Politics.* London: Oxford University Press.

Musashi. 2005. "*Yellow Menace* Review of *The Red Spectacles.*" <http://www.yellow-menace.com/modules/zmagazine/article.php?articleid=114>.

Napier, S.J. 2001. *Animé from Akira to Princess Mononoke.* New York: Palgrave.

Oberth, P. 2004. "*Shakefire.com* Interview with Mamoru Oshii." <http://www.shakefire.com/interview-mamoruoshii.html>.

Oshii, M. 1993. "Around the Movie *Patlabor 2*: To Put an End to the Era." (Dialogue: Mamoru Oshii versus Hayao Miyazaki.) *Animage* 184. Trans. R. Toyama, ed. D. Goldsmith. <http://www.nausicaa.net/miyazaki/interviews/m_oshii_patlabor2.html>.

Oshii, M. 1997. "*Production I.G.* Interview with Mamoru Oshii." <http://dan42.com/jinroh/e/interviews.html#OshiiProdIG>.

Oshii, M. 2002. "*Fluctuat.Net* Interview with Mamoru Oshii." (In French.) <http://www.fluctuat.net/cinema/interview/Oshii2.htm>.

Oshii, M. 2003. Interview in *WXIII: Patlabor* Ultimate Edition. Disc three. Pioneer Entertainment. DVD.

Oshii, M. 2004a. "Oshii talks softly, but carries a big script: Interview for *The Japan Times.*" 17 March. <http://202.221.217.59/print/features/film2004/ff20040317a2.htm>.

Oshii, M. 2004b. "Cannes Film Festival Official Website: *Ghost in the Shell 2: Innocence* Press Kit." PDF downloadable from <http://www.festival-cannes.fr/films/>.

Oshii, M. 2004c. "*Midnight Eye* Interview with Mamoru Oshii." <http://www.midnighteye.com/interviews/mamoru_oshii.shtml>.

Panzner, C. 2005. "V-Cinema and OVA: No Mosaics, No Blurred Details, No Missing Bits." *Animation World Magazine.* <http://mag.awn.com/index.php?article_no=2445>.

Patten, F. 2000. "The Animé Debate." *Animation World Magazine.* <www.awn.com/mag/issue5.09/5.09pages/osmondanime4.php3>.

Patten, F. 2004. "The *Ghost* Rises Again." *Animation World Magazine.* <http://mag.awn.com/?article_no=2229>.

Pointon, S. 2000. "Orgasm as Apocalypse." <http://www.nzwritersguild.org.nz/>.

Poitras, G. 2001. *Animé Essentials: Every Thing A Fan Needs To Know.* Berkeley, Cal.: Stone Bridge Press.

Robinson, T. 1998. "*Patlabor: The Mobile Police—* The TV Series: one *mecha* series on rye, hold the *mecha.*" *Science Fiction Weekly.* <http://www.scifi.com/sfw/issue76/anime.html>.

Robinson, T. 2003. "Review of *Stray Dog: Kerberos Panzer Cops.*" <http://avclub.com/content/node/7538/print/>.

Roche, J. 1999. *Comedy Writing.* London and Chicago: Hodder.

Rosenstone, R.A., ed. 1995. Introduction to *Revisioning History: Film and the Construction of a New Past.* Princeton, N.J.: Princeton University Press.

Rucka, N. 2004. "Samurai Cinema 101." *Midnight Eye.* <http://www.midnighteye.com/features/samurai_cinema_101.shtml>.

Sandman, I. 2000. *The Basset Hound Mamoru Oshii Website.* <http://www.igorsandman.net/thebassethound/>.

Schilling, M. 2003. "Five Bullets on Killer: Shoot 'em up, in bits." *DVD Forum Online.* <http://forum.dvd-forum.at/showthread.php?t=11933>. Originally published in *The Japan Times,* 25 June 2003.

Server, L. 1999. *Asian Pop Cinema.* San Francisco, Cal.: Chronicle Books.

Shaye, R. 1996. "The Crime of Monsieur Lang." In *Film Policy: International, National and Regional Perspectives,* edited by A. Moran. London: Routledge.

Shirow, M. 2004. *Ghost in the Shell.* Trans. F. L. Schodt and T. Smith. 2nd Edition. Milwaukee: Dark Horse Comics.

"*Sigillum Dei Aemaeth (Emeth).*" <http://www.geocities.com/peripsol/Enoch/5SigilumAmeth.htm>.

Smith, L. 2005. "Stolen Innocence." Review of *Blood+* for *Animéfringe.com.* <http://www.animefringe.com/magazine/2005/11/feature/02.php>.

Sobshack, T. 1996. "Bakhtin's 'Carnivalesque.'" *Journal of Popular Film and Television,* winter.

Sontag, S. 1979. *On Photography.* London: Penguin.

Sterling, B. 1993. From a contribution to the Convocation on Technology and Education, National Academy of Sciences, Washington D.C., 10 May. <http://www.eff.org/pub/Publications/William_Gibson/Sterling_gibson_nas.speeches>.

Sterling, B. 1995. Preface to *Burning Chrome,* by W. Gibson. London: Harper Collins.

Suchenski, R. 2004. "Mamoru Oshii." <http://www.sensesofcinema.com/contents/directors/04/oshii.html>.

"*Tachigui*: Overview." <http://www.productionig.com/contents/works_sp/35_/index.html>.

Takayama, F. 2003. "Production Notes," booklet accompanying the *WWIII: Patlabor* Ultimate Edition DVD (Pioneer Entertainment, 2003).

Tanaka, S. 2003. Interview in *WXIII: Patlabor* Ultimate Edition. Disc three. Pioneer Entertainment. DVD.

Telotte, J.P. 1995. *Replications: A Robotic History of Science Fiction Film.* Urbana and Chicago: University of Illinois Press.

Terrorism: Questions and Answers 2004. Council on Foreign Relations (in cooperation with the Markle Foundation). <http://cfrterrorism.org/groups/aumshinrikyo.html>.

Tetsuya, N. 1997. "*Production I.G.* Interview with Tetsuya Nishio." <http://dan42.com/jinroh/e/interviews.html#NishioProdIG>.

Tom, T. 2004. "Review of *Avalon.*" <http://www.jeremysilman.com/movies_tv_tt/avalon.html>.

Tomobiki on Rumiko Takahashi. <http://www.furinkan.com/uy/intro/takahashi.htm>.

Tori, M. 2003. "Production Notes," booklet accompanying the *WWIII: Patlabor* Ultimate Edition DVD (Pioneer Entertainment, 2003).

Twelve Hawks, J. 2005. *The Traveller.* London: Bantam Press.

The Twilight Zone. "*SciFi.com* Review." <http://www.scifi.com/twilightzone/>. 2004.

Ultra Q: "Review, *Godzilla and Other Monster Music.*" <http://www.godzillamonstermusic.com/VPCD81294.htm>.

Wells, P. 1998. *Understanding Animation.* London: Routledge.

Whitley, M. 2003. *Schaft Enterprises: A Patlabor Website.* <http://members.iimetro.com.au/~mwhitley/aboutpat.htm>.

Williams, R. 2001. *The Animator's Survival Kit.* London: Faber and Faber.

Wittgenstein, L. 1973. *Philosophical Investigations.* Trans. G.E.M. Anscombe. Oxford: Blackwell.

Wu, G. 1998. "CultureVulture.net Review of *Jin-Roh: The Wolf Brigade.*" <http://www.culturevulture.net/Movies2/Jin-Roh.htm>.

Zipes, J. 1993. *The Trials and Tribulations of Little Red Riding Hood.* London: Routledge.

Index

245